Leeds Studies in English

New Series XLVII

© *Leeds Studies in English* 2017
School of English
University of Leeds
Leeds, England

ISSN 0075-8566
ISBN 978-1-84549-726-2

Copyright

All rights reserved. No part of this publication may be reproduced in any material form (including photocopying or storing it in any medium by electronic means, and whether or not transiently or incidentally to some other use of this publication) without the written permission of the copyright owner, except in accordance with the provisions of the Copyright, Designs and Patents Act 1988, or under terms of a licence issued by the Copyright Licensing Agency Ltd, 33-34, Alfred Place, London WC1E 7DP, UK. Applications for the copyright owner's permission to reproduce part of this publication should be addressed to the Publishers.

Printed in the UK

Publishing Office
Abramis Academic
ASK House
Northgate Avenue
Bury St. Edmunds
Suffolk
IP32 6BB

Tel: +44 (0)1284 700321
Fax: +44 (0)1284 717889
Email: info@abramis.co.uk
Web: www.abramis.co.uk

Leeds Studies in English

New Series XLVII

2016

Edited by

Alaric Hall

Leeds Studies in English

<www.leeds.ac.uk/lse>
School of English
University of Leeds
2016

Leeds Studies in English

<www.leeds.ac.uk/lse>

Leeds Studies in English is an international, refereed journal based in the School of English, University of Leeds. *Leeds Studies in English* publishes articles on Old and Middle English literature, Old Icelandic language and literature, and the historical study of the English language. After a two-year embargo, past copies are made available, free access; they can be accessed via <http://www.leeds.ac.uk/lse>.

Editorial Board:
    Catherine Batt, *Chair*
    Venetia Bridges
    Marta Cobb
    Alaric Hall, *Editor*
    Paul Hammond
    Oliver Pickering
    Helen Price
    N. Kıvılcım Yavuz *Reviews Editor*

Notes for Contributors

Contributors are requested to follow the *MHRA Style Guide: A Handbook for Authors, Editors, and Writers of Theses*, 2nd edn (London: Modern Humanities Research Association, 2008), available at <http://www.mhra.org.uk/Publications/Books/StyleGuide/download.shtml>.

    Where possible, contributors are encouraged to include the digital object identifiers or, where a complete free access text is available, stable URLs of materials cited (see *Style Guide* §11.2.10.1).

    The language of publication is English and translations should normally be supplied for quotations in languages other than English. Each contributor will receive a free copy of the journal, and a PDF of their article for distribution. Please email all contributions to <lse@leeds.ac.uk>.

Reviews

Copies of books for review should be sent to the Editor, *Leeds Studies in English*, School of English, University of Leeds, Leeds LS2 9JT, United Kingdom.

Contents

Diachronic Development of the Order of Prenominal Adjectives in English: The Case of AGE and SHAPE Semantic Categories — 1
    Łukasz Stolarski   *Jan Kochanowski University in Kielce, Poland*

Honour, Humour, and Women in the Romance of *Yder* — 15
    Jane Bliss   *Independent scholar, Oxford*

The Structure of the Exeter Book: A Reading Based on Medieval Topics — 29
    Jan-Peer Hartmann   *Freie Universität Berlin*

Reading Scribal Intervention in the Squire-Wife of Bath Link of MS Lansdowne 851 — 63
    Jeremy DeAngelo   *Carleton College*

'Do not Give that which is Holy to Dogs': Noble Hunting, the *Curée* Ritual, and the Eucharist — 77
    Andrew Pattison   *University of Oulu*

Sexual Sin and 'Anxieties of Outreach' in Thirteenth-Century England: Two Manuals for Penitents and their Adaptations — 99
    Krista A. Murchison   *Leiden University*

Affective Wounding in *Ancrene Wisse* and the *Wooing Group* — 115
    A. S. Lazikani   *University of Oxford*

Diachronic Development of the Order of Prenominal Adjectives in English: The Case of AGE and SHAPE Semantic Categories

Łukasz Stolarski

Introduction

In English there may be several adjectives in the attributive position and their order seems to follow particular patterns. For instance, the phrase 'a funny red hat' sounds more natural than 'a red funny hat' and the expression 'an intriguing, small, round, yellow toy' is more appropriate than 'a yellow, round, small, intriguing toy'. Because of such tendencies to favour one pattern over others, numerous grammar books for foreign learners of English propose ready solutions on the order of adjectives in the attributive position.[1] In many such publications it is suggested that the patterns are only strong tendencies and alternative orders may also be found in English. Moreover, many details of particular solutions differ from each other and, ultimately, it may be difficult for a foreigner to apply the patterns in practice. Suggestions on particular orders are also presented in the scholarly linguistic literature. A summary of the adjective patterns proposed in a selection of publications is provided in Table 1.

The phenomenon under discussion has been explained by referring to distinctions along 'general – specific', 'extrinsic – intrinsic' or 'subjective – objective' continua.[2] To give a few

---

[1] For example, Louis Alexander, *Longman English Grammar Practice for Intermediate Students* (Harlow: Longman, 1996); Virginia Evans, *CPE Use of English* (Newbury: Express Publishing, 2008) and *FCE Use of English* (Newbury: Express Publishing, 2010); Martin Hewings, *Advanced Grammar in Use* (Cambridge: Cambridge University Press, 2002); J. Hill, R. Hurst, M. Lewis, C. Blissett and C. Hallgarten, *Grammar and Practice* (Hove: Language Teaching Publications, 1995); N. Hopkins and D. Hopkins, *Developing Grammar in Context* (Cambridge: Cambridge University Press, 2009); E. Mańczak-Wohlfeld, A. Niżegorodcew, and E. Willim, *A Practical Grammar of English* (Warsaw: Wydawnictwo Naukowe PWN, 1996); Martin Parrott, *Grammar for English Language Teachers* (Cambridge: Cambridge University Press, 2011); Fiona Scott-Barrett, *New Proficiency Use of English* (Harlow: Longman, 2002); Michael Swan, *Practical English Usage* (Oxford: Oxford University Press, 1995); George Yule, *Oxford Practice Grammar* (Oxford: Oxford University Press, 2011).

[2] Cf. Brian Byrne, 'Rules of Prenominal Adjective Order and the Interpretation of "Incompatible" Adjective Pairs', *Journal of Verbal Learning and Verbal Behavior*, 18 (1979), 73–78; J. H. Danks and S. Glucksberg, 'Psychological Scaling of Adjective Orders', *Journal of Verbal Learning & Verbal Behavior*, 1.10 (1971), 63–67; William Frawley, *Linguistic Semantics* (Hillsdale: Lawrence Erlbaum, 1992); Robert Hetzron, 'On the Relative Order of Adjectives', in *Language Universals*, ed. by Hans Sauer (Tubingen: Narr, 1978), pp. 165–84; Hill and others, *Grammar and Practice*; James Martin, 'Semantic Determinants of Preferred Adjective Order', *Journal of Verbal Learning and Verbal Behavior*, 8 (1969), 697–704 and 'Some Competence-Process Relationships in

examples, Hill and others claim that 'usually the more specific the adjective is, the closer it comes to the noun. In other words, the order is often: general adjective – specific adjective – noun'. However, Teschner and Evans suggest that 'the more intrinsic the adjective is to the nature of the noun, the closer it will be to the noun'.[3] Such proposals are discussed by Danks and Glucksberg, who suggest an additional interpretation. They claim that adjectives which are more intrinsic to a modified noun are less likely to discriminate the noun referent from other potential referents. As a consequence, such adjectives tend to appear close to the noun. Conversely, adjectives which are less intrinsic to a modified noun are more suitable for discriminating the noun referent from other referents and this is why they tend to appear further away from the noun. For instance, in the phrase 'a large red car' the word 'red' is closer to the head than 'large' because it may easily be understood without reference to other objects. The notion of COLOUR tends to be more inherent to the noun 'car' then the notion of SIZE because the latter is more relative and a comparison to other cars is necessary for correct interpretation. Therefore, adjectives denoting SIZE are frequently more appropriate for discriminating objects and are placed further away from nouns than adjectives referring to COLOUR. Obviously, this may change in a situation in which one is referring to several large vehicles and wants to discriminate one of them by their colour. In such a case the more appropriate order would be 'a red large car'.[4]

Other explanations involve various systems based on 'zones'.[5] In general, it is claimed that the position of a particular adjective within a noun phrase depends on which 'modification zone' it is placed in. Three of these are usually distinguished. The first one involves specifying adjectives which 'help single out or quantify the referent of the construction in relation to some context'.[6] They tend to have determiner-like properties. An example of a specifying adjective is 'main' in 'his main reason' and 'former' in 'my former colleague'. Such items are placed furthest from the noun, although, obviously, they may be preceded by determiners. The second modification zone, called 'descriptive', encompasses the most central adjectives, that follow all the main criteria for adjectival status (they may occur in both the attributive and predicative position, can serve as conjoints in linked coordination, are gradable, etc.). The investigation discussed in the following sections of this article focuses on two types of adjectives belonging to the 'descriptive zone'. Finally, 'classifying' adjectives 'subcategorise

---

Noun Phrases with Prenominal and Postnominal Adjectives', *Journal of Verbal Learning and Verbal Behavior*, 8 (1969), 471–80; James Martin and T. Ferb, 'Contextual Factors in Preferred Adjective Ordering: A Critique', *American Journal of Psychology*, 88 (1973), 201–15; R. Quirk, S. Greenbaum, G. Leech, and J. Svartvik, *A Comprehensive Grammar of the English Language* (London: Longman, 1985); Meredith Richards, 'The Pragmatic Rule of Adjective Ordering: A Critique', *American Journal of Psychology*, 88 (1975), 201–15; R. Teschner and E. Evans, *Analyzing the Grammar of English* (Washington, D.C.: Georgetown University Press, 2007); Benjamin Whorf, 'Grammatical Categories', *Language*, 21 (1945), 1–11.

[3] Hill and others, p. 192; Teschner and Evans, p. 147.
[4] J. H. Danks and S. Glucksberg, 'Psychological Scaling of Linguistic Properties', *Language and Speech*, 13 (1970), 118–40.
[5] Cf. Carl Bache, *The Order of Premodifying Adjectives in Present-day English* (Odense: Odense University Press, 1978); C. Bache and N. Davidsen-Neilsen, *Mastering English* (Berlin: Mouton de Gruyter, 1997); David Kemmerer, 'Selective Impairment of Knowledge Underlying Prenominal Adjective Order: Evidence for the Autonomy of Grammatical Semantics', *Journal of Neurolinguistics*, 13 (2000), 57–82; D. Kemmerer, C. Weber-Fox, K. Price, C. Zdanczyk, and H. Way, 'Big Brown Dog or Brown Big Dog? An Electrophysiological Study of Semantic Constraints on Prenominal Adjective Order', *Brain and Language*, 100 (2007), 238–56; D. Kemmerer, D. Tranel and C. Zdanczyk, 'Knowledge of the Semantic Constraints on Adjective Order can be Selectively Impaired', *Journal of Neurolinguistics*, 22 (2009), 91–108; Quirk and others.
[6] Bache and Davidsen-Neilsen, p. 458.

the head they modify — e.g. "a medical dictionary" is a special kind of dictionary and "solar energy" is a special kind of energy. Classifying adjectives thus help establish precisely what sort of thing is involved in the expression'.[7]

In addition to the order resulting from the zone a given adjective belongs to, there are also rules that apply within zones. This is particularly noticeable among 'descriptive' adjectives. Still, Kemmerer provides empirical evidence that the level of inter-zone organisation has priority over intra-zone organisation.[8] In his experiment on brain-damaged subjects mistakes were more frequent inside the 'descriptive' zone than between zones. This was also true for normal control subjects and it suggests that the two types of rules are stored in distinct neural networks and inter-zone distinctions are more recognisable than intra-zone distinctions. It is also worth adding that only some semantic features are visible to syntax, as was initially proposed by Pinker in his Grammatically Relevant Semantic Subsystems Hypothesis and later substantiated by Kemmerer in a series of publications through the first decade of this century.[9] For instance, the fact that adjectives denoting age usually precede adjectives referring to colours proves that these semantic categories constrain linear order. On the other hand, the distinction between 'red' and 'green' is invisible to syntax and there are no preferences for one of them to follow the other. It is, therefore, apparent that many semantic differences do not influence linear sequence.

Table 1. Sequential orders proposed in selected publications. '–' separates different slots in the sequence and '/' denotes that no particular order for a given pair or group of adjectives was suggested.

Author(s)	Suggested sequential order of prenominal adjectives
Alexander[10]	opinion – size – age – shape – colour – origin/past participle – noun
Campbell[11]	opinion – shape – age – colour – origin – material
Cinque[12]	quantification – quality – size – shape – colour – nationality

---

[7] Bache and others, p. 458.
[8] Kemmerer, 'Selective Impairment of Knowledge'.
[9] Steven Pinker, *Learnability and Cognition* (Cambridge, MA: MIT Press, 1989); David Kemmerer, 'Grammatically Relevant and Grammatically Irrelevant Features of Verb Meaning can be Independently Impaired', *Aphasiology*, 14 (2000), 997–1020; 'Selective Impairment of Knowledge'; 'Neuropsychological Evidence for the Distinction between Grammatically Relevant and Irrelevant Components of Meaning' (Commentary on R. Jackendoff 'Precis of Foundations of Language"), *Behavioral and Brain Sciences*, 26 (2003), 684–85; 'Why Can you Hit Someone on the Arm but not Break Someone on the Arm? A Neuropsychological Investigation of the English Body-Part Possessor Ascension Construction', *Journal of Neurolinguistics*, 16 (2003), 13–36; 'Action Verbs, Argument Structure Constructions, and the Mirror Neuron System', in *From Action to Language via the Mirror Neuron System*, ed. by Michael Arbib (Cambridge: Cambridge University Press, 2006), pp. 347–73; D. Kemmerer and S. K. Wright, 'Selective Impairment of Knowledge Underlying Un-prefixation: Further Evidence for the Autonomy of Grammatical Semantics', *Journal of Neurolinguistics*, 15 (2002), 403–32; Kemmerer and others, 'Big Brown Dog or Brown Big Dog?'; Kemmerer and others, 'Knowledge of the Semantic Constraints on Adjective Order'.
[10] *Longman English Grammar Practice*.
[11] Doug Campbell, *Professor Grammar's Rule Book* ([London]: BBC, 1991)
[12] Guglielmo Cinque, 'On the Evidence for Partial N-movement in the Romance DP', in *Paths towards Universal*

Author(s)	Suggested sequential order of prenominal adjectives
Hare and Wayne[13]	size – colour – material
Dixon[14]	value – dimension – physical property – speed – human propensity – age – colour
Evans[15]	opinion – size/weight – age – shape – colour/temperature – participle – origin/nationality – material
Evans[16]	opinion – size – age – shape – colour – origin – material – used for/be about (purpose)
Hewings[17]	gradable – ungradable opinion – size/physical quality/shape/age – colour – participle – origin – material – type – purpose
Hill and others[18]	general adjective – specific adjective
Hopkins and Hopkins[19]	describers – classifiers describers: opinion – size – age – shape – colour classifiers: nationality – material – type
Kemmerer and others[20]	value – size – dimension – various physical properties – colour
Kingsbury and Wellman[21]	subjective comment – size – age – shape – colour – nationality/origin – material
Lockhart and Martin[22]	high-ranking (less definite meaning) – low-ranking (more definite meaning)
Mańczak-Wohlfeld and others[23]	opinion – size – shape – age – colour – origin – substance – gerund
Parrott[24]	size – shape – colour – origin – material – use
Scheffehn[25]	size – colour – material (although 'colour – size – material' also encountered)

Grammar: Studies in Honor of Richard S. Kayne, ed. by G. Cinque and others (Washington, DC: Georgetown University Press, 1994), pp. 85–110.

[13] V. C. Hare and O. Wayne, 'Development of Preferred Adjective Ordering in Children, Grades One to Five', *The Journal of Educational Research*, 71.4 (1978), 190–93.
[14] Robert Dixon, *Where Have All the Adjectives Gone?* (Berlin: Mouton de Gruyter, 1982).
[15] *CPE Use of English*.
[16] *FCE Use of English*.
[17] *Advanced Grammar in Use*.
[18] *Grammar and Practice*.
[19] *Developing Grammar in Context*.
[20] 'Big Brown Dog or Brown Big Dog?' and 'Knowledge of the Semantic Constraints'.
[21] *Longman Advanced English*.
[22] R. Lockhart and J. Martin, 'Adjective Order and the Recall of Adjective-Noun Triples', *Journal of Verbal Learning and Verbal Behavior*, 8 (1969), 272–75.
[23] *A Practical Grammar of English*.
[24] *Grammar for English Language Teachers*.
[25] Margaret Scheffelin, 'Children's Understanding on Constraints upon Adjective Order', *Journal of Learning Disabilities*, 4 (1971), 34–42.

Author(s)	Suggested sequential order of prenominal adjectives
Scott[26]	comment – size – length – height – speed –width – weight – temperature – age – shape – colour – nationality/origin – material
Scott-Barrett[27]	judgement – dimensions – colour – origin – material
Swan	age/shape/size/temperature – colour – origin – material – purpose
Yule[28]	describing – classifying describing: opinion – size – physical quality – age/time – shape – colour classifying: location – origin/source – material – type – purpose

2 Aims of the project

Among the linear orders summarised in Table 1 one may find various discrepancies. Firstly, different authors use different semantic categories. Secondly, there are instances in which the semantic categories are the same but labelled differently. Moreover, in some cases the patterns do not specify the preferred order for a given category, while in others such an order is explicitly proposed. Additionally, there are also instances in which selected semantic categories are placed in different slots in the sequential order. Of particular interest to the present study is the case of adjectives referring to the notions of AGE and SHAPE. Authors such as Alexander, Evans, Hopkins and Hopkins, Kingsbury and Wellman, Scott, and Yule suggest that the preferred order is AGE – SHAPE, while Campbell and Mańczak-Wohlfeld and others propose that the sequence SHAPE – AGE is more natural. Because of such discrepancies the initial aim of the research described in the following sections of this article is to establish the actual linear sequence of the adjectives denoting AGE and SHAPE in contemporary English. The second and primary aim of this publication concentrates on a more general problem: if both of the proposed orders appear in contemporary English (which is suggested by the results of the first part of the research described below), it may indicate a diachronic change. Therefore, it is necessary also to investigate possible trends in the historical development of the two adjective orders. Any consistent patterns observed in such a diachronic investigation may contribute to our understanding of the way languages change over time.

3 Methods

In order to accomplish the aims of this project, the preferred order of adjective types under discussion must be tested in a large corpus of English which allows diachronic analysis. One

---

[26] Gary-John Scott, 'Stacked Adjectival Modification and the Structure of Nominal Phrases', in *Functional Structure in DP and IP*, ed. by Cinque Guglielmo (New York: Oxford University Press, 2002), pp. 91–120.
[27] *New Proficiency Use of Enlish*.
[28] *Oxford Practice Grammar*.
[29] Mark Davies, *The Corpus of Historical American English: 400 Million Words, 1810–2009* (2010–),

possibility would be to use *COHA* (*The Corpus of Historical American English*).[29] It is based on 400 million words from 1810 to 2009. Even though the corpus seems large, however, pilot studies revealed that it is still too small of statistically sound evaluation of both the synchronic distribution and the historical development of the two orders of adjectives. Therefore, the American version of the *Google Books Corpus*, based on the *Google Books Ngram Corpus*, was chosen instead.[30]

The first edition of the *Google Books Ngram Corpus* has been available online since 2010.[31] The first suggested application was the study of culture and several papers investigating such aspects with the use of *Google Books Ngrams* have recently been published.[32] J. B. Michel and others have also given examples of the ways in which the corpus may be utilised in lexicography and in the analysis of the evolution of grammar.[33] Since their publication, numerous studies focusing on the use of *Google Books Ngrams* for linguistic purposes have been conducted. This includes disciplines such as syntax,[34] semantics,[35] and psycholinguistics.[36] Moreover, the Ngrams have been used in several studies on the diachronic development of English. For instance, Demetris Koutsoyiannis analysed the historical development of several expressions with the word 'change',[37] while R. Mihalcea and C. Nastase have conducted a diachronic study of 200 words chosen to represent the four basic parts of speech: nouns, verbs, adjectives and adverbs.[38] Furthermore, K. Gulordava and M. Baroni proposed an automatic detection system for semantic change.[39] They applied the

---

http://corpus.byu.edu/coha/ [accessed 15 July 2013].

[30] Mark Davies, *Google Books Corpus, Based on Google Books N-grams* (2011–), http://googlebooks.byu.edu [accessed 15 July 2013].

[31] It structure and basic use is described by J. B. Michel and others, 'Quantitative Analysis of Culture Using Millions of Digitized Books', *Science*, 331 [6014] (2011), 176–82.

[32] Patrick Juola, 'Using the Google N-Gram Corpus to Measure Cultural Complexity', *Literary and Linguistic Computing*, 28 (2013), 668–75; Martin Ravallion, 'The Two Poverty Enlightenments', *The World Bank Policy Research Working Paper*, 5549 (2011); D. S. Soper and O. Turel, 'An N-gram Analysis of Communications 2000–2010', *Communications of the ACM*, 55.5 (2012), 81–87.

[33] 'Quantitative Analysis of Culture'.

[34] Y. Goldberg and J. Orwant, 'A Dataset of Syntactic-Ngrams over Time from a Very Large Corpus of English Books', in *Proceedings of the Second Joint Conference on Lexical and Computational Semantics*, 2 vols (Stroudsberg, PA: Association for Computational Linguistics, 2013), I 241–47.

[35] K. Gulordava and M. Baroni, 'A Distributional Similarity Approach to the Detection of Semantic Change in the Google Books Ngram Corpus', in *Proceedings of the GEMS 2011 Workshop on Geometrical Models of Natural Language Semantics* (Stroudsburg, PA: Association for Computational Linguistics, 2011), pp. 67–71; C. Joubarne and D. Inkpen, 'Comparison of Semantic Similarity for Different Languages Using the Google N-gram Corpus and Second-Order Co-occurrence Measures', in *Proceedings of the 24th Canadian Conference on Advances in Artificial Intelligence* (Berlin: Springer, 2011), pp. 216–21; A. Islam, E. Milios and V. Kešelj, 'Comparing Word Relatedness Measures Based on Google N-grams', in *Proceedings of COLING 2012 International Conference on Computational Linguistics: Posters* (Mumbai: The COLING 2012 Organizing Committee, 2012), pp. 495–506; H. Agt and R. D. Kutsche, 'Automated Construction of a Large Semantic Network of Related Terms for Domain-Specific Modeling', in *Advanced Information Systems Engineering* (Berlin: Springer, 2013), pp. 610–25.

[36] M. Brysbaert, E. Keuleers and B. New, 'Assessing the Usefulness of Google Books' Word Frequencies for Psycholinguistic Research on Word Processing', *Frontiers in Psychology*, 2 (2011), https://doi.org/10.3389/fpsyg.2011.00027; E. Keuleers, M. Brysbaert and B. New, 'An Evaluation of the Google Books Ngrams for Psycholinguistic Research', *Lexical Resources in Psycholinguistic Research*, 3 (2011), 23–26.

[37] Demetris Koutsoyiannis, 'Hydrology and Change', *Hydrological Sciences Journal*, 58 (2013), 1177–97.

[38] R. Mihalcea and V. Nastase, 'Word Epoch Disambiguation: Finding How Words Change over Time', in *Proceedings of the 50th Annual Meeting of the Association for Computational Linguistics*, 2 vols (Stroudsberg, PA: Association for Computational Linguistics, 2012), II 259–63.

[39] 'A Distributional Similarity Approach'.

distributional semantics model suggested by P. D. Turney and P. Pantel and used the portion of the corpus that includes American English 2-grams.[40]

Since its initial launch in 2010, *Google Books Ngrams* have undergone numerous changes. Y. Lin and others describe an improved edition of the corpus which is larger and includes tagging of basic parts of speech as well as syntactic annotations.[41] The Ngrams have also been integrated into the interface created by Mark Davies.[42] This version of the corpus, which in this paper is referred to as the *Google Books Corpus*, makes it possible to search the data in a more flexible manner because it uses the same advanced part-of-speech tagging system as Davies's aforementioned *Corpus of Historical American English* and his *Corpus of Contemporary American English*.[43]

The investigation described in Section 4 was conducted on the *Google Books Corpus*, but it must be stressed that even the advanced interface created by Mark Davies does not include semantic annotation, so it was not possible, for example, to search for 'any adjective' referring to AGE followed by 'any adjective' denoting SHAPE. Instead, selected pairs of adjectives needed to be typed in manually. As a consequence, a list of such possible pairs was compiled. It included five adjectives denoting AGE (or TIME — the distinction between these two semantic categories is not made in the literature): 'new', 'ancient', 'modern', 'current' and 'contemporary'. Many other adjectives were rejected for various reasons. Some of them were likely to have two (or more) very dissimilar meanings, as in the case of the word 'old', which basically refers to any entity which has existed for many years, but may also be used in expressions such as 'an old friend' with the meaning 'very familiar'. Another problem concerned the fact that many adjectives referring to AGE (or TIME) are also used as other parts of speech. For instance, 'present' is an adjective in 'a present moment', a noun in 'a birthday present' or a verb in 'to present the results'. Such problems could theoretically be solved by a detailed qualitative analysis of individual examples, in which case adjectives such as 'old' or 'present' could still be included in the investigation. However, for technical reasons, such a solution proved impossible. The *Google Books Corpus* is based on only a part of the *Google Books* depository; the latter is constantly changing and new items are being continually added to it. This means that any query run from the *Google Books Corpus* search engine will give a potentially smaller number of tokens than the ones found in the current *Google Books* depository. As a result, individual examples of combinations of adjectives such as 'old' and 'present' with other adjectives found in the *Google Books Corpus* cannot be effectively evaluated qualitatively. There is also a mismatch between the results obtained in the *Google Books Corpus* and the *Google Books* site resulting from the fact that the former uses only one set of data (American English in our case), while the latter provides extracts from all available books it has access to. As a consequence of all these inconsistencies, a systematic, qualitative analysis was unfeasible and the final decision was made to choose only the adjectives which referred to the notion of AGE in the least ambiguous way. Still, it must be stressed that even a very careful selection of examples does not guarantee the appropriateness of the tokens found

---

[40] P. D. Turney and P. Pantel, 'From Frequency to Meaning: Vector Space Models of Semantics', *Journal of Artificial Intelligence Research*, 37 (2010), 141–88.

[41] Y. Lin and others, 'Syntactic Annotations for the Google Books Ngram Corpus' in *Proceedings of the ACL 2012 System Demonstrations* (Stroudsberg, PA: Association for Computational Linguistics, 2012), pp. 169–74.

[42] *Google Books Corpus*.

[43] Mark Davies, *The Corpus of Contemporary American English: 520 Million words, 1990–present* (2008–), available online at http://corpus.byu.edu/coca/ [accessed 15 July 2013].

in the corpus. Other unpredictable factors may influence the results. For example, it is difficult to decide whether the adjective 'modern' could not in some cases be interpreted as evaluative, since in some contexts 'modernity' is regarded as something positive in contrast to anything which is 'old-fashioned'. For such reasons, a potential degree of error of the results must be presumed.

As far as the semantic category of SHAPE is concerned, some examples were excluded from the analysis for reasons similar to those described in the previous paragraph (e.g. the words 'square' and 'oblong' may function as nouns as well as adjectives), and, eventually, the following seven were chosen: 'rectangular', '*x*-shaped', 'jagged', 'triangular', 'curved', 'conical' and 'spherical'. According to the online search engine *wordandphrase.info*, which provides information on the relative frequencies of words in English based on data from the *Corpus of Contemporary American English*, these were the most frequent adjectives from among the possible candidates.[44] Other possible adjectives, such as 'ovate', were too rare for the purposes of the current project.

All of the selected adjectives denoting AGE were juxtaposed with all of the adjectives referring to SHAPE in both of the tested word orders, resulting in 70 searches (35 for each order). Nevertheless, only some of the combinations used in the investigation were actually present in the corpus (see Section 4).

The combinations were typed in the main search box of the corpus as pairs of words without any additional annotation. The only exception was the group of adjectives of the '*x*-shaped' type which involve any lexical element preceding 'shaped' (e.g. 'heart-shaped', 'diamond-shaped', etc.). In order to obtain all possible combinations of the AGE adjectives with such compounds, the symbol used in the investigation was '*-shaped', which is interpreted by the corpus search engine as 'any word' before '-shaped'.

Finally, it should be pointed out that for the purposes of calculating the percentages from the empirical part of the paper, the corpus samples were divided by 2. For instance, for the most recent decade in the American version of the Google Books Corpus, which was used in Section 4.1, the percentages were calculated out of 13441150000, rather than 26882300000 tokens. This solution does not change the relative differences between individual results, but it provides a more realistic picture of frequencies, since the items under analysis are pairs of words, not single words.

4 Results and Discussion

4.1 Synchronic analysis

As stated in Section 2, before conducting a diachronic investigation on the development of the two adjective orders under discussion, an analysis of the synchronic distribution of the two proposals in contemporary English was performed. The results of this brief investigation are shown in Table 2.

It is immediately visible that the order AGE – SHAPE is more frequent than SHAPE – AGE. While the former was found in as many as 12 out of the 70 different combinations investigated, the latter was encountered in only 1 combination. Moreover, 437 tokens exhibited the prevailing order, which is almost 100 times more frequent than the 5 cases

---

[44] http://www.wordandphrase.info/frequencyList.asp.

Order AGE – SHAPE		Order SHAPE – AGE	
new rectangular	120	rectangular new	5
new {x}-shaped	14		
new triangular	103		
new curved	93		
new conical	19		
new spherical	26		
ancient rectangular	11		
ancient triangular	6		
modern rectangular	11		
modern curved	15		
modern conical	5		
current rectangular	11		
sum	437	sum	5

Table 2. The two adjective orders in contemporary American English

of the SHAPE – AGE pattern. In terms of percentages, the two results may be expressed as 0.000003258649744% and 0.000000037199198%, respectively. The 95% confidence interval for the difference between them is 0.000003221450546% ± 0.000000306917394%, and the p-value for this difference is smaller than 0.0001. Therefore, the predominance of the AGE – SHAPE adjective order in contemporary American English is beyond any doubt.

It is worth noting at this point that the number of tokens for examples with 'new' is relatively higher than for other combinations encountered in the *Google Books Corpus* and constitutes around 80% of all the tokens listed in Table 2. One possible explanation for such a popularity of combinations with 'new' is that the adjective is generally very common in English. The list of the top 5000 words available at *wordfrequency.info*, which is based on the *Corpus of Contemporary American English*, indicates that 'new' is the second most frequent adjective after 'other'.

It must be added that the small number of SHAPE – AGE tokens does not necessarily mean that they are that infrequent on the *Google Books* site. One of the restrictions imposed on *the Google Books Corpus* is that it is based on the n-grams which occur at least 40 times or more. They are, in fact, the same n-grams which are available on the *Google Books N-gram Viewer*. Any number of tokens below this threshold is not displayed in the *Google Books Corpus* (the result for 'rectangular new' was 5, but it was established on the basis of all the examples for the last two centuries, and their total number exceeded 40), which may cause bias in the results, especially as regards pairs that represent rare phenomena in the English language. Consequently, the order SHAPE – AGE may be used more often in contemporary English than the data in Table 2 suggest.

4.2 Diachronic analysis

Table 3 summarises the raw occurrences of the two adjective orders in the American portion of the *Google Books Corpus* over the last two hundred years. As in the synchronic analysis discussed in Section 4.1, the pattern SHAPE – AGE was found only for the example 'rectangular

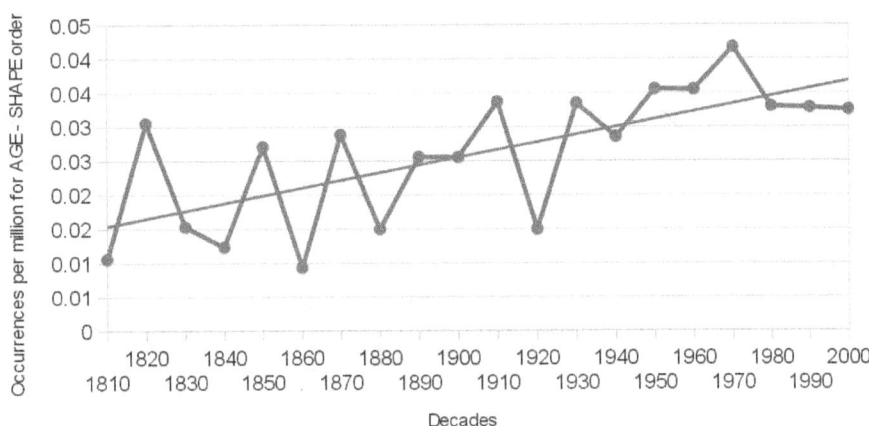

Figure 1. Normalised frequencies of the pairs of adjectives following the order AGE – SHAPE. The slanting line in the middle represents linear regression.

new'. None of the other pairs was encountered in this order, but, similarly to the problem encountered in the previous section, some of the tokens were inevitably missed due to the threshold limitation of 40 tokens. Nevertheless, the preference for the order of AGE – SHAPE is beyond any reasonable doubt.

Among the pairs of adjectives representing the AGE – SHAPE pattern, combinations involving 'new' were the most frequent. Out of the 9 different combinations, as many as 7 contained this adjective. This distribution is the result of the general high frequency of the adjective "new" mentioned in the previous section.

The data in Table 3 present raw frequency counts and they must be normalised before any valid conclusions may be drawn. This has been done in Figure 1, which summarises the relative occurrences of the pairs of adjectives representing the AGE – SHAPE pattern in the decades from 1810 to 2000. Although the line showing the frequency of use of this adjective order meanders, the graph suggests an overall upward trend. This may be tested statistically in at least two different ways. Firstly, it is possible to calculate the percentages of occurrence for all the tokens for the nineteenth century (0.00000207985395%, or 0.0207985395 per million) and the tokens for the twentieth century (0.00000335089772%, or 0.0335089772 per million). It is plainly visible that the AGE – SHAPE adjective order was less common in the former than in the latter. The 95% confidence interval for this difference is 0.00000127104377% ± 0.00000007563067995%, and the p-value is lower than 0.0001, which leaves no doubt as to the statistical significance of the difference between the two results. The AGE – SHAPE pattern was less popular in the nineteenth century than in the twentieth. Secondly, the chi-squared test for trend in proportions also indicates that there is a statistically relevant change: the obtained p-value is smaller than 0.0001.

Due to the limited number of examples, the opposite tendency for the SHAPE – AGE order is more difficult to ascertain. While the distribution of the 42 examples of 'rectangular new'

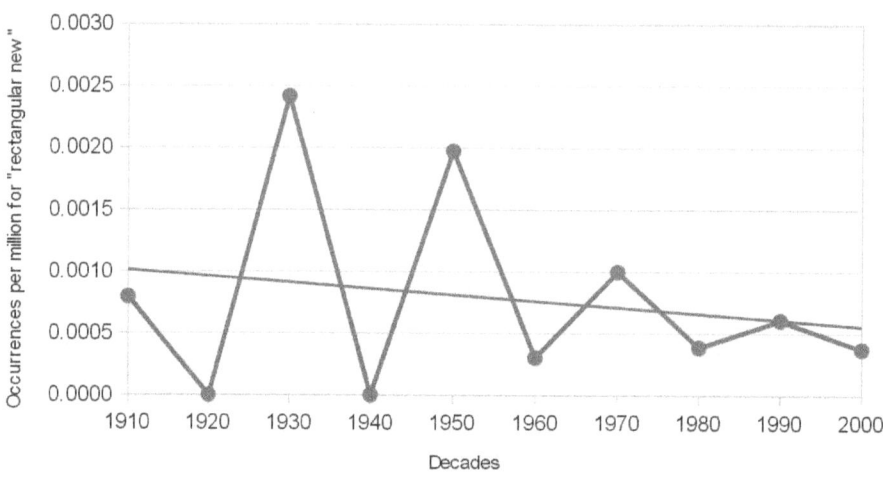

Figure 2. Normalised frequencies of 'rectangular new'. The slanting line in the middle represents linear regression.

in the twentieth century indicate a downward trend (see Figure 2), the chi-squared test for trend in proportions does not yield a statistically significant result in this case (p = 0.1145). The limitation of 40 tokens imposed on *the Google Books Corpus* resulted in a small number of examples of the SHAPE – AGE pattern and the diachronic development of this word order could not be adequately investigated.

On balance, the results of the present investigation confirm an increase in the use of the AGE – SHAPE adjective pattern over the last two centuries. It must be emphasised, though, that this claim does not imply that the pairs of adjectives of the AGE – SHAPE type are becoming more popular in absolute terms. Even though the opposite trend to use the SHAPE – AGE order less frequently could not be proven statistically, the assumption that it is happening is more reasonable than concluding that American writers have been mentioning more and more objects which are, for instance, new and triangular. This would suggest that there are proportionally more new triangular objects in existence now than a hundred years ago, or that such objects are noticed more often. With the methodology applied in the present study, this interpretation is theoretically also possible and cannot be completely excluded; however, Figures 3 and 4 provide additional evidence against such an explanation. Figure 3 presents the diachronic development of nine pairs of adjectives of the AGE – SHAPE type. All of them reveal an upward trend, although it is easily noticeable only for 'new rectangular', 'new triangular' and 'new curved'. The results of the chi-squared test for trend in proportions confirm these observations. The p-values for all nine cases are below 0.0001. The pair 'new conical' is not included in Figure 3 because its diachronic development does not follow any consistent pattern, but the three remaining pairs shown in Figure 4 seem to exhibit a downward trend. It is especially evident in the case of the pair 'new spherical'. The chi-squared test for trend in proportions confirms this observation (p < 0.0001), but in the other two examples, the weak

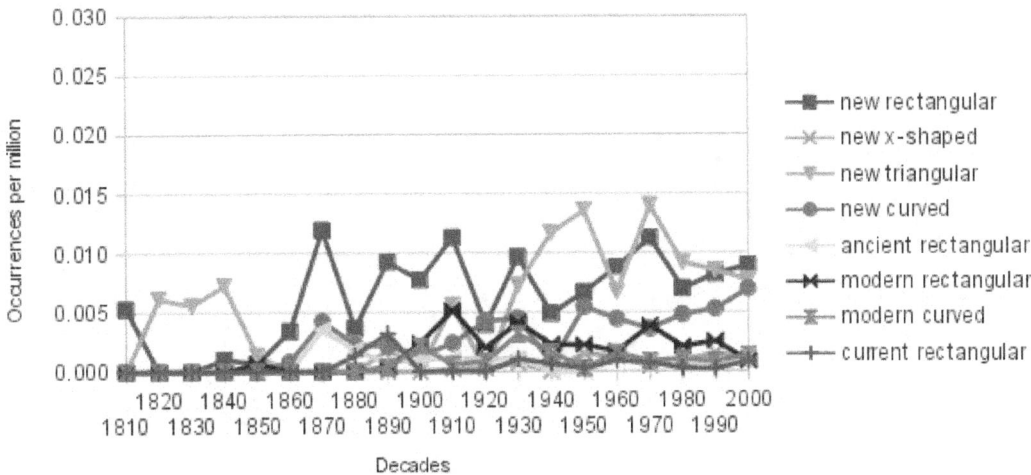

Figure 3. Normalised frequencies of individual adjective pairs exhibiting an upward trend.

negative trend cannot be statistically validated. The p-values for both 'ancient triangular' and 'modern conical' are clearly above the alpha level of 0.05 (0.1067 and 0.2903, respectively). This leads to the conclusion that the general tendency to use the AGE – SHAPE pattern applies to the majority of the adjective pairs investigated in the current study and not just selected examples. The alternative 'absolute interpretation', according to which there are more objects with the qualities indicated by the adjective pairs in existence now than a hundred years ago, would have to assume an increase in the number of objects which are 'new rectangular', 'new x-shaped', 'new triangular', 'new curved', 'new oblong', 'ancient rectangular', 'modern rectangular', 'modern curved' and 'current rectangular', and explain why only the objects which are 'new spherical' have decreased in popularity. The ultimate interpretation proposed in this paper is, therefore, less controversial. It is more reasonable to assume that we are dealing with a change in the order of adjectives rather than an increase in frequencies of individual word pairs.

Conclusion

The present study has found that the adjective order AGE – SHAPE is prevalent in contemporary American English. This agrees with most of the proposals put forward by the authors discussed in Section 2. The only exceptions were the suggestions expressed by Campbell and Mańczak-Wohlfeld and others,[45] according to whom the preferred order should be SHAPE – AGE. The question which arises is why these two authors' position was different from those expressed in other publications. Firstly, it must be stressed that the SHAPE – AGE order is also found in contemporary English. The claim that it should be used is, therefore, not entirely

---

[45] Campbell, *Professor Grammar's Rule Book*; Mańczak-Wohlfeld and others, *A Practical Grammar of English*.

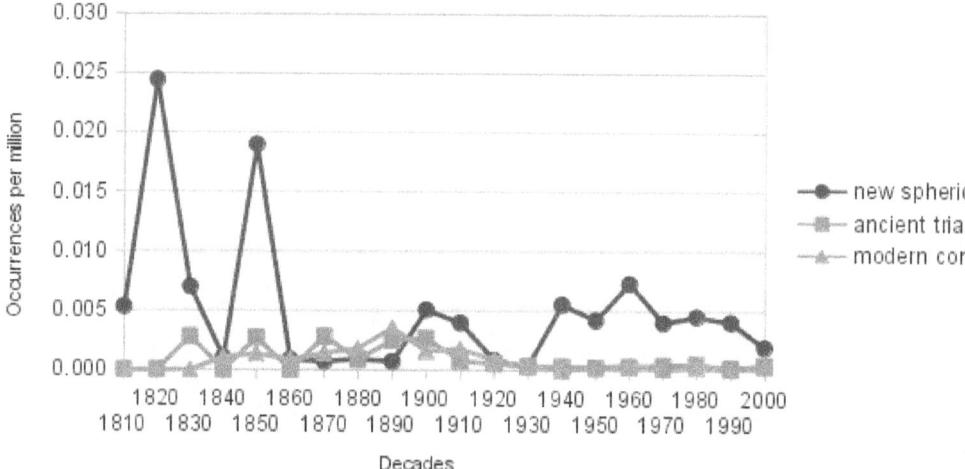

Figure 4. Normalised frequencies of individual adjective pairs exhibiting a downward trend.

unsubstantiated. The problem is that this pattern is clearly less popular than AGE – SHAPE and advising use of the opposite is, ultimately, wrong. A possible reason for such a mistake could be the fact that both Campbell and Mańczak-Wohlfeld and others did not rely on empirical data. At the time of their publications, the use of electronic corpora was severely limited and the corpora which were available were significantly smaller than the ones used in this project. Therefore, claims made at the time about a given grammatical rule tended to rely on author's intuition. Thus, these results also point to the superiority of empirical methods over introspection.

It has also been shown that the AGE – SHAPE pattern has increased in popularity over the nineteenth and twentieth centuries. Such an observation enhances our understanding of language change. The preferred orders of adjectives in the attributive position may alter in time just as is the case with many other aspects of human communication. While some facets of the phenomenon under discussion tend to be universal across languages (cf. Svenonius 2008), others may be more language specific and change in the course of diachronic development.

The reverse order SHAPE - AGE was only observed a few times. As a result, its historical decline was impossible to prove statistically with the methodology applied above, but the additional aspects discussed in Section 4.2 support such an interpretation.

One of the possible aims for the future is to investigate this issue with the use of methods which would not be hampered by the restrictions described in Section 4.1. Such a solution requires new advances in corpus linguistics resources. Furthermore, it would be interesting to study the diachronic development of selected adjective orders in dialects of English other than American. This could be partially accomplished with the use of some currently available corpora, but, again, in order to obtain statistically reliable results on both adjective orders under discussion, larger corpora are required.

Table 3. Raw frequencies of the pairs of adjectives under analysis in the *Google Books Corpus*

AGE – SHAPE	Total	1810	1820	1830	1840	1850	1860	1870	1880	1890	1900	1910	1920	1930	1940	1950	1960	1970	1980	1990	2000
new rectangular	620	1			1	1	4	17	8	26	29	57	14	28	15	27	58	79	54	81	120
new X-shaped	57		2	4	7	2						1	1	2		6	8	3	7	15	14
new triangular	561									5	1	28		21	36	55	44	98	71	84	103
new curved	323						1	6	5	6	5	12	15	13	2	22	29	25	37	52	93
new oblong	59									3	1		5	1	6	2	7	2	9	22	1
new conical	104		8	5		2	4	6	5	3	5	5	1	3	3	4	7	12	16	7	19
new spherical	303	1			1	28	1	1	2	2	19	20	3	1	17	17	48	28	35	40	26
ancient rectangular	63							5	4	2	4	5	4	3		1	8	5	4	8	11
ancient triangular	55			2		4		4	2	7	10	4	2	1	1		2	3	4	2	6
modern rectangular	162					1				1	9	26	7	12	7	9	11	27	16	25	11
modern curved	80									1	8	3	3	9	5	1	10	6	8	8	18
modern conical	52				1	2	1	2	4	10	6	9	3	1		1	3	1	2	1	5
current rectangular	44								3	9				3	2	1	6	5	2	2	11
SHAPE – AGE																					
rectangular new	42											4		7		8	2	7	3	6	5

Honour, Humour, and Women in the Romance of *Yder*

Jane Bliss[1]

Introduction

This article examines the Arthurian *Romanz du reis Yder*, to shed light upon an apparently misogynistic passage: the hero kicks a lady who is trying to seduce him.[2] It contextualises the incident with an examination of humour in the romance and examples from other texts which could be considered comparable. In order to examine the role of this lady, it sketches that of every woman in the story to show how each is important to the plot, developing a more general understanding of attitudes to women in the romance. The lady's actions, which facilitate a key plot development at the beginning of the romance, are seen as dishonourable and therefore comic by the other characters. This could modify any suspicion that the poet's view is anti-feminist *per se*, because the theme of honour and dishonour is central to the whole romance. The analysis of the text's humour presented here aims at an understanding, and enjoyment, of how humour is used in *Yder*, providing an aid to interpreting a rather disturbing passage. As far as I can discover, nobody has looked at the treatment of Ivenant's wife in *Yder* by comparing it with the treatment of women in the anti-feminist fabliaux. This comparison, together with discussion of the attempted seduction of Sir Gawain in *Sir Gawain and the Green Knight* and a look at another English 'anti-feminist' Gawain romance, concludes the article.

Yder and its context.

Little work has been devoted to *Yder*, and as far as I can discover, nobody has looked at humour or antifeminism in *Yder* at all, let alone studied this episode of kicking the lady in any

---

[1] Thanks are due to members of the Oxford Anglo-Norman Reading Group, whose discussions of *Yder* fostered my interest in this romance. Further thanks are due to colleagues whose sensitive reading has helped the shaping of this article.

[2] Citations in this article are from *The Romance of Yder*, ed. and trans. by Alison Adams (Cambridge: Brewer, 1983), with any alternative readings from *Le Romanz du reis Yder*, ed. and trans. by Jacques Ch. Lemaire (Brussels: Editions Modulaires Européennes, 2010) in brackets or added in my text. Lemaire's edition is more recent, and has been considered better than Adams's (see for example Keith Busby, review of *Le Roman du reis Yder*, ed. by Jacques C. Lemaire, *The Modern Language Review*, 107 (2012), 1250–51). But Adams is easier to use for English readers because Lemaire's translation and notes are in modern French. Every citation has been checked against both versions.

detail. The romance was omitted from Dean's *Anglo-Norman Literature*,[3] but may arguably be considered Anglo-Norman. Dean's criteria for selecting works for inclusion were to do with the provenance of manuscripts and the subject-matter of the texts. The single copy of *Yder* is insular, and the story takes place in Britain rather than in Continental France; therefore it could reasonably have been included.[4] The manuscript, Cambridge CUL Ee. 4. 26, is believed to be Anglo-Norman and from the second half of the thirteenth century;[5] as noted above, it lacks the beginning of the story. The romance may have originated in the western part of mainland France, around the end of the twelfth century or the beginning of the thirteenth. Recurrent dialect features identify the scribe's dialect as Anglo-Norman. We lack the first part of the romance, the single manuscript copy being acephalous. Although the events therein can be deduced from the following narrative, we can only guess at the writer's style in the missing part or what narratorial comments might have been included.

The hero Yder appears here and there across medieval literature, from William of Malmesbury to *Claris et Laris*.[6] But studies of *Yder* are few, compared to many other romances. The International Arthurian Society's *Bibliographical Bulletin* shows a currently low level of interest. The entry for Yder in the *Dictionary of Medieval Heroes* says that although he is the leading character in one romance his fame was too small to inspire later writers or visual artists; it lists only three studies.[7] Further investigation has turned up only a short piece on 'Geography in *Yder*' by A. H. W. Smith.[8]

In spite of *Yder*'s comparative obscurity, reviews of Adams's edition and translation were broadly welcoming when it appeared. Tony Hunt calls it a careful and useful edition of a 'delightful text'.[9] Gilles Roques remarks that the introduction of this 'elegant volume' insists on 'l'humour contenu dans quelques passages'.[10] A. J. Holden confesses a liking for this unusual and interesting romance, remarking on its 'tendances satiriques et sarcastiques'.[11]

There has, however, been some debate about the date and place of *Yder*'s composition. Beate Schmolke-Hasselmann argues that, because the figure of Arthur is shown to be weak and unsympathetic, the romance must have been written during the reign of the unpopular King John; and she says the writer's anti-clerical views are evidence that it was written at the abbey of Glastonbury.[12] This account has been found unconvincing. Holden considers that the efforts made to attach the romance to particular historical circumstances are 'parfaitement gratuites'.[13] Both M. Jacques Charles Lemaire, *Yder*'s most recent editor, and Linda Gowans

---

[3] Ruth Dean, with Maureen Boulton, Anglo-Norman Text Society, o. p. 3 (London: Anglo-Norman Text Society, 1999).
[4] See below, and Tony Hunt's review of Dean in *Medium Ævum*, 70 (2001), 340–43.
[5] The following notes in this paragraph are from Adams's introduction (pp. 1–7).
[6] See Lemaire, pp. 7–8.
[7] Willem P. Gerritsen and Anthony G. van Melle, *A Dictionary of Medieval Heroes: Characters in Medieval Narrative Traditions and their Afterlife in Literature, Theatre, and the Visual Arts*, trans. by Tanis Guest, repr. (Woodbridge: Boydell, 2000 [first publ. 1998]); the entry for *Yder* is pp. 299–302.
[8] *Ceridwen's Cauldron* (Michaelmas 2000 to Hilary 2001), 12–15.
[9] Tony Hunt, review of *Chrétien de Troyes and the Troubadours: Essays in Memory of the Late Leslie Topsfield*, ed. by Peter S. Noble and Linda M. Paterson, *The Modern Language Review*, 80 (1985), 932–33, judges there is no firm philological evidence for Schmolke-Hasselmann's thesis (see below).
[10] Review of *The Romance of Yder*, ed. and trans. by Alison Adams, *Zeitschrift für romanische Philologie*, 100 (1984), 712–13.
[11] Review of *The Romance of Yder*, ed. and trans. by Alison Adams, *Romania*, 107 (1986), 130–35 (p. 130).
[12] Schmolke-Hasselmann, 'King Arthur as Villain in the Thirteenth-century Romance *Yder*', *Reading Medieval Studies*, 6 (1980), 31–43.
[13] Holden, p. 130. He is referring to Schmolke-Hasselmann's arguments about the romance's date and place of

have expressed their reservations about Schmolke-Hasselmann's conclusions.[14] Evidence to question Schmolke-Hasselmann's arguments further is set out here and in the pages below. My purpose in challenging her argument is not to offer alternative opinions about the romance's provenance, but to demonstrate that her arguments have distracted readers' attention from what two important themes of the romance are really intended to achieve: the anti-monastic satire is part of the poet's comic purpose throughout, and the portrait of an unsatisfactory king is part of the poet's overall critique of dishonourable behaviour.

Satire, directed at the pursuit of wealth and the worldly life, is identified by Adams in two passages: general satire at 1678–745, and of monks specifically at 3681–717. Although anti-clerical satire is one of the humorous elements of the romance, and therefore of interest to my argument, it is no indication of the romance's source. Satire on monastic life is a medieval commonplace, therefore it is hardly likely to help us locate the composition of the romance.[15] The setting is England, and one of Dean's criteria for including texts in the Anglo-Norman canon is that their matter should be insular. However, as Smith points out, an abbey, identified as Glastonbury by scholars, is shown in the romance to be a house of entirely benevolent nuns; this weakens Schmolke-Hasselmann's argument that it must have been written at Glastonbury or that it satirizes the monks there.[16]

Schmolke-Hasselmann also argues that the despicable Arthur is modelled on King John, thus aiming to date the romance rather precisely. Arthur's behaviour is directly responsible for the main thrust of the romance's plot: he is the most important of the characters who behave dishonourably, even though he is not mocked as the seductive lady is. It must be stressed, however, that the theme of a king behaving badly is not unusual in romance. In *Four Sonnes of Aymon*, Charlemagne behaves atrociously because of the needs of the plot.[17] In the *lai* of *Lanval* the king is 'inadequate'; Lemaire notes other negative characterizations of Arthur, and of Charlemagne, and is not convinced by Schmolke-Hasselmann's arguments.[18] A recent article by Elizabeth Archibald, on the *Historia Meriadoci*, discusses the topos of Arthur as an unsatisfactory king, but does not insist that the romance must therefore have been written in the time of King John.[19] Rather, she suggests that it may be reflecting Welsh traditions in which Arthur is not always an idealized king. This could equally be true of *Yder*, so other factors (than an unsatisfactory king) must be sought if one wished to research *Yder*'s sources. Meanwhile, for the figure of King John as model for an unsatisfactory Arthur, Lemaire points out that his groundless jealousy in *Yder* hardly matches what is known about the real monarch John. Arthur is forgetful (John may have been so), and murderously jealous (not something

---

composition. If it was written in Western France, as suggested by Adams (see p. 17, above), one does ask oneself whether King John was as unpopular there as he is supposed to have been in England.

[14] M. Jacques Charles Lemaire, 'Originalités thématiques et textuelles du *Romanz du reis Yder* (circa 1210): Communication de M. Jacques Charles Lemaire à la séance mensuelle du 12 décembre 2009', *Le Bulletin de l'Académie royale de langue et de littérature françaises de Belgique*, 87 (2009), 195–211; Linda Gowans, *Cei and the Arthurian Legend* (Cambridge: Brewer, 1988), pp. 104–7 and, especially, p. 182 fn 11.

[15] Adams pp. 11–13.

[16] Smith, 'Geography in *Yder*'.

[17] See for example *The Right Plesaunt and Goodly Historie of the Foure Sonnes of Aymon. Englisht from the French by William Caxton*, ed. by Octavia Richardson, in *The English Charlemagne Romances*, Early English Text Society, extra series 34–41, 43–45, 50 (London: Trübner, 1879–87), parts X–XI.

[18] Lemaire, *Le Romanz*, pp. 11–15.

[19] 'Variations on Romance Themes in the *Historia Meriadoci*', *Journal of the International Arthurian Society*, 2 (2014), 3–19.

John was notorious for). Therefore, even if John was generally unpopular, it is unlikely that *Yder* was written specifically as an anti-monarchical polemic.

Adams has much to say about the *Yder* poet's sense of humour, a topic of fundamental importance to this article. She points especially to the episode of the lady, Ivenant's wife, in which everybody laughs at the lady's failure to seduce the hero; she also points to the slapstick tug-of-war over a horse (2308–19). She notes a down-to-earth attitude that debunks any suggestion of the marvellous: a bear that Yder has to deal with in the queen's chamber is not wild but has merely escaped from its handlers. Further, the miraculous cure of Yder, after he has been poisoned by Kei towards the end of the romance, is effected not by magic but by an emetic. Arthur is not portrayed as specially funny, although several other characters (especially Kei) are roundly mocked.[20] The mocking of Kei parallels the mocking of the seductive lady.

The notorious incident of the lady who tries to seduce the hero is picked out by Adams as comic. It may be thought, at first reading, to resemble a very important incident in a more famous romance, *Sir Gawain and the Green Knight*,[21] in which the lady succeeds only in eliciting kisses and persuading the hero to accept her girdle (to be discussed further below). The episode of the seductive lady in *Yder* could be seen as distasteful: in order to escape her attentions, Yder kicks her in the stomach. This seems to go directly against the knightly code of good behaviour towards women, and is brutally violent. However misogynistic this punishment of a woman may seem, there are numerous passages about women in *Yder* that show them all to be strong and decisive ladies whose actions, and words, are important to the plot. Given that there are divergent ways of reading the episode, in the context of other women in the romance, I deemed that an article about these women, and the comedy that colours one of them, might be an acceptable addition to *Yder* studies.

Women in *Yder*

Yder proves himself fit to be dubbed as knight by kicking a lady, wife of King Ivenant, hard in the stomach. At the beginning of the romance as it survives, while Yder is visiting Ivenant's court, Ivenant warns the hero that he will be tested by his wife's attempt to seduce him (at 202–10); this test has in the past been the downfall of other aspiring young men, and the courtiers are all aware of the situation. Before Yder first meets her, Ivenant jokes about her naughty tricks. This joking on the part of her husband underlines both the importance of the episode and the importance of humour for interpreting the poem. Ivenant's wife appears (at 260), together with her maid and an old woman. After the maid's enthusiastic description of the fine young stranger, the lady goes to look at Yder for herself (315). The pair then discuss who ought properly, because of rank, to love whom. Yder resists her advances energetically, and kicks her in the stomach (374–80):

---

[20] Adams, pp. 19–24.
[21] *Sir Gawain and the Green Knight*, ed. by J. A. Burrow (Harmondsworth: Penguin, 1972). A parallel with the Joseph and Potiphar's wife story from the Old Testament, in which a lady tempts the young man and cries rape when she is repulsed, is adduced by Jana Lyn Gill, 'Gawain's Girdle and Joseph's Garment: Tokens of "Vntrawþe" ', *Journal of the International Arthurian Society*, 2 (2014) 46–62, but the story is so common as to be referred to familiarly as 'the badger game' among medievalists; it also appears in Classical literature (for example, the story of Phaedra and Hippolytus). Neither of ladies in question, either in *SGGK* or in *Yder*, cries rape.

> Quanque il puet se treit ariere,
> Més ele se treit tot dis soentre.
> Yder la fiert del pié al ventre,
> Si qu'el cheï ariere enverse
> E qu'el en devint tote perse.
> Jo nel sai pas de ça reprendre,
> Kar il ne se poeit defendre.

> Yder pulled away as best he could, but she kept moving closer. So he kicked her in the stomach, so that she fell back and turned pale. I can't blame him for that, because there was nothing else he could do to defend himself.

People overhearing the scene laugh heartily, as if all this is a well-known joke. By his resistance, Yder shows himself worthy to be made a knight. However, he promises the lady that he will speak to her before he leaves; he keeps his promise by shouting to her rather than going into her room.

The romance contains three queens: Guinevere, Guenloie, and this lady who is the wife of King Ivenant and thus also a queen. We are not told what her name is, even though she is such a prominent character. Her anonymity could be seen as distinguishing: she differs from the other queens by her bad behaviour, which is set up and exploited by the poet. Apart from the bear which appears later, this disgraceful incident is the only thing that many of its readers can remember about the romance. These female figures call for close attention: because they are all important to the plot, the episode of this lady is no isolated anti-feminist passage. I argue that her importance is in her comic role: the romance's pervasive humour and joking quickly stand out as characteristic. Humour's part in the romance is to underline what the poet has to say about honour and dishonour, especially as embodied in the episode under discussion.

The episode in which Yder kicks the lady is comedy. Yder is justified because the lady's behaviour is dishonourable, and she becomes the butt of everybody's mirth. The king warns Yder about what is going to happen, but although he explains that it is a joke for him (the king), he has not instructed his wife to behave like this (see esp. 203–8). It is paralleled by episodes in which Kei, the king's favourite, likewise behaves dishonourably; he is frequently a laughing-stock in spite of the fact that he nearly kills Yder twice. Because neither he nor the seductive lady succeeds, the comedy remains comic throughout the romance. Neither the narratorial voice nor any character spouts forth the usual outburst of complaint at women's faithlessness and frailty that is found in anti-feminist passages elsewhere. The nearest to anti-feminist sentiment among the characters occurs in only one passage: Arthur remarks that women resort to grief as a vengeance (6292), but that men ought not to do so. But his is an untrustworthy voice for such sentiments; this speech is placed in the mouth of somebody whom we know to be unsympathetic and unpleasant, late in the romance, so that we are not at all inclined to believe him. The writer as narrator betrays no misogynistic tendency anywhere else, and shows misogyny as a vice in the person of Arthur.

The reaction of characters in *Yder* is to regard what happens to the lady as comic, and to laugh heartily. Why would this be? I argue that it is because the story is about honour and dishonour, with emphasis on the destructiveness of jealousy. Arthur's jealousy nearly destroys the hero; Kei is mocked for envy and for dishonourable behaviour. If anything, the lady achieves a kind of parity with an important male character, in that she too is the butt of amusement when she behaves badly. If this is anti-feminism, it is of a very unusual kind.

Before exploring the failed seduction attempt by Ivenant's wife further, I now set out an account of each female figure of the story in order of appearance: what they have to say, and how they behave. This analysis attempts to set that lady's unusual role into the context of other women in the story, whose roles are more traditional for a narrative of this kind.

Their importance is marked in a number of ways: many are given direct speech, or are shown taking part equally in conversations with men. Their feelings are usually described sympathetically; some are shown making jokes. Some are shown to be powerful in their own right, and they all play a crucial part in the plot. Listing them in this way allows readers to review the female figures one after another, removing any necessity to group them in order of importance.

i) The Maidens' Castle damsel (70–122) addresses Arthur very confidently, using the familiar 'tu',[22] and she is furious at Arthur's refusal to help her mistress against her attacker, in spite of his earlier promises to the lady. Arthur explains that he wants to defeat the knight Talac de Rougement first. This sets the scene for the king's untrustworthiness and its ensuing consequences. Later, when the situation has changed, Arthur says he will not help Talac until after he has defeated that same Black Knight who besieges the same 'orgoillose pucele' of Maidens' Castle (3485). The latter never appears in person, but she is important because she is among the female characters who advance the plot.

ii) Ivenant's wife, whose encounter with Yder I have described above.

iii) A key development in Yder's story is his acquistition of a squire, Luguain. Luguain's mother is first mentioned at 576. The family is poor but generous; she gives Yder her own cloak because there is no other in the house. Luguain had warned her that a lot of people were coming to visit, but in fact Yder comes alone. She longs to be able to entertain lavishly, as is honourable. Luguain's parents discuss his future, worrying what will become of him. Luguain had intended to ask his mother's advice about what to do (722), which indicates her wisdom, although in the end he makes plans with his father.[23] Later there is a welcome given by both parents; the mother gets direct speech (6119). If minor figures are given a voice when it is not strictly necessary for them to have one, it suggests that the writer nevertheless wishes to stress their importance to the plot or to its themes.

iv) Yder's mother. Yder says that he is looking for a knight who seduced a poor girl twenty-five years ago (918). These are, predictably, his own father and mother. She is described as 'a poor girl' again at 4794. At 4911 the knight, Nuc, vows he will marry none but Yder's mother. Yder goes to look for his mother at 6649, also for his grandmother if she is still alive.[24] Yder then arranges the marrriage of his own father and mother, as well as that of Cliges and his lady (who will appear later in the story).

v) Talac's sister (1007), even wiser than she is beautiful, gives Yder a fine cloak. Later she is named Guilladon, and again she is seen giving fine clothes. It is stated that this is no dishonour, because it is for Talac's sake. It is curious that such gift-giving should have

---

[22] Except for this lady, to Arthur, people use the 'vos' form to one another.
[23] There is a nice leave-taking scene at 892; Luguain is not named until 908.
[24] This late arrival in the story is alive, but we don't see much of her.

to be justified; here, extra talk about a character seems to be a way of underlining her importance.

vi) Guinevere, and her ladies. One of the many who come to watch the fight, at Arthur's siege of Talac's stronghold Rougemont, is Guinevere (1053). At 1495 she praises Yder. At 1873, the watching ladies have given their wimples as pennants to their favourites; they want to know who Yder is. Guinevere tries to stop Yder jousting with the great Gawain (2192); it is a brief but thoughtful conversation, showing that Guinevere is no mere figurehead. Further, by establishing Guinevere as a person of consequence, the poet valorizes her dislike of the dastardly Kei.

Everybody is heart-broken at Yder's wounding by Kei (2338). When Guinevere hears that Yder has recovered, she wants to go with Arthur (3156–61) to fetch him to the Round Table. Arthur is angry that she is praising him (3173), because he is jealous. The narrator suggests that if she asked Yder to stay he might do so; but she tactfully whispers to Gawain to ask him, so that Arthur will not hear or suspect her wish (3247). The bear episode (3301–98), which happens in Guinevere's room, is not explained in the text, but it has become significant for scholars because of Yder's conventional association with a bear. It is possibile that Yder's bear could, in the present romance at least, be an *alter ego* of the jealous and aggressive king himself.[25] The bear, which has escaped the dogs baiting it, tries to attack Guinevere and her company; Yder conquers it and throws it out of the window. Guinevere's messengers include, surprisingly, a daughter of the King of Ireland.[26] She jokes as she summons Gawain, Ywain, and Yder, but we never find out why because of the bear's sudden appearance. There is a long passage where Arthur cross-questions Guinevere, out of jealousy (5136–220). Later he pretends not to know who Yder is; he says 'the one the ladies are so keen on' (5263). Towards the end of the romance Guinevere appears accompanied by knights; it will be seen that Guenloie, by contrast, is accompanied by ladies. This is a nice way of differentiating the two queens.

vii) Guenloie, the lady on whom Yder sets his heart and whom he eventually marries. The ladies surrounding Guinevere are joined by Guenloie (1185), the central female figure of the romance. During an important battle, Guinevere sends a girl to fetch this heroine to her side. Guenloie is afraid she will be unable to recognize Yder, not knowing what arms he wears nor which side he is fighting on. She had first met him during the opening section of the romance, which is lacking, so we have no details of the meeting. She suffers terribly in case he, the one she is looking at, is not Yder. Later, after a long passage about Yder's love-suffering, we are given Guenloie's own thoughts (1754–832), spoken aloud. She raves at length (2532), citing tragic women from antiquity. But she acts positively, giving orders, going to the look-out, in spite of preparing to kill herself out of despair, thinking she will never be united with her lover. Ready to die bravely and alone, she sees Luguain (2662). There follows a long episode with conversation and action; she is strong

---

[25] E. C. Southward, 'The Knight Yder and the Beowulf Legend in Arthurian Romance', *Medium Ævum*, 15, 1946, 1–47. See Natalia Tikhonov, 'The King, the Goddess and the Bear', *Ceridwen's Cauldron* (Trinity 1998), xix–xxi, for the supposed meaning 'bear' of the name *Arthur*.

[26] Miroet and Kamelin (5840–42), who appear as if miraculously to heal Yder of the poison administered by Kei, are sons of a King of Ireland called Alfred. There may be a connection with this messenger, daughter of an Irish king; if so it is not stated. Perhaps they were on their way to visit their sister when they happened upon the moribund hero.

enough to realise that she can heal Yder. Later she is happy at his cure, and at his honour. She decides to besiege Talac as a way of getting Arthur and his knights, including Yder, to come to her (she has Talac watched, for this purpose).[27] In a conversation between Guenloie and a messenger-girl there is a long description of the battle (reported speech 5005). Guenloie shows her clenched fist to Yder at 5371. This powerful but curious detail is later explained as both an instruction and a gesture of confidence. When she arrives to meet King Arthur towards the end of the romance, with her train of lovely ladies (cf. Guinevere's knights), she sends a messenger to announce herself (6453). She has been discussing her marriage with her anxious barons. Because she is a queen, Yder must be crowned before he can marry her.

viii) The Nuns. There is a central monastic element in the story, as important incidents are set in one or more friendly nunneries. This argues against anti-monastic satire being crucial to identifying the place of the romance's composition.[28] Although the poet complains about monks elsewhere in the text, the nunnery is portrayed as a benevolent and important place; female religious, at least, are not the object of mockery or satire in the romance. Yder gives one prize horse to a convent. And it is a convent or abbey, implicitly the same one, where Luguain takes the wounded Yder after Kei's first attack on him (2878); he gives them Gawain's horse and some money. The hosteler, a lady named Esotil (3003) welcomes them. The doctor, by contrast, is a man; his method is described enthusiastically by the hosteler (3069–93). When Arthur and his party visit to enquire after Yder, the abbess is given a longish speech (3195–213).

Yder is not healed by a woman: Guenloie starts the first healing process, but the convent doctor is male. No woman helps with the later healing, by the sons of Alfred (5837–922). However, women nurture their dead or wounded men in the romance: Guenloie and the nuns help Yder, as explained above; a lady will not abandon her dead lover (below).

ix) The lady with a dead lover. Yder, left behind by his companions, finds this lady, whose lover (set upon and killed by seven assailants) had been one of Talac's men (3583). She is very vocal, and long speeches include talk about the value of confession. Here, a woman is allowed to discuss important matters pertaining to the Church. They go to the house with the dwarf (see next paragraph), where later the lady is given a bed after the events of the evening have been resolved. When Yder leaves, he charges Cliges to see to the body's burial and also to return the lady to her father (4379).

x) The mistress of the house with the dwarf is clever (3899), but Yder tricks her into pleading with her lover for lodging and hospitality (3994). There is some light-hearted play with Yder's name (4072–89). It turns out that the mistress of the house's own lady is Guenloie. The mistress of the house reconciles Yder with her lover, the dwarf's master,[29] whose

---

[27] This is the first we hear that Guenloie is Arthur's niece (3469); nothing special is made of it but it adds to the lady's status as queen in her own right. When Arthur and his companions meet her on their way to seek adventures (5285) he calls her 'niece' again.

[28] See Schmolke-Hasselmann for this view.

[29] In Chrétien's *Erec et Enide*, Yder has an aggressive dwarf of his own. Motifs of this kind are very mobile; although if a really famous attribute such as a named sword were to appear in the wrong hands then the writer responsible would be forced to explain how it got there (presumably because an oral performance of the text in question, if it happened later than the sword's becoming famous in previous romances, would be loudly heckled by the audience).

name is Cliges (4290). He is Guenloie's vassal, although Guenloie took his lands away because of his unwelcome advice to her about love. However, at the end of the romance, on the occasion of his marriage which Yder arranges, she gives him back his lands and more besides. At a later visit to Cliges's house, Yder and the mistress of this house joke together; she is not forgotten (5110) at the leave-taking of Yder and Nuc.

xi) The lady with the plaits, whom Yder finds in Guenloie's tent (at 4464–72), seems to be one of Guenloie's servants. She explains about her nameless suitor, and laughs when the very man appears behind Yder's back (4551). She is able to look on as Yder fights him (4670), so that part of the scene is described as if through her eyes. Thanks to her insistence on discovering Nuc's name, he and Yder are reunited and go off together. She is very happy, and will tell Guenloie about Yder's father (4894).

It will be clear that the women in *Yder* are an active and talkative lot compared to typical female characters in some other romances. Their presence in *Yder* helps to build a romance in which the misogyny found in so many medieval texts is here subordinated to other themes. Significantly, a main theme of *Yder* is the foolish destructiveness of jealousy, especially in men; the poet deals with it by poking fun at this kind of jealousy. The hero and heroine are not guilty of such feelings, but Arthur most certainly is; others, Kei especially, behave badly because of envy.

The romance contains much talk about love and how painful it is; it is tempting to see this as humorous because so very exaggerated. The light-hearted treatment of love itself supports a view that the romance is shot through with humour, even if some of it is rather grim: scenes such as the hero's encounter with Ivenant's wife set the tone for later adventures. Later events include the comic discomfiting of Kei, the jealous knight (detailed below). Witnesses at the royal court laugh at Kei; witnesses at Ivenant's court laugh at this king's wife. Yder is tested, and succeeds, at the beginning of his career. The scene is clearly intended to be funny, at least to everybody in the story, because they laugh uproariously; Ivenant himself warns the hero, quite without any jealousy, as if something hilarious is going to happen to him. The passage in which Ivenant warns Yder does not say that he has instructed his wife to test the hero; rather, he says he knows about her little ways and this situation amuses him immensely: 'Huem ne se puet de lui defendre: | Sa druerie l'i feit prendre | Qu'il ne la prent delivrement [...] Jo en faz mon gab, si m'en dedui' (Nobody can defend himself against her: her passion takes hold so that she is left with no choice ... I make a joke of it, and enjoy it (203–8, my translation)).

When she complains that 'he brings me shame for his amusement' (334) she does not mean he has told her to behave like this, only that he sends young men to her and then laughs at the outcome. However unpleasant modern readers may find the episode, it would seem that the lady has taken no harm from being kicked; at least her reply to Yder's parting words seems cheerful enough (457–58). For this later exchange, Yder is careful to keep out of her way while still keeping his promise to speak to her before leaving. No doubt she will try her wiles on the next young man who comes along.

The Romance as Comedy

The theme of humour is well established, and may have been set up at the very beginning of the romance. Light-heartedness is apparent from the start (as we have it), when the king's huntsman meeting the hero simply cannot believe Yder doesn't know who Arthur is. There is a comic scene, cited above among examples of humour noted by Adams, of knights pulling desperately at a rather annoyed horse; the narrator also chuckles at Gawain's fall (2281–91). This happens immediately before Kei's dastardly attack at 2320–32 ff.

The words and phrases picked out in this section, and the kinds of humour identified, range from narrator's comments through to characters' open laughter. They include everything from gentle fun through to irony and sarcasm, merriment and joking to explicit comic game. The following is an analysis of every example of any kind of humour, reading straight through the romance in order of appearance, because in this way it can be observed how the comic effect builds up. It may be noticed that some of the humour is the kind enjoyed by the characters, some by the narrator, and some intended for the enjoyment of the audience (although it is difficult to gauge how a medieval audience, whose idea of humour might differ from ours, would respond). We are therefore on safer ground if we analyze passages where characters make and enjoy jokes; passages where the narrator is having fun at the characters' expense certainly appear to be intended to amuse the audience.

I have not included examples of word-play in my list because they are so very common in this kind of romance; many sidelong comments from the narrator are likewise very common. All build a picture of a poet enjoying himself at the expense of bad or excessive behaviour. An example of the narrator winking, so to speak, at the audience is his gentle fun at 2071–75: we are told that had Yder wanted a love-affair, now that the ladies were all so admiring of him, he could have had ten!

29	'gabast'. The huntsman thinks Yder is joking when the latter asks who Arthur is; there follows, rather ironically, an encomium of Arthur.
118	'or ad son (il) bon meritement' (see also 114–15). This, meaning 'he's got what he deserves' (in the context of a reported dispute), is sarcasm.
159	'qu'il rient'. Yder gives horses to a young man who is apparently not being helped by Arthur; when he tells his companions they chatter and laugh (merriment), and Arthur is embarrassed when he hears his lack of generosity being reported.
208	'Jo en faz mon gab si m'en dedui'. It is Ivenant's game to send Yder to be tempted by his wife: if Yder loses he will be tonsured like a criminal.[30] There may be a further joke in the line 'La verrez li meistre del chastel' (230), as if Ivenant is pretending his wife is the boss (You'll see the 'master' there).
293–97	The short exchange between Ivenant's lady and her maid is certainly humorous. It is to be noted that the lady is under-dressed, ostensibly because of the heat but obviously in order to look seductive.[31]
334	'honte me feit pur son deduit'. The lady is aware of her husband's amusement, but complains that he is shaming her for his own fun. The narrator, meanwhile, explains that Yder has absolutely no choice but a kick to get out of her clutches.

---

[30] Lemaire, *Le Romanz*, p. 448 n. to 213, notes that this kind of tonsure was especially applied to adulterers.
[31] The lady in *SGGK* is likewise under-dressed (lines 1740–41).

382–90   These lines are about the amusement throughout Ivenant's household; the lady knows they are all laughing at her (403). It is stressed how cleverly Yder manages not to touch her — at least, not with his hand (418).

465–66   'Li reis s'en rist [...] E li chevaliers'. The king and the knights are also amused at how cleverly Yder manages to keep his promise to speak to the lady before leaving — without actually having to see her.[32]

618–24   'tricher ... gabé ... fausé'. These words close together (trick, joke, fool) suggest a teasing exchange between Luguain and his mother.[33]

1144–66   'fu Quois bon chevaliers / A poi de mos vos a conté / Quanqu'il out en lui bonté ...' This is heavily sarcastic, and the narrator goes on to explain just what a bad knight (and bad man) Kei is: that is, he has no good qualities and therefore they can be told in few words. The list of his vices includes envy, and this explains but does not excuse his dreadful behaviour.

1249–55   This is a passage in which Kei is mocked. Because of his disloyalty, the onlookers have no pity when he is beaten.

1278   '... set ke Bedoer le gabe'. Kei knows, in spite of Bedoer's 'reasonable' words, that he is being laughed at. Guinevere emphatically does not like Kei, and laughs after his third fall (1317–24); nor does anybody like him except Arthur (fortunately for Kei, in the circumstances).[34] There is more mockery at 1330–44. This treatment of Kei undermines what looks like a negative portrait of Ivenant's wife: both are being punished for dishonourable behaviour. If the medieval audience laughs at Kei's discomfiture, as well they might because it is refreshing to be allowed to mock a character often portrayed as negative, then they may also have laughed at the importunate lady and her failure to seduce the hero.

2573   'dedire'. Guenloie is on the verge of killing herself, and accuses Love of having fun at her expense. This point is underlined by the narrator's rather sarcastic comment, that the boy sent to fetch a knife for her managed to find one so quickly (2624–27).

2908–12   The narrator remarks with apparent amusement that Luguain addressed the prioress incorrectly.

3026–28   Yder asks Luguain whether he is teasing him, in response to his news.

3166–71   Arthur's expression, and his laugh, are evidence of his felony.[35] Arthur's laugh is at the expense of other characters, and the audience would be more alarmed than amused by such behaviour.

---

[32] It is thanks to Yder's winning the 'game' that Ivenant agrees to dub him. Note at this point a detail not (to my knowledge) commonly found in romances: the practice of putting one's sword on the altar and then 'buying it back' by means of a donation to the religious house in question.

[33] It was noted earlier that the young man is not named here, but at a later and significant point in the story. Naming is a way of pointing up the important moments of a character's role.

[34] Arthur does admit Kei's bad influence at 2460.

[35] Who will fetch Yder to the Round Table? Adams, according to his note on the line, thinks that line 3165 is the

3238–46 Yder reacts, at first with sarcasm, to the king's invitation to the Round Table.

3313–21 There is a joke about a bishop immediately before the scene with the bear.

3465 Talac will be a laughing-stock if Arthur won't help him.[36]

All this shows the frequency of words and phrases expressing humour. The narrator is clearly enjoying the frequent comic turns of the plot, and portrays the characters reacting light-heartedly to many of them. The audience may be reluctant to laugh directly at a hero's suffering, even if it is portrayed as ludicrous; but they are more likely to laugh against bad characters.

Even the last lines of the poem are a tease: the poet insists repeatedly that the book is not for anybody, for nobody at all, but clergy and noblemen and their ladies. This is a very wide group of people who will enjoy the romance and laugh at or with the characters. Adams's translation of the final couplet ('Ici finist le romanz du reis Yder | Com il esteit bon chevaler') keeps this feeling: 'Here ends the Romance of King Yder and what a fine knight he was'. This makes the narrator sound cheerful and as if amused by the story we have just heard; compare Lemaire's less spirited 'Ici s'acheve le roman du roi Yder qui était un bon chevalier' ('... who was a good knight').

Humour is an important theme or element in the romance, because it underlines what the poet has to say about honour and dishonour. People laugh at Kei just as they laugh at Ivenant's wife: quite simply, both are perceived as behaving dishonourably. In other romances the same figure (Kay, or similarly spelt) behaves badly and is punished by taking a fall or a beating from other characters. In this romance his punishment is public shaming and mockery. Everybody knows the worst about Kei, so the theme is not unexpected, but it is unusual for a woman to be so treated in a romance. Interestingly, in view of *Yder* 's theme of jealousy, Ivenant is not in the least jealous about his wife; he says most knights fail the test, but there is no suggestion that he minds when she succeeds in seducing them. Nobody laughs at Ivenant; this is not a jealous husband! The narrator has much to say about jealousy, including that there is no need to guard a good woman — in fact, it is a stupid thing to do. The passage is intended as a disparaging comment on Arthur's jealousy because Guinevere admires Yder; the narrator goes on to say that a bad woman (presumably Ivenant's wife) brings shame upon herself (5447–78). In fabliaux, however, there is a perceived need to guard women: the good ones in case of male predators, and the bad ones to prevent them preying on males.

There seems to be little irony in the long disquisitions about love that recur several times. Such musing seems to be standard stuff for romances of this type and period. It is treated light-heartedly, however, and it is also remarked that anybody who pursues what is worthwhile may laugh at those who pursue riches (1690–92). There may indeed be a shade of irony when, after one such passage (1633–1746), Yder appears to have had enough ... of the narrator going on and on? 'Yder out ja dis bien assez' (1747) begins a new paragraph that describes the hero's suffering, but it could be read as a wry comment by the poet.

---

narrator wishing he (Gawain?) would leave the subject; Lemaire's commentary interprets the line as part of the queen's speech where she is hoping that Yder is still at the abbey.

[36] This is where Arthur at last resolves to go and help the lady whom he refused to help before (the first of the female characters, above).

Jane Bliss

Yder's Context, Conclusions

Any text containing apparently hostile attitudes to women immediately invites comparison with the fabliaux, those notoriously misogynistic short stories whose classification or interpretation continues to challenge critics. Here I focus on just two examples of the genre, known as *De l'engin de femme: del velous* ('pulling the wool over his eyes') and *De l'espee: autre engin de femme* ('the sword — more women's trickery').[37] There is no such thing as a typical fabliau, but the two I have chosen show elements which are common in many. In both, the ladies are shown as winning the battle of the sexes, saving the lover from detection and fooling the husband. Of the ladies, the younger needs the help of her crafty mother; the latter is responsible for the trick that saves the situation. Neither woman is mocked. The lover cuts, in both cases, a poor figure; he hides behind the women and is saved by them. The laugh, if there is one, is against only the husband: in both cases he looks foolish for being so easily taken in. Because he is a good man in both these cases (the husband is not portrayed as 'good' in all fabliaux), it is possible to feel sorry for him and to blame the wickedness of women.

Neither the lady in *Yder* nor the lady in *SGGK* fits even remotely into this kind of pattern. For one thing, neither of them 'wins', even though the latter appears to achieve her somewhat mysterious aim when the hero accepts her girdle. For another, neither hero is mocked for being taken in by the lady in question. Yder is not taken in at all; the reaction of characters in the story to Gawain's predicament is hardly mockery, and a modern audience at least would be unlikely to laugh at him. However, although the romance episodes just examined both differ from fabliau situations in the way the women are treated by the writers, they differ from each other in equally important ways.

Any parallel with *SGGK*, as was suggested earlier in this article, is not a very close one. Although the episodes are analogous in their object of testing the hero, they cannot be seen as comparable once we examine them.

Talk with the lady is about love in both stories, but in *SGGK* there is much play about 'which' Gawain it is: the famous warrior known to British romance, or the famous lover notorious in French romance. It is not about rank in the context of love, as it is in *Yder*. The Gawain scenes with the lady take place in comparative privacy, although the kisses are 'handed over' publicly; by contrast, Yder is warned jovially and openly about the wiles of the lady in question, and everybody is gleefully aware of what is going on. The lady in *SGGK* is acting on instructions from her husband and from Morgan le Fay; the lady in *Yder* is acting according to her own devices. Yder touches the lady with a foot (to kick), not with a hand; he certainly does not kiss. Gawain achieves kisses without succumbing further, and also without repulsing the lady. The lady is not mocked by the poet, nor by anybody in the story.

Yder passes the test at the beginning of his career as a knight, and there is no question about his success. Gawain, by contrast, has been a knight for long enough to establish his reputation, and the test is not about his suitability for knighthood. It comes towards the end of the story rather than at the beginning, and it includes the ambiguous girdle as well as kisses. He himself is uncertain about his success, whatever anybody else thinks at the conclusion of the romance. The *Yder* version is entirely light-hearted, with no ominous aftermath; nor is there any suggestion that the lady and her husband are other-world figures.

---

[37] Numbers 6 and 7 respectively in *Eighteen Anglo-Norman Fabliaux*, ed. by Ian Short and Roy Pearcy, Anglo-Norman Text Society, Plain Texts Series 14 (London: Anglo-Norman Text Society, 2000). They will also be included in my forthcoming anthology, *A Book of Anglo-Norman*; the anthology is currently in draft form.

A further search for comparable episodes in romance leads us to a differently misogynistic text: *Le Chevalier à l'épée*.[38] In this, the well-known hero Gawain moves out of an identifiably Arthurian space into a world of burlesque or fabliau.[39] But such texts vary profoundly in their apparent dispraise of women; here again the comedy is differently targeted.

In *Chevalier*, as in other Gawain romances, a hero who won his knighthood long ago (unlike Yder) has become famous throughout the fictional world he inhabits, and throughout the literary world of numerous stories about him — an audience's knowledge of these is assumed by authors who build upon this fund of tales. Accordingly, 'most of the humour is applied to a slight deflation of Gauvain.'[40] He is so inadequate as a lover that the lady in question abandons him for another man, hoping the latter will prove worthy and valiant, as soon as possible (983–97). He behaves 'unchivalrously' by dispatching the man; the 'misogynistic tirade' is spoken by Gauvain and not by the author; the narratorial voice says that the story started well but has become 'laide et anuiose' (1202). We, the audience, are invited to laugh at the hero's inadequacy. Nobody laughs at the woman, either inside or outside the story; she is punished by being abandoned in her turn. Gauvain tries to tell us how faithless women are, but we are not encouraged to sympathize with him.

The main point here is that Yder does not complain about the faithlessness of women, he shows no inadequacy as a lover, the woman in the episode we are examining is entirely unlike the woman in *Chevalier*: she is a test of Yder's worthiness and no more. It is she, not the hero, who is 'deflated' by mockery.

General Conclusion

The distasteful episode in which the hero kicks a lady in the stomach is, unlikely as this may at first seem, set up as a piece of comedy. All the women in the story are portrayed as talkative and powerful; the actions of this one are especially necessary to the plot because her success would prevent the hero becoming a knight and thus stifle the story at its outset. However, her behaviour is dishonourable, and therefore she is the butt of everybody's mirth when she fails to seduce the hero.

Kei likewise behaves dishonourably, and he is frequently a laughing-stock in spite of — indeed, because of — the fact that he nearly kills the hero twice. Because he does not succeed either time the comedy, surprisingly again to our modern feeling, remains comic as far as the romance is concerned. For a male character to be the butt of a poet's humour is not uncommon; in this romance a female character is untypically mocked, for trying to destroy the hero. If either had succeeded, there would be no comedy — and no romance.

---

[38] *Two Old French Gauvain Romances, Part I: Le chevalier à l'Épée and La mule sans frein*, by R. C. Johnston and D. D. R. Owen (Edinburgh: Scottish Academic Press, 1972).
[39] See Jane Bliss, *Naming and Namelessness in Medieval Romance* (Cambridge: Brewer, 2008), p. 54.
[40] *Two Old French Gauvain Romances*, p. 5.

The Structure of the Exeter Book: A Reading Based on Medieval Topics

Jan-Peer Hartmann[1]

Introduction: the structure of the Exeter Book – old and new approaches

MS 3501 in the library of the Dean and Chapter of Exeter Cathedral, more commonly known as the Exeter Book, is often thought to be referred to by an entry in the list of books and religious objects that Bishop Leofric intended to leave to the cathedral and its community: 'i mycel englisc boc be gehwilcu[m] þingu[m] on leoðwisan geworht', 'one big English book on various things in verse'.[2] Modern scholarship since the nineteenth century has by and large echoed this characterization with its emphasis on diversity of content rather than coherence. 'The Exeter Book differs from the other three [Old English] poetic codices in that it is a poetic miscellany in which there does not appear to have been a recognizable principle of selection,' says N. F. Blake in his edition of *The Phoenix*.[3] John C. Pope calls it 'the most varied' of the four poetic codices[4] and Kenneth Sisam maintains that 'the order of contents is generally haphazard', wondering whether 'we [shall] ever know more about the way in which this miscellany was compiled'.[5] But why have scholars been so keen on trying to detect order in the Exeter Book anyway? After all, might we not just content ourselves to see the Exeter

---

[1] I thank Alaric Hall and the two anonymous reviewers for *Leeds Studies in English*, from whose comments this article has profited considerably. I would also like to thank Kirsten Middeke for reading the article prior to submission and, most importantly, Andrew James Johnston, who not only made invaluable suggestions but also directed my attention to encyclopaedias in the first place.

[2] Titles and quotations from *The Exeter Anthology of Old English Poetry: An Edition of Exeter Dean and Chapter MS 3501*, ed. by Bernard J. Muir, 2nd edn, 2 vols (Exeter: Exeter University Press, 2000), II; unless otherwise noted, translations from the Old English are my own. The list, which is usually referred to as 'Leofric's donation list' in modern scholarship, is now prefixed to Exeter, Cathedral Library, MS 3501, the Exeter Book, as folios 1–2. While most modern scholars think it at least 'reasonable' to infer that the entry refers to the Exeter Book (e.g. Bernard Muir in *The Exeter Anthology*, I, 3; Patrick W. Conner, *Anglo-Saxon Exeter: A Tenth-Century Cultural History*, Studies in Anglo-Saxon history, 4 (Woodbridge: Boydell, 1993), p. 34; John C. Pope, 'Paleography and Poetry: Some Solved and Unsolved Problems of the Exeter Book', in *Medieval Scribes, Manuscripts & Libraries: Essays Presented to N. R. Ker*, ed. by M. B. Parkes and Andrew G. Watson (London: Scolar Press, 1978), pp. 25–65 (p. 65) goes as far as stating this as a fact), we cannot, of course, be certain of this.

[3] *The Phoenix*, ed. by N. F. Blake (Manchester: Manchester University Press, 1964), p. 2.

[4] Pope, p. 25.

[5] Kenneth Sisam, *Studies in the History of Old English Literature* (Oxford: Clarendon Press, 1953), p. 97.

Book as a loose collection of texts whose order may well have been determined by practical constraints, such as the availability of the material or the predetermined structure of different exemplars?

Yet the majority of scholars working with the Exeter Book have felt that the compiler not only chose the texts with care, but also structured various sections of the manuscript, possibly even altering individual texts so as to better fit their environment.[6] Table 1 summarises the contents of the manuscript, giving the titles as they appear in Muir's edition and in the Anglo-Saxon Poetic Records.[7] I also provide some descriptive comments: these are naturally simplistic and cannot do justice to the complexity of the poems. I have included them to make it possible to trace the various thematic, formal or functional sequences discussed here, but also to highlight their fuzziness.[8]

Careful handling of the texts on part of the compiler is suggested, for instance, by the textual and thematic coherence of the three *Christ*-poems, the following sequence of poems concerning saints and Old Testament righteous (*Guthlac A* and *B*, *The Canticles of the Three Youths, The Passion of Saint Juliana*), the three successive *Physiologus*-poems (*The Panther, The Whale, The Partridge*) and the two collections of riddles toward the end of the manuscript. A scan of the Exeter Book's contents will reveal further sequences that exhibit at least some degree of formal or thematic coherence. Thus, many of the poems between *The Passion of Saint Juliana* and the *Physiologus*-group are either presented as catalogues listing pieces of advice or items of knowledge (*God's Gifts to Humankind, Precepts, Widsith, The Fates of Mortals, Maxims I*) or are otherwise didactic in tone (*Vainglory, The Order of the World*). Likewise, the section of poems between the two groups of riddles has been observed to show a strong concern for penitential and paschal themes.[9] That these last two groups are interspersed with the so-called 'elegies' (*The Wanderer, The Seafarer, The Riming Poem, Deor, Wulf and Eadwacer, The Wife's Lament, The Husband's Message, The Ruin*) may indicate that these poems were not perceived as a homogeneous group by the compiler(s) of the codex, which might in turn potentially undermine the thesis of a sequential arrangement just presented.

Pope has drawn attention to the fact that all the longer poems (up to and including *The Passion of Saint Juliana*) are assembled in the first half of the manuscript, while the second half comprises shorter poems, with the split occurring within the tenth of the codex's seventeen quires.[10] The manuscript's size and the care and skill with which it was written, as well as the extensive corrections made by the scribe, likewise indicate that some thought went into the manuscript's production.[11] Moreover, modern scholars' desire for some kind of organising principle is also prompted by the relative coherence of other contemporary compilations in Old English, such as the Blickling Homilies or the Junius and Vercelli

---

[6] For the last claim, see for instance Roy M. Liuzza, 'The Old English *Christ* and *Guthlac* Texts, Manuscripts, and Critics', *Review of English Studies*, 41 (1990), 1–11 (p. 5) and the discussion below.

[7] *The Exeter Book*, ed. by George Philip Krapp and Elliott van Kirk Dobbie, The Anglo-Saxon Poetic Records, 3 (New York: Columbia University Press, 1936).

[8] See also Table 5.1 in Michael D. C. Drout, *Tradition and Influence in Anglo-Saxon Literature: An Evolutionary, Cognitivist Approach* (New York: Palgrave Macmillan, 2013), p. 139.

[9] See *Two Literary Riddles in the Exeter Book. Riddle 1 and The Easter Riddle: A Critical Edition with Full Translations*, ed. by James E. Anderson (Norman and London: University of Oklahoma Press, 1986) and Muir's introduction in *The Exeter Anthology*, I, 23.

[10] Pope, p. 40; *The Exeter Anthology*, p. 22.

[11] Richard Gameson calls it 'a handsome codex, [...] of large dimensions for one written in the vernacular' and 'a major work written by a skilful scribe at a centre that was not short of resources and that had access to an interesting range of texts both in Latin and the vernacular' (Richard Gameson, 'The Origin of the Exeter Book of

manuscripts.[12] Why should the Exeter Book have been different? And indeed, variety does not by necessity entail randomness. As James E. Anderson remarks, 'Even if the Exeter Book is a poetic miscellany, [...] it is not necessarily of wholly arbitrary or random order. Like many other medieval collections it was probably assembled on some more or less definite but unstated plan.'[13] Speaking of medieval manuscripts in general, Fred C. Robinson likewise encourages modern readers to look beyond the individual text:

> [W]hen we read an Old English literary text we should take care to find out what precedes it in its manuscript state and what follows it. [...] For medieval books often constituted composite artifacts in which each component text depended on its environment for part of its meaning. If a text is detached from its codicological environment (as texts normally are in our modern editions), we risk losing that part of its meaning.[14]

More recent studies of the Exeter Book from the 1980s onward have accordingly tended to stress the coherence rather than the variety of the collection. Thus Bernard Muir, the manuscript's most recent editor, states:

> I was prompted to undertake this new edition by a feeling that it was time to focus attention on the collection as an anthology. I have found in my own study of the texts that there is much to be gained by reading the manuscript from beginning to end, and recent scholarship suggests that the anthologist's design and intention can sometimes be perceived in the texts as they are preserved today.[15]

Old English Poetry', *Anglo-Saxon England*, 25 (1996), 135–85 (pp. 135, 179)). On alterations and corrections, see *The Exeter Anthology*, I, p. 32, 'The large number of deliberate alterations and corrections made to the texts in *The Exeter Anthology* [...] indicates that the scribe is a much more conscientious worker than has previously been thought. He (and others) made numerous alterations to the text, sometimes systematically, indicating that what appears in the manuscript is for the most part what he (or they) wanted to be there.'

[12] This is not to say that these manuscripts have not raised considerable discussion. Thus, while the structure of the Junius manuscript is comparatively straightforward in gathering a number of paraphrases of Biblical texts in verse (*Genesis, Exodus, Daniel, Christ and Satan*), arranged chronologically, the Vercelli Book, containing prose homilies as well as poetry, has been censured for its intermingling of prose and verse and its lack of thematic development as compared to other collections of homilies. Nevertheless, as Elaine Treharne has shown, the Vercelli texts are all related by their homiletic function and their applicability as didactic and devotional meditations for specific Church feasts, especially with respect to lay audiences (Elaine Treharne, 'Form and Function of the Vercelli Book', in *Text, Image, Interpretation: Studies in Anglo-Saxon Literature and Its Insular Context in Honour of Éamonn Ó Carragáin*, ed. by Alastair Minnis and Jane Roberts, Studies in the Early Middle Ages, 18 (Turnhout: Brepols, 2007), pp. 253–66). This 'pragmatic unity' resonates with the present paper's engagement with the formal and functional characteristics of the Exeter Book poems. The Nowell Codex, the fourth major poetic manuscript in Old English, in spite of containing far fewer texts, would seem to rival the Exeter Book in its thematic eclecticism, mixing materials associated with Christianity (*Saint Christopher, Judith*), classical antiquity (*Letter of Alexander to Aristotle*), Germanic heroic legend (*Beowulf*), and a description of marvellous creatures (*The Wonders of the East*), as well as mingling verse and prose. It has long been noted, however, that all of these texts engage with marvels and monstrous creatures, and if *Judith* originally preceded *Saint Christopher*, as Peter Lucas has argued, the first four texts were arranged in thematically and geographically related pairs (*Judith* and *Saint Christopher*; *The Wonders of the East* and *Letter of Alexander*), resulting in thematic echoes between consecutive texts (Andy Orchard, *Pride and Prodigies: Studies in the Monsters of the 'Beowulf'-Manuscript* (Cambridge: Brewer, 1995)). For a comprehensive study of all four poetic codices see Gunhild Zimmermann, *The Four Old English Poetic Manuscripts: Texts, Contexts, and Historical Background*, Anglistische Forschungen, 230 (Heidelberg: Winter, 1995).

[13] *Two Literary Riddles*, p. xii.

[14] Fred C. Robinson, 'Old English Literature in Its Most Immediate Context', in *Old English Literature in Context: Ten essays*, ed. by John D. Niles (Cambridge: Brewer, 1980), pp. 11–29 (p. 11).

[15] *The Exeter Anthology*, I, ix–x.

Table 1. The contents of the Exeter Book

Folios	Titles in *The Exeter Anthology*	Titles in *ASPR* III	Comments
8r–14r	The Advent Lyrics (Christ I)	Christ (I)	biblical history: Christ's birth (translation of Latin antiphons for advent)
14r–20v	The Ascension (Christ II)	Christ (II)	biblical history: Christ's ascension
20v–32r	Christ In Judgement (Christ III)	Christ (III)	biblical history: Christ's Second Coming
32v–44v	Life of Saint Guthlac A	Guthlac (I)	saint's life
44v–52v	Life of Saint Guthlac B	Guthlac (II)	saint's life
53v–55v	Canticles of the Three Youths	Azarias	Old Testament righteous: the three youths in the furnace (Daniel 3)
55v–65v	The Phoenix	The Phoenix	nature allegory
65v–75r	Passion of Saint Juliana	Juliana	saint's life
76v–78v	The Wanderer	The Wanderer	'elegy' (spiritual biography, homiletic exemplum)
78v–80r	God's Gifts to Humankind	The Gifts of Men	'wisdom poem' (catalogue)
80r–81r	Precepts	Precepts	'wisdom poem' (catalogue)
81v–83v	The Seafarer	The Seafarer	'elegy' (spiritual biography, homiletic exemplum)
83r–84v	Vainglory	Vainglory	'wisdom poem' (minor catalogue element)
84v–87r	Widsith	Widsith	'wisdom poem' (catalogue, biographical element)
87r–88v	The Fates of Mortals	The Fortunes of Men	'wisdom poem' (catalogue)
88v–92v	Maxims I (A–C)	Maxims I	'wisdom poem' (catalogue)
92v–94r	The Order of the World	The Order of the World	'wisdom poem'
94r–95v	The Riming Poem	The Riming Poem	'elegy' (spiritual biography?)
95v–96v	The Panther	The Panther	nature allegory (Christ)
96v–97v	The Whale	The Whale	nature allegory (Satan)
97v	The Partridge	The Partridge	nature allegory (Satan/Man)
98r	Homiletic Fragment III	[treated as part of *The Partridge*]	homiletic
98r–100r	Soul and Body	Soul and Body II	soul-body allegory (homiletic)

Folios	Titles in *The Exeter Anthology*	Titles in ASPR III	Comments
100r–100v	Deor	Deor	'elegy'
100v–101r	Wulf and Eadwacer	Wulf and Eadwacer	'elegy'
101r–115r	Riddles (1–59)	Riddles (1–59)	riddles
115r–115v	The Wife's Lament	The Wife's Lament	'elegy'
115v–117v	Judgement Day I	The Judgment Day I	homiletic
117v–118v	Contrition A	Resignation	penitential prayer
119r–119v	Contrition B	[treated as part of *Resignation*]	
119v–121v	The Descent into Hell	The Descent into Hell	Christian history: the harrowing of hell
121v–122r	Almsgiving	Alms-Giving	homiletic
122r	Pharaoh	Pharaoh	biblical history: the drowning of the Egyptians in the Red Sea (Exodus 14); dialogic (question-answer)
122r	The Lord's Prayer I	The Lord's Prayer I	verse adaptation of Lord's prayer
122r–122v	Homiletic Fragment II	Homiletic Fragment II	homiletic
122v	Riddle 30	Riddle 30b	riddle
122v–123r	Riddles 60	Riddle 60	riddle
123r–123v	The Husband's Message	The Husband's Message	'elegy'
123v–124v	The Ruin	The Ruin	'elegy' (no biographical element)
124v–130v	Riddles (61–94)	Riddles (61–95)	riddles

Muir does not give any further indication as to what this design might have been, and other studies have mainly focused on short poetic sequences or thematic links between individual poems and refrained from giving an interpretation of the collection as a whole.[16] Indeed, as Gunhild Zimmermann points out, 'the number and diversity of texts make it difficult to discern a wholly satisfying structural concept behind this amalgam of Old English texts.'[17] Thus, while it seems possible to detect a sort of coherence at the micro-level, in that the immediate succession of two or more poems can often — though not always — be explained by a similarity of subjects or general themes, it has proved more difficult to detect a more general principle or plan on the macro-level of the manuscript. Zimmermann, who has undertaken the most comprehensive study of the collection, comes to the conclusion that the poems are all concerned with the human individual and the social and religious aspects of his or her earthly life:[18] 'Man's fundamental experience is defined as the constant threat of loneliness and of a meaningless life.'[19] The Exeter Book, she argues, 'proposes rules and models of identification' through which religious and social integration can be achieved.[20]

While Zimmermann's reading is in many respects helpful and persuasive, it tends to require stretching as soon as the actual order of the poems is considered. Her theory suggests a thematic unity that is sufficiently general to encompass all of the texts, but it throws no light on the principles of arrangement, the way in which the collection is organized.[21] This deficiency is evidenced by her practice of discussing individual poems out of sequence, often in relation to other poems not found in their immediate manuscript vicinity.

The search for thematic coherence, this paper proposes, has to some extent obscured an understanding of other structural features that can help shed a light on the principles that organize the Exeter Book as a collection. As I will argue in the next section, it is important to take into consideration formal and functional aspects, such as a text's genre, structure, style,

---

[16] See for instance *Two Literary Riddles*; Karma Lochrie, 'Wyrd and the Limits of Human Understanding: A Thematic Sequence in the Exeter Book', *Journal of English and Germanic Philology*, 85 (1986), 323–31; Liuzza; Patrick W. Conner, 'Four Contiguous Poems in the Exeter Book: A Combined Reading of *Homiletic Fragment III*, *Soul and Body II*, *Deor*, and *Wulf and Eadwacer*', in *The Genesis of Books. Studies in the Scribal Culture of Medieval England in Honour of A. N. Doane*, ed. by Matthew T. Hussey and John D. Niles (Turnhout: Brepols, 2011), pp. 117–36.

[17] Zimmermann, p. 91.

[18] Zimmermann, pp. 98–99.

[19] Zimmermann, p. 180.

[20] Zimmermann, pp. 179, 281–82.

[21] To my knowledge, the only studies to have focused on the actual structure of the Exeter Book were undertaken by Patrick W. Conner, 'The Structure of The Exeter Book Codex (Exeter, Cathedral Library, MS. 3501)', *Scriptorium*, 40 (1986), 233–42 and Conner, *Anglo-Saxon Exeter*. Conner saw palaeographical and codicological evidence for the assumption that the Exeter Book is in fact made up of three distinct booklets, copied by the same scribe but over a prolonged period of time (for a discussion of the evidence, see Conner, *Anglo-Saxon Exeter*, pp. 112–28). According to Conner, the first booklet in the sequence (comprising folios 8–52, i.e. *The Advent Lyrics* through *Guthlac B*) was the last to have been written, while the second (comprising folios 53–97, *The Canticles of the Three Youths* through *The Partridge*) was written first. This order of composition, Conner claims, is paralleled by a difference in subject matter reflecting the tastes of different periods: the second booklet, which he believes to have been copied first, is supposed to have been compiled from Continental, possibly Carolingian models, whose content ceased to be appropriate in a monastic context after the Benedictine Reform (Conner, *Anglo-Saxon Exeter*, pp. 148, 150–51). The other two booklets supposedly reflect the return to stricter monastic ideals after the minster of Exeter's reform in 968 under abbot Sidemann (Conner, *Anglo-Saxon Exeter*, pp. 148–50; Conner believes the Exeter Book to have been composed at Exeter; cf. Conner, *Anglo-Saxon Exeter*, p. 94). Muir, who had the opportunity to study the manuscript in its unbound state, refutes Conner's booklet theory, arguing that it is not supported by the codicological evidence (*The Exeter Anthology*, I, pp. 7–8).

rhetorical strategies or manner of presentation, or the ends to which the text may have been employed. More importantly, the Exeter Book shows extensive use of catenulate links between poems and sections that connect otherwise only vaguely related texts via their less obvious or subsidiary aspects. Taking this observation as its point of departure, this paper attempts to trace the Exeter Book's seemingly conflicting combination of catenulate and category-based textual links to late antique and early medieval principles of organizing knowledge based on mnemonic and topical practices, as reflected in contemporary florilegia, encyclopaedias and inventories.[22] Rather than constituting a rigid and inflexible order, topical organization — the practice of systematizing by reference to an item's properties or characteristics — highlights and actively employs the material's polysemous character in order to shift focus or introduce new ordering principles without having to renounce preceding ones. The collection's seeming diversity and patchiness can thus be linked to medieval semiotic procedures, which allow for the concurrence of multiple meanings and multi-dimensional structural principles.

Form, function and catenulate linking

For the past thirty-odd years, scholars have become increasingly aware of the fact that, to a certain extent at least, medieval texts rely on their material presentation to generate meaning.[23] This may include paratextual features such as layout, form, illuminations or rubrics, as well as intertextual relations with the surrounding texts. 'Medieval books often constituted composite artifacts in which each component text depended on its environment for part of its meaning'.[24] These intertextual relations, Peter von Moos notes in his study of the historical exemplum, do not necessarily appear on the level of content. He urges us, therefore, to scrutinize aspects such as form, function, methods or categories in order to understand the way texts were read during the Middle Ages:

> Medieval studies ought to address *a fortiori* the forms, functions, methods, rules, signs, mathematical categories of the Middle Ages: not so much the individual statements of the 'parole' as the general figures of the 'langue' that recur in variation; not so much aspects of the 'literary' in its modern sense (for instance, the genuineness of subjectivity) as the structures of rhetoric as it is shaped by society; not so much the narrative material [...] as narration itself as a means of entertainment and argumentation; not so much the

---

[22] I take this opportunity to cite Mercedes Salvador-Bello, *Isidorean Perceptions of Order: The Exeter Book Riddles and Medieval Latin Enigmata*, Medieval European Studies, 17 (Morgantown, WV: West Virginia University Press, 2015), who traces the arrangement of medieval Latin and Old English riddle collections, including the Exeter Book riddles, to medieval encyclopaedic principles, with Isidore's *Originum seu Etymologiarum libri XX* constituting a major model. Salvador-Bello's observations in many respects corroborate my own, for instance with regard to the way the compiler(s) employed different principles in structuring the collection, such as association, analogy/contrast and organisation by subject matter. This important study was published when the present article was already in the review process, so that I have not been able to discuss its observations in any detail. I thank Alaric Hall for giving me the opportunity to include a few references.

[23] See Matthew J. Driscoll, 'The Words on the Page: Thoughts on Philology, Old and New', in *Creating the Medieval Saga: Versions, Variability and Editorial Interpretations of Old Norse Saga Literature*, ed. by Judy Quinn and Emily Lethbridge (Odense: University Press of Southern Denmark, 2010), pp. 87–104 for a discussion of scholarly approaches that stress the material aspects of the transmission of medieval literature. The classic examples are, of course, Bernard Cerquiglini, *In Praise of the Variant: A Critical History of Philology*, trans. by Betsy Wing (Baltimore, MD: Johns Hopkins University Press, 1999) [first publ. *Éloge de la variante: Histoire critique de la philologie* (Paris: Seuil, 1989)], and Stephen G. Nichols, 'Introduction: Philology in a Manuscript Culture', *Speculum*, 65 (1990), 1–10. For the specific context of the Exeter Book, see Liuzza, pp. 8–11.

[24] Robinson, p. 11.

brilliant achievements of great thinkers as the forms of thought and the logical instruments through which knowledge is constituted; not so much the contents of consciousness within historical experience (this is what the historians' 'history of events' never seems to be capable of escaping from) as the 'habits of consciousness' within the perception and appraisal of reality.[25]

Formal aspects, von Moos argues, are integral to the way texts were perceived during the Middle Ages, as are the means to which a text could be employed, in other words, its perceived function. 'Function', of course, is a problematic term, dangerously close to a notion of 'authorial intention' as famously criticized by the New Criticism.[26] As far as medieval literary categories are concerned, however, we often find a convergence of function and form that seems to have been traditionally agreed on. This is not to say that texts could only be interpreted in a single way, but that certain formal features would have evoked specific contexts in which a particular text might be read. This is true for instance of didactic or hortatory texts which employ certain stylistic and formal features instantly recognizable by a contemporary audience. Lists and catalogues, to name two examples that feature heavily throughout the Exeter Book, and especially in the sequence of poems following *The Wanderer*, were known as mnemonic tools frequently used in didactic and educational contexts. Even in contexts that are not primarily educational, the presence of lists often lends the respective texts an appearance of authoritative knowledge, wisdom and learning.[27] One well-attested form is the glossary, used for learning vocabulary. As Nicholas Howe points out,

> an Anglo-Saxon reader who had worked his way through various glossaries would have come to regard the list as an entirely respectable and efficient didactic form. He would, for this reason, bring to a poem such as *The Gifts of Men* [Muir's *God's Gifts to Humankind*] an immediate understanding of and appreciation for the list as a form.[28]

---

[25] Peter von Moos, *Geschichte als Topik: Das rhetorische Exemplum von der Antike zur Neuzeit und die 'historiae' im 'Policraticus' Johanns von Salisbury*, Ordo. Studien zur Literatur und Gesellschaft des Mittelalters und der frühen Neuzeit, 2 (Hildesheim: Olms, 1988), p. xliii (my translation): 'Die Mediävistik [...] sollte sich *a fortiori* auf Formen, Funktionen, Methoden, Regeln, Zeichen, mathematische Kategorien des Mittelalters richten: weniger auf die individuellen Aussagen der „parole" als auf die allgemeinen, variiert wiederkehrenden Figuren der „langue"; weniger auf Aspekte des „Literarischen" im heutigen Sinn (etwa Echtheit der Subjektivität) als auf die Struktur des gesellschaftlich geprägten Rhetorischen; weniger auf Erzählstoffe [...] als auf das Erzählen selbst als Mittel des Unterhaltens und Argumentierens; weniger auf die genialen Leistungen großer Denker als auf die Denkformen und logischen Instrumente der Wissensbildung; weniger auf die Bewusstseinsinhalte der geschichtlichen Erfahrung (daran klebt die „Ereignisgeschichte" der Historiker) als auf die „Bewußtseinsgewohnheiten" der Wirklichkeitswahrnehmung und Wirklichkeitsbewertung.' See also Martin Irvine, 'Medieval Textuality and the Archaeology of Textual Culture', in *Speaking Two Languages: Traditional Disciplines and Contemporary Theory in Contemporary Medieval Studies*, ed. by Allen J. Frantzen (Albany, NY: State University of New York Press, 1991), pp. 181–210, who proposes a model of analysis based on Foucauldian archaeology, reception theory and semiotic theory.

[26] See, for instance, René Wellek and Austin Warren, *Theory of Literature*, 2nd edn (New York: Harcourt, Brace & World, 1956), pp. 135–38. Treharne discusses Paul E. Szarmach's notion of the 'intended function' of the Vercelli Book — for instance, as a form of personal book or as a book with a public, liturgical function — but also draws attention to the manuscript's 'pragmatic unity', that is, its functionality in devotional or homiletic contexts. Pointing out the applicability of texts has the advantage of stressing *possible* rather than (hypothetical) actual or intended uses. See Treharne, pp. 260, 264–65 and Katherine O'Brien O'Keeffe, *Visible Song: Transitional Literacy in Old English Verse*, Cambridge Studies in Anglo-Saxon England, 4 (Cambridge: Cambridge University Press, 1990), pp. 14–21 for reception-based approaches to Old English manuscripts.

[27] On this issue, see for instance Tobias Bulang, *Enzyklopädische Dichtungen: Fallstudien zu Wissen und Literatur in Spätmittelalter und früher Neuzeit*, Deutsche Literatur. Studien und Quellen, 2 (Berlin: Akademie Verlag, 2011).

[28] Nicholas Howe, *The Old English Catalogue Poems*, Anglistica, 23 (Copenhagen: Rosenkilde and Bagger, 1985),

There is a connection between function and form, established through convention, which can help us recognize links between otherwise unrelated texts. This convergence has long been recognized in modern scholarship, which has employed, for want of a better term, the label 'didactic' or 'wisdom poetry' to characterize the respective 'catalogue' poems.[29] Poems like *God's Gifts to Humankind*, *Precepts* and *Widsith*, in spite of their differences in content, can thus be seen as linked through their form, an aspect which, if we follow von Moos, may have had greater significance for the medieval compiler than subject matter.

In addition, even formally dissimilar texts may still be related functionally. For instance, the 'wise narrator' figures that introduce teachings, maxims and even narrative in poems like *Precepts*, *Vainglory*, *The Order of the World* or, for that matter, *The Wanderer*, likewise evoke a didactic context: indeed, the narrator figures of *The Wanderer* and *The Seafarer*, as well as of several other so-called 'elegies' such as *Deor* or *The Riming Poem*, can be understood as passing on a form of ethical knowledge not fundamentally different from that presented in *Precepts* or *Vainglory*, the main difference being that the former combine their teachings with hints of a personal story that is never actually spelled out but largely stays on a general or metaphoric level.[30] Yet this is perhaps more a question of emphasis than of actual difference since indeed most of the 'wisdom' poems maintain a fiction of oral deliverance, either by presenting their catalogues as the speech of a 'wise man' or by feigning a direct dialogue with the reader, as in the case of *Maxims I*:[31]

> Frige mec frodum wordum. Ne læt þinne ferð onhælne,
> degol þæt þu deopost cunne. Nelle ic þe min dyrne gesecgan,
> gif þu me þinne hygecræft hylest ond þine heortan geþohtas.
> Gleawe men sceolon gieddum wrixlan. (*Maxims I*, lines 1–4)

> Interrogate me with learned words. Don't let your mind be hidden, the mysteries that you know most deeply. Nor will I tell you my secrets if you hide from me your intellect and the thoughts of your heart. Wise men should exchange wise words/riddles.

The structural similarity between 'elegies' and 'wisdom poems' is perhaps most apparent in *Widsith*, a poem that consists chiefly of long and often apparently disconnected lists of peoples and rulers that the eponymous narrator, a wandering poet, has supposedly visited or at least heard of. Because of the catalogue format, the poem has often been assigned to the category of wisdom poems. Yet the main part of the poem, presented as the protagonist's speech, is not merely introduced and concluded by a general narrator, as it is in the other 'catalogue poems'

---

p. 23.

[29] See, for instance, *Poems of Wisdom and Learning in Old English*, ed. T. A. Shippey (Cambridge: Brewer, 1976); Thomas D. Hill, 'Wise Words: Old English Sapiental Poetry', in *Readings in Medieval Texts: Interpreting Old and Middle English Literature*, ed. by David F. Johnson and Elaine Treharne (Oxford: Oxford University Press, 2005), pp. 166–79; Michael D. C. Drout, *How Tradition Works: A Meme-Based Cultural Poetics of the Anglo-Saxon Tenth Century* (Tempe, AZ: ACMRS, 2006), pp. 219–92.

[30] Cf. T. A. Shippey, 'The Wanderer and The Seafarer as Wisdom Poetry', in *Companion to Old English Poetry*, ed. by Hendrik Aertsen and Rolf H. Bremmer, Jr. (Amsterdam: Vrije University Press, 1994), pp. 145–58.

[31] This combination of formal and stylistic features suggestive of oral delivery with subject matter seemingly derived from both ecclesiastical literary and (presumably) lay oral contexts illustrates Irvine's assertion that 'Old English poetic texts are constituted by an interplay between the textual memory of an oral culture, known to us only as a dialectical inverse of textual culture inscribed as a trace or absence within a text, and the culture of *grammatica* [i.e., Latin-influenced literary culture]' (Irvine, p. 185). The only poems of the group that lack such features of feigned orality are *God's Gifts to Humankind* and *The Fates of Mortals*, although the former could well be read as a continuation of *The Wanderer* and hence the protagonist's speech; see below.

that employ a narrator-figure; here, as in *The Wanderer*, it is the speaker himself who interrupts his enumeration of peoples and rulers in order to refer to his personal experiences. These, indeed, provide a striking echo of the loneliness and separation from friends and relatives lamented by *The Wanderer*'s and *The Seafarer*'s protagonists:

> Swa ic geondferde fela fremdra londa
> geond ginne grund — godes ond yfles
> þær ic cunnade cnosle bidæled,
> freomægum feor folgade wide. (*Widsith*, lines 50–53)

> So I journeyed through many foreign lands throughout the wide earth — good and evil there I experienced, bereft of family, distant from kinsmen, I served far and wide.

Conversely, both *The Wanderer* and *The Seafarer* include long sections of teachings and statements so general that, to paraphrase Pope, 'they could be attached to almost any edifying poem.' In *The Seafarer*, some of these statements echo *Maxims I*.[32]

Bearing these observations in mind, it is thus possible to group these poems together, irrespective of whether they use the catalogue format or not: the one feature they all share is their engagement with — and, indeed, transmission of — various forms of knowledge. This sequence, starting with *The Wanderer*, can even be extended to include the three poems usually referred to as the 'Old English *Physiologus*', *The Panther*, *The Whale* and *The Partridge*, which immediately follow the 'catalogue poems' and 'elegies' just mentioned and likewise belong to a tradition associated with knowledge and wisdom, the medieval bestiary.[33] Indeed, in its specific selection of animals whose allegorical interpretations refer to God, Satan and Man's choice between the two,[34] the Exeter Book *Physiologus* presents a form of ethical knowledge that fits well with the teachings presented, on the one hand, in *The Wanderer* and *The Seafarer* and, on the other, in such poems as *Precepts* or *Vainglory*. At the same time, the *Physiologus* purports to explicate phenomena of the natural world (the behaviour of animals).[35] Similarly, the two collections of riddles that take up most of the last third of the Exeter Book playfully engage with questions of knowledge, exploiting school texts and bestiaries for their subject matter and often presenting their subject by recourse to Pliny's *Historia naturalis* or Isidore's *Etymologiae*.[36] There is also an obvious formal resemblance between the dialogic question-answer structure of the riddles and interrogative dialogues in didactic contexts, such as Alcuin's

---

[32] Pope, p. 33.

[33] Cf. Florence McCulloch, *Medieval Latin and French Bestiaries*, University of North Carolina Studies in the Romance Languages and Literatures, 33 (Chapel Hill: University of North Carolina Press, 1962), p. 15: 'From the early centuries of our era through the Middle Ages the *Physiologus* and its later, expanded form, the bestiary, were among the most popular and important of Christian didactic works.' Cf. also Nikolaus Henkel, *Studien zum Physiologus im Mittelalter*, Hermaea, germanistische Forschungen, 38 (Tübingen: Niemeyer, 1976).

[34] Pope, pp. 34–35.

[35] This latter concern links the Exeter Book *Physiologus* to the two preceding poems, *The Order of the World* and *The Riming Poem*, the former of which celebrates the greatness of God's creation, while the narrator of the latter has been interpreted as God's will personified: Ruth P. M. Lehmann, 'The Old English Riming Poem: Interpretation, Text and Translation', *Journal of English and Germanic Philology*, 69 (1970), 437–49 (p. 444). See further footnote 138.

[36] Dieter Bitterli, *Say What I am Called: The Old English Riddles of the Exeter Book and the Anglo-Latin Riddle Tradition*, Toronto Anglo-Saxon Series, 2 (Toronto, ON: University of Toronto Press, 2009), p. 19. The indebtedness of the Exeter Book riddles to Isidore's *Etymologiae*, not only with regard to subject matter and treatment but also to their internal structuring, is discussed in detail by Salvador-Bello, according to whom the Exeter Book riddles evince a 'manifest didactic intent' (p. 343). Riddles, she argues, 'permitted authors to effectively channel knowledge of grammar, rhetoric, encyclopedic lore, lexicography, metrics and other

Disputatio Pippini cum Albino or Ælfric's *Colloqui*. The opening of *Maxims I*, 'Frige mec frodum wordum [...] Gleawe men sceolon gieddum wrixlan' ('Interrogate me with learned words. [...] Wise men should exchange wise words/riddles'), with the term *gied* covering a semantic range from 'song', 'poem', 'tale', 'speech' to 'proverb', 'maxim' and 'riddle',[37] followed by a catalogue of proverbs and commonplace wisdom, gives a good illustration of this overlap. Indeed, Patrick Murphy's observation that a 'sense of the miraculous in the mundane is at the heart of Old English riddling', with many of the Exeter Book riddles revealing 'the great wonder of a commonplace thing'[38] could well apply to many of the 'wisdom' poems, whose contents likewise frequently border on the banal.

If we follow this line of argument, a substantial section of the Exeter Book emerges as being devoted primarily to the transmission of knowledge, its elements connected by formal and functional features rather than content.[39]

Von Moos' injunction that we address aspects such as form, function, method, style or rhetorical strategy is important for studying the Exeter Book in its entirety because the search for thematic coherence has biased our understanding of the manuscript's arrangement and hindered a clearer perception of some of the structural principles behind the compilation as a whole.[40] If we consider the Exeter Book poems according to formal and functional criteria, it is striking that a great number of them can be assigned quite easily to a set of well-established medieval genres, such as the riddle, the bestiary, the homiletic exemplum or hagiography. And yet, assigning poems to genres or categories cannot adequately explain the make-up of

disciplines into a compact literary format' and thus constituted an 'ideal vehicle for didactic and instructional purposes' (p. 448). There is ample evidence that riddling was perceived as related to other forms of knowledge transmission in Anglo-Saxon England. Several Anglo-Saxon ecclesiastics (Aldhelm, Tatwine, Eusebius) are known to have composed and exchanged collections of riddles in Latin as well as in the vernacular, although the latter have not survived, and collections of riddles are often transmitted in medieval manuscripts together with proverbs, fables and dream interpretations (Patrick J. Murphy, *Unriddling the Exeter Riddles* (University Park, PA: Pennsylvania State University Press, 2011), p. 36).

[37] Joseph Bosworth and T. Northcote Toller, *An Anglo-Saxon Dictionary Based on the Manuscript Collections of the Late Joseph Bosworth* (Oxford: Oxford University Press, 1898), s. v. *giedd*. The word is related to Old English *gieddan* 'speak', 'sing', 'recite'.

[38] Murphy, p. 7.

[39] Cf. Shippey, 'The Wanderer' and *Poems of Wisdom and Learning*, pp. 3–4; Michael D. C. Drout, *Tradition and Influence*, pp. 135–69.

[40] In his most recent monograph, Michael D. C. Drout suggests a similar strategy for analysing part of the Exeter Book, based on 'smaller units of form, content and style' as opposed to 'presumed themes' (Drout, *Tradition and Influence*, p. 251). Drout, in his analysis of the distribution of vocabulary and features such as style and structure in the Exeter Book wisdom poems (Conner's booklet II), makes observations similar to mine regarding the generic ambivalences in this part of the Exeter Book. He, however, attributes these generic ambivalences to the ambiguities of a new genre in the process of evolving (cf. e.g. Drout, *Tradition and Influence*, p. 148), whereas my approach highlights the ambiguities inherent in literary texts per se. While I find Drout's analysis highly suggestive, I feel somewhat uncomfortable with its strong reliance on methods that seem to emulate procedures more typical of the natural sciences than of the humanities. Nor am I sure that biology and literature can be compared quite as easily as Drout's 'evolutionary, cognitivist' approach suggests. As Drout himself remarks in his earlier book *How Tradition Works*, the memetic theory is weakened by its inability to adequately explain the workings of memory or account for literary aesthetics (Drout, *How Tradition Works*, p. 294), a problem he hopes will be solved by future psychological and neurobiological research (a confidence I do not share). Such a hope is by no means new: already in 1924 I. A. Richards was referring to future neurological research 'as insuring the solutions of all literary problems', as René Wellek and Austin Warren observe (Wellek and Warren, p. 4). Another point where my approach diverges from Drout's is his contention that 'it is extremely difficult for us, using only current literary theory, for us [sic] to interpret works whose genres we cannot identify' (Drout, *Tradition and Influence*, p. 167). It is worth quoting here von Moos's critique of the modern preoccupation with genres, which he thinks obscures the actual formal principles that guided the medieval way of categorizing texts: 'The actual [...] theoretical

the collection, in spite of the fact that poems falling into these categories tend to occur in sequence. This is because these sequences are neither fully coherent internally nor clearly delimited — were this the case, it would be possible, even reasonable, to assume the existence of different exemplars from which the respective sections were copied. As it is, it often proves difficult to pin-point precisely where one category ends or where another starts,[41] nor can a division according to categories explain why some sequences are interrupted by poems that cannot properly be assigned to the same category, as in the case of the two riddle collections or the hagiographic sequence of *Guthlac A* and *B*, *The Canticles of the Three Youths* and *The Passion of Saint Juliana*, the last of which poems is preceded by the bestiary allegory *The Phoenix*. However, a closer look at the respective passages often reveals striking textual or thematic links, if not between complete poems, then at least between the adjoining ends and opening passages. *The Wanderer*, for instance, is linked both to the preceding encomium of the hagiographic *Passion of Saint Juliana* and the opening lines of the following catalogue poem *God's Gifts to Humankind* in that all three allude to God's mercy and grace.[42] It is only in *The Wanderer*, however, that the theme plays a central role; both *The Passion* and *God's Gifts* give it no more than a passing allusion. *The Wanderer*, to adopt Thomas P. Dunning and Alan J. Bliss's interpretation, can be read as a spiritual biography, an *exemplum* of how an individual came to find God's grace, and thus fits into the sequence of hagiographical poems that precede it.[43] The link to the preceding *Passion* is established through that poem's encomium, 'forgif us mægna god, | þæt we þine onsyne [...] | *milde* gemeten' ('grant us, God of powers, that we find your face mild [i.e. mercyful]', lines 629b–631a, my emphasis), which is followed by *The Wanderer*'s opening line, 'oft him anhaga are gebideð, | metudes *miltse* [...]' ('often the lonely one awaits for himself grace, the Measurer's mildness [i.e., God's grace or mercy]', lines 1–2a, again my emphasis). Similarly, *God's Gifts* takes its cue from *The Wanderer*'s closing words ('wel bið þam þe him are seceð, | frofre to fæder on heofonum', 'it will be well for the one who seeks grace for himself, comfort from the Father in heaven', lines 114b–15a), asserting that God's grace can be seen in the many gifts he dispenses among mankind:

> Fela bið on foldan forðgesynra
> geongra geofona, þa þa gæstberend
> wegað in gewitte, swa her weoruda god,
> ... monnum dæleð. (*God's Gifts to Humankind*, lines 1–4).

> Many there are, visible on earth, the fresh gifts that the spirit-carriers [i.e., human beings] carry in their minds, which the God of multitudes here deals out to men.

---

question about the principles, formal laws, methods of presentation, *modi tractandi* valid in the Middle Ages themselves remains largely unanswered. Medieval forms of narrative, for instance, are treated morphologically, according to the narrative material, not functionally, according to situational intentions and strategies. This can be seen in the studies of the fable, the parable and the exemplum, which were conducted quite independently from each other: the discussion revolves around problems of definition and assignment with regard to content, hardly around rhetorical aspects' (von Moos, pp. XLIV–XLV, my translation). 'Demgegenüber bleibt die eigentliche [...] theoretische Frage nach den im Mittelalter selbst gültigen Prinzipien, Formgesetzen, Darstellungsmethoden, *modi tractandi* weitgehend unbeantwortet. Mittelalterliche Typen der Erzählung etwa werden morphologisch nach Stoffen, nicht funktional nach situativen Absichten und Strategien betrachtet. Dies zeigen die ziemlich unabhängig voneinander durchgeführten Untersuchungen zur Fabel, zur Parabel und zur Beispielgeschichte: Die Diskussion kreist um Definitions- und Zuordnungsprobleme nach inhaltlichen Merkmalen, kaum um rhetorische Aspekte.'

[41] Note, for instance, Murphy's observation that 'even today the defined boundaries of the [riddle] collection remain somewhat in flux' (p. 27).
[42] See the commentary in *The Wanderer*, ed. T. P. Dunning and A. J. Bliss (London: Methuen, 1969), p. 79.
[43] Dunning and Bliss, pp. 80–81.

God's Gifts continues as a catalogue enumerating the various gifts that God has dispensed amongst mankind, ignoring the preceding poem's actual theme and form.

An even more striking example of this associative way of sequencing can be seen in the linking passage between *Christ in Judgement* and *Guthlac A*, in which the closing theme of the former, the coming of the souls of the blessed into heaven, is taken up and related to various ways of leading a virtuous life, one of which — monastic life — is then treated in the following poem, *Guthlac A*. The passage connects equally well to either of the two poems and has consequently been assigned to either by different scholars, although the manuscript division makes it clear that the scribe treated it as part of *Guthlac A*.[44] In any case, the similarities between the two descriptions of the soul's entrance into heaven suggest that the passage may have prompted the poems' order in the manuscript, as Jane Roberts argues.[45] One might even surmise that it was especially written for the purpose of joining the two poems, a possibility implied by Roy M. Liuzza.[46]

There are more examples of this kind scattered throughout the Exeter Book.[47] Zimmermann draws attention to the same phenomenon when she observes that many of the poems are linked in an associative way, by a principle of concatenation, with individual poems taking up phrases, themes or ideas from those preceding or following them and developing them into new directions, resulting in differences of genre or mode of presentation.[48] A similar term is used by Fred C. Robinson when he describes the arrangement of lists and catalogues as 'catenulate'.[49] The Exeter Book, one might argue with Zimmermann, resembles medieval lists and catalogues in so far as many of the poems are likewise arranged in a 'series of joined rather than unified elements'.[50]

Robinson's term 'catenulate' echoes, whether deliberately or not, the mnemonic tool of the chain or *catena*, employed as a means of structuring items stored in one's memory and, by extension, the contents of written lists and catalogues. Indeed, late antique and early medieval florilegia and encyclopaedias — genres that by the time the Exeter Book was compiled had gained new popularity through Carolingian works like Hrabanus Maurus's *De universo* — frequently employed a combination of categories and associative links between individual subjects.[51] The Exeter Book is no encyclopaedia, but it shares with the genre a number

---

[44] Cf. the discussion and literature cited in *The Guthlac Poems of the Exeter Book*, ed. by Jane Roberts (Oxford: Clarendon, 1979), pp. 49–51; Liuzza, pp. 1–4.

[45] *The Guthlac Poems*, p. 49.

[46] Liuzza, p. 5. He similarly draws attention to the transitional nature of *The Ascension*, which may have been written or at least reworked in order to conjoin the two other *Christ*-poems, possibilities first entertained by, respectively, Dolores W. Frese, 'The Art of Cynewulf's Runic Signatures', in *Anglo-Saxon Poetry: Essays in Appreciation*, ed. by Lewis Nicholson and Dolores Warwick Frese (Notre Dame: University of Notre Dame Press, 1976), pp. 301–11 and Colin Chase, 'God's Presence through Grace as the Theme of Cynewulf's *Christ II* and the Relation of this Theme to *Christ I* and *Christ III*', *Anglo-Saxon England*, 3 (1974), 87–101 (Liuzza, p. 6).

[47] Cf. for instance Bitterli's discussion of the 'storm' and 'bird' riddles (pp. 35–36) and the many verbal echoes in the Exeter Book wisdom poems observed by Michael D. C. Drout (Drout, *How Tradition Works*, pp. 239–86; Drout, *Tradition and Influence*, pp. 138–69) and Brian O'Camb, 'The Inscribed Form of *Exeter Maxims* and the Layout of Quire XI of the Exeter Book', in *The Genesis of Books: Studies in the Scribal Culture of Medieval England in Honour of A. N. Doane*, ed. by Matthew T. Hussey and John D. Niles (Turnhout: Brepols, 2011), pp. 137–59.

[48] Zimmermann, p. 159. Brian O'Camb similarly surmises that 'the Exeter Book scribe or compiler crafted thematic and verbal connections' in order to arrange the texts 'into thematically meaningful sequences' (p. 158).

[49] Robinson, p. 26.

[50] Howe, p. 27.

[51] For an argument that the compilation of the Exeter Book is at least partly influenced by Continental, Carolingian models, see Conner, *Anglo-Saxon Exeter*, pp. 148, 150, and footnote 21 above. I have not studied Latin poetic

of structural principles that can ultimately be traced to classical and medieval methods of organization as discussed in the theories of mnemonics and topics.[52] As a compilation of miscellaneous poetry, some of which seems to have been reworked or abridged in order to fit the manuscript context, the Exeter Book may indeed have been planned as a kind of florilegium of vernacular poetic texts, perhaps because these could be quoted in hortatory or wisdom-related contexts or were at least thought worth preserving for posterity. Yet whatever the actual or intended function(s) of the Exeter Book, it is not unreasonable to assume that methods of organisation known from Latin models may have influenced the compilation of Old English manuscripts. As Martin Irvine points out,

> *grammatica* [i.e., the discipline that governed literacy, the study of literary language, the interpretation of texts, and the writing of manuscripts] and the technology of book production were the historical preconditions for the culture of the monastery and church, and, consequently, this culture was the historical precondition for the appearance of Old English texts. [...] The very fact that Old English poems were recorded in manuscripts signifies that they functioned within the library of textual culture.[53]

In order to gain a better understanding of the way the Exeter Book is organized, we will have to look more closely at these collections and the theories that shaped them.

Mnemonic and dialectic topics and the organization of encyclopaedic knowledge

Florilegia, compilations of excerpts from larger works, served both as textbooks and memorial aids. They usually contained texts on a variety of topics, from maxims and the sayings of great writers to exempla of virtuous behaviour and even divine learning and natural history. While florilegia did not necessarily aspire to the same universal scope as encyclopaedias, there were overlaps, as in the case of Hrabanus Maurus's encyclopaedia *De universo*, whose stated purpose is essentially that of a florilegium. In the prefatory address to his friend, bishop Haimon, for whom the work was compiled, Hrabanus states: 'cogitabam, quid Tuæ Sanctitati

---

collections in any detail, but at least some of them likewise arrange their material into categories. For instance, the *Carmina* of Venantius Fortunatus, which appear four times in Helmut Gneuss, *Handlist of Anglo-Saxon Manuscripts: A List of Manuscripts and Manuscript Fragments Written or Owned in England up to 1100*, Medieval and Renaissance Texts and Studies, 241 (Tempe, AZ: Arizona Center for Medieval and Renaissance Studies, 2001), in manuscripts dated to the ninth and tenth centuries (with one possible eleventh-century exception), are divided into thematically coherent books, with some inconsistencies and overlaps. It is not unlikely that Latin encyclopaedic compilations were used as models for vernacular collections, given that all of them were produced or at least copied in the same literary environment.

[52] A related approach that the present paper does not follow is Katherine O'Brien O'Keeffe's thesis of 'residual orality' that would allow for a concomitance of primarily 'oral' and 'literary' techniques in Anglo-Saxon textual culture. According to O'Brien O'Keeffe, Old English texts and manuscript differ from Latin ones in showing a higher frequency of 'oral' traces, such as a lack of punctuation and stress marks, which suggests 'a strong overlay of oral habits of transmission in the copying of Old English formulaic verse' as well as a certain amount of familiarity with Old English poetic rhetorical strategies on part of the reader (O'Brien O'Keeffe, pp. 21–22). While the rhetorical strategies discussed in the present contribution parallel O'Brien O'Keeffe's argument in that both the mnemonic and the dialectical topical method were originally developed for 'oral' contexts (debates and orations) yet were quickly integrated into practices of literary composition and compilation, they would have been known to Anglo-Saxons compilers and readers of manuscripts via Latin literary works, and indeed recent studies have traced the 'formulaic' characteristics of the 'wisdom' poems to Latin models (see the studies by Howe and Drout mentioned above).

[53] Irvine, p. 186.

gratum et utile in scribendo conficere possem: quo haberes ob commemorationem in paucis breviter adnotatum quod ante in multorum codicum amplitudine [...] legisti' ('I considered what I could produce in writing that would be welcome and useful to Your Holiness: through which you would have for your recollection in briefly annotated selections that which you have previously read in the abundance of great codices').[54] As compilations of extracts, florilegia reflected the excerpting habits of medieval scholars who, while reading, would make mental notes or even memorize whole passages of text.[55] As Mary Carruthers points out: 'A florilegium is basically the contents of someone's memory, set forth as a kind of study-guide for the formation of others' memories.'[56] Consequently, the arrangement of florilegia was often based on the same structural principles as those used by scholars to memorize texts. These could vary depending on subject matter; some florilegia arrange their excerpts by moral topic, others in alphabetical order according to subject, incipit or author's name.[57] Some compilations show no discernible order at all, which does not mean that they were wholly unstructured. As Carruthers points out, 'An unorganized compilation could hardly be used unless it were to cue an already-formed *memoria*, readers slipping the material into their own basic schemes, as they had been taught to do.'[58] Indeed, classical and medieval texts on the art of memorizing constantly stress the benefits of using one's own schemes rather than ready-made ones.[59] Nevertheless, Carruthers adds, 'collections that come with their own organization were also designed to stock or cue the memories of their users'.[60]

Encyclopaedias likewise follow a variety of different ordering principles, sometimes even within one and the same work. Works like Pliny's *Historia naturalis*, Cassiodorus' *Institutiones divinarum et humanarum lectionum* or Isidore's *Originum seu Etymologiarum libri XX* are arranged categorically according to fields of knowledge, that is, they place their contents in categories like geography, zoology, medicine, mineralogy, astronomy, houses, peoples, the heavenly hierarchies and so on.[61] Within these fields, subjects may be arranged alphabetically (as in the case of Book x of Isidore's *Originum seu Etymologiarum*, where etymologies and word-formation are discussed) or in descending cosmological or utilitarian importance, and the fields themselves may similarly follow various kinds of order, according to cosmological significance or the order of the trivium and the quadrivium, to give just two examples. The principles of arrangement can even vary within one and the same work, depending on the subject and the arrangement most suitable to it.[62]

---

[54] B. Rabani Mauri Fuldensis abbatis et Moguntini archiepiscopi opera omnia: Variis praeterea monumentis quae suppeditarunt Mabillonii, Martenii et Dacherii collectiones memoratissimae aucta et illustrata, ed. by J.-P. Migne, Patrologiae cursus completus: Patrologia latina, series secunda, 111 (Paris: Migne, 1852), pp. 11–12 (my translation).

[55] A discussion of medieval practices of mentally excerpting material from books can be found in Mary J. Carruthers, *The Book of Memory: A Study of Memory in Medieval Culture*, Cambridge Studies in Medieval Literature, 70, 2nd edn (Cambridge: Cambridge University Press, 2008), pp. 105 and 136–37.

[56] Carruthers, p. 218.

[57] Carruthers, p. 220.

[58] Carruthers, p. 221.

[59] Carruthers, p. 180.

[60] Carruthers, p. 221.

[61] See Robert Collison, *Encyclopaedias. Their History Throughout the Ages: A Bibliographical Guide with Extensive Historical Notes to the General Encyclopaedias Issued throughout the World from 350 B.C. to the Present Day* (New York: Hafner, 1964), pp. 21–73 for an overview of classical and medieval encyclopaedias.

[62] Howe, pp. 19–21.

Usually the principles employed had some foundation in general or traditional practice. Pliny's *Historia naturalis*, for instance, begins with the universe and ends with the minerals, which are again arranged according to the traditional hierarchical order.[63] Similarly, Hrabanus Maurus's *De universo*, albeit arranged by key-words, is organized not alphabetically but 'logically', starting with God and the angels.[64] Hrabanus is thus following the advice of Saint Augustine, who had criticized the arrangement of the contents of Varro's encyclopaedia on the grounds that he had placed secular matters before things divine.[65] (It might be noted here that the Exeter Book, too, begins with matters divine by opening with a trinity of poems on the Incarnation, the Ascension and the Last Judgement, in a poetic sequence centring on man's relations to Christ.[66]) But while this arrangement is called 'logical' in the quotation above, it must be stressed that it is not uniquely so. Christian writers might prefer to put divine matters before secular ones, but this is a question of ideology or convention: Hrabanus or Augustine would have readily conceded that Varro's arrangement is equally 'logical' — logical here meaning 'systematic', i.e. by subject rather than by schemes unrelated to the topic, like alphabetical or numerical ones.

To a great extent, the order actually employed is determined by the material in the collection, but even here the compiler is free — indeed required — to make innumerable choices. The variability of these structural schemes — as opposed to the predictable but inflexible alphabetical order usually employed in modern encyclopaedias — can be traced to two distinct yet related traditions of structuring knowledge: the dialectic, which promoted systematic order, and the mnemonic, which worked on principles of association.[67] We have seen earlier how both categorical and associative principles contribute to shaping the order of the Exeter Book poems. Both the dialectic and the mnemonic tradition involve the use of so-called *loci* (Greek *topoi*), literally 'places' in which information can be stored and from which it can be drawn. This coincidence of terminology suggests to Eleonore Stump that the use of *loci* has its origin in the ancient methods of memorization, in which a 'topic' literally denotes a place that the memorizer pictures in his mind in order to store or retrieve information.[68]

---

[63] Howe, pp. 35–39.
[64] Carruthers, p. 219.
[65] Collison, p. 44.
[66] Salvador-Bello, p. 342, notes that the first of the two riddle sequences in the Exeter Book likewise starts with a cosmological theme (wind in its various manifestations), while the last of the Exeter Book riddles bar one is one of three 'creation' riddles. Even more importantly, the first group of riddles at least initially follows a twofold pattern (also found in the second decade of books in Isidore's *Originum seu Etymologiarum*) of *opera-dei* and *opera-hominis* themes.
[67] The following, very much simplified discussion will focus on the way these methods were understood at around the time the Exeter Book was compiled. I will treat historical developments only where necessary. I direct the reader to the following excellent works, from which my discussion is mainly drawn: Carruthers, *The Book of Memory*; Niels Jørgen Green-Pedersen, *The Tradition of the Topics in the Middle Ages: The Commentaries on Aristotle's and Boethius' 'Topics'* (München: Philosophia Verlag, 1984); *Boethius's 'De topicis differentiis'*, ed. by Eleonore Stump (Ithaca, NY: Cornell University Press, 1978); *Boethius's 'In Ciceronis topica'*, ed. by Eleonore Stump (Ithaca, NY: Cornell University Press, 1988); Wilhelm Schmidt-Biggemann, 'Sinnfülle, Einsicht, System. Bemerkungen zur topischen Arbeitsweise im Humanismus', in *Entwicklung der Methodenlehre in Rechtswissenschaft und Philosophie vom 16. bis zum 18. Jahrhundert: Beiträge zu einem interdisziplinären Symposium in Tübingen, 18.–20. April 1996*, ed. by Jan Schröder, Contubernium. Tübinger Beiträge zur Universitäts- und Wissenschaftsgeschichte, 46 (Stuttgart: Franz Steiner Verlag, 1998), pp. 27–46; Frances A. Yates, 'The Ciceronian Art of Memory', in *Medioevo e Rinascimento: Studi in onore di Bruno Nardi*, ed. by G. C. Sansoni (Florence: Pubblicazioni dell' Instituto di Filosofia dell' Università di Roma, 1955), pp. 871–903; Frances A. Yates, *The Art of Memory* (Chicago: University of Chicago Press, 1966).
[68] *De topicis differentiis*, p. 16.

During the Middle Ages, one of the most influential mnemonic techniques was the architectural method described in Cicero's *De oratore*, Quintilian's *De institutione oratoria* and the anonymous first-century B.C. *Rhetorica ad Herennium*, a work attributed to Cicero during the Middle Ages.[69] According to Cicero's *De oratore* (II, 86),

> [E]is qui hanc partem ingeni exercerent locos esse capiendos et ea quae memoria tenere vellent effigenda animo atque in eis locis collocanda: sic fore ut ordinem rerum locorum ordo conservaret, res autem ipsas rerum effigies notaret, atque ut locis pro cera, simulacris pro litteris uteremur.
>
> ([P]ersons desiring to train this faculty [of memory] must select localities and form mental images of the facts they wish to remember and store those images in the localities, with the result that the arrangement of the localities will preserve the order of the facts, and the images of the facts will designate the facts themselves, and we shall employ the localities and images respectively as a wax writing tablet and the letters written on it.)[70]

The fullest account of this method is given in Book III of the *Rhetorica ad Herennium*. According to this account, the memorizer associates the imaginary *loci* with real places, e.g. corners, columns or arches in a building. If he cannot find a suitable building, he can also devise an imaginary sequence of places.[71] In these *loci* he stores images, forms, marks or simulacra (ideally striking or unusual ones, since these are easier to remember), with which he associates the pieces of knowledge he wishes to remember.[72] As Richard Sorabji notes, the two sets of images have the advantage that 'one will remember not only the points in one's speech, but also, thanks to the background places, their order. [...] The background places can supply a connexion in cases where the items one is memorizing have no memorable connexion of their own.'[73] Ideally, of course, the parts of a particular speech will already follow an inherent train of thought that makes it easier to memorize their order, but this is not necessarily the case with unconnected items of knowledge: Seneca the Elder, for instance, claimed he could repeat two thousand names after a single hearing or two hundred disconnected lines of verse either in the order given or in reverse order,[74] and similar accounts abound in classical and medieval sources.[75]

Methodologically, the architectural method represents a whole chain of associations: items of knowledge are associated with images, images with *loci*, and *loci* with real or imagined

---

[69] According to Carruthers, p. 87, the treatise was written *circa* 86–82 B.C., possibly by someone who had the same teacher as Cicero. The treatise is directed at someone named Herennius, hence the title. It was referred to by Thomas Aquinas and others as 'Tullius's [i.e., Cicero's] Second Rhetoric' (the first being Cicero's *De inventione*) and thought to present the author's mature views on rhetoric (Yates, 'The Ciceronian Art of Memory', p. 881). Although Carruthers maintains that 'there is little evidence of anyone, classical or medieval, systematically teaching the *Rhetorica ad Herennium* before the end of the eleventh century' (p. 154), this does not mean that the method was discontinued or forgotten in the earlier Middle Ages. For instance, the same practice seems to be referred to in St. Augustine's *Confessions*, another highly influential text in the period under discussion, who speaks of 'the fields and palaces of memory (*campos et lata praetorian memoriae*) where are the treasures of innumerable images, brought into it by things of all sorts perceived by the senses' (Yates, 'The Ciceronian Art of Memory', p. 880).

[70] Text and translation from *Cicero: De oratore*, ed. by E. W. Sutton and H. Rackham, The Loeb Classical Library, 348, 2 vols (London: Heinemann, 1948), I, 254–55.

[71] Yates, 'The Ciceronian Art of Memory', p. 877.

[72] Yates, *The Art of Memory*, p. 6.

[73] Richard Sorabji, *Aristotle on Memory* (Providence: Brown University Press, 1972), p. 24.

[74] Sorabji, p. 22.

[75] Cf. for instance Carruthers, pp. 21, 133, 143.

architectural constructions. Quintilian notes that it is easier to link pieces of knowledge to the images if there is some resemblance or associative link between the two, such as, for instance, an anchor which can serve as a reminder of navigation.[76] This idea goes back to Aristotle's discussion in *De memoria* of the process of recollection, which is said to work like a chain of associations: a starting image gives rise to a train of thought which leads through a number of steps to the idea one wishes to recollect. *De memoria* was not available at the time the Exeter Book was compiled, but the idea of developing ideas through an associative process can be detected in many other works on mnemonics.[77]

The architectural mnemonic was not the only mnemonic method known during the Middle Ages; others make use of the alphabet, numbers or key-words — the latter being especially relevant in the light of the Exeter Book's way of sequencing poems via verbal or phrasal echoes. But what unites all these different memory schemes is the way they use various levels of association in order to keep together and structure what is supposed to be remembered. A recurring image is that of the *catena* or chain that binds together the various images or ideas. Carruthers quotes Quintilian's remark that 'however large the number [of items] we must remember, all are linked one to another like dancers hand in hand, and there can be no mistake since they join what precedes to what follows, no trouble being required except the preliminary labor of memorizing'.[78] The emphasis on correct sequential order is very characteristic of classical and medieval treatises, whose writers seem to have been impressed not so much by the ability to memorize items, but to arrange and re-arrange them in various kinds of order, like the ability to recite poetry backwards that Augustine lauds in *De natura et origine animae*.[79]

Nicholas Howe has shown how in classical and late antique encyclopaedias the order of items within categories often follows catenulate principles, that is, as a series of joined rather than unified elements, and how these principles recur in Old English catalogue poems like *Gods's Gifts to Humankind* or *Widsith*.[80] There is every reason, then, to likewise link the catenulate method of sequencing poems that we have observed, for instance, between *Christ in Judgement* and *Guthlac A* or *The Passion of Saint Juliana*, *The Wanderer* and *God's Gifts to Humankind* to the mnemonic techniques reflected in the encyclopaedic tradition.

Due to their usefulness in composing and remembering speeches, mnemonic methods were taught as a part of rhetoric,[81] although in practice they could be used for any effort at

---

[76] Carruthers, p. 135.
[77] Yates, 'The Ciceronian Art of Memory', p. 885; Carruthers, pp. 80–81.
[78] Carruthers, p. 78.
[79] Carruthers, p. 21; Yates, 'The Ciceronian Art of Memory', p. 879. This does not, however, preclude digressions or excursive developments. Indeed, an associative development of ideas is especially apt for digressions, since associations can work in all sorts of directions. Carruthers illustrates this with the tree-model Hugh of St. Victor employs in his *De archa Noe*. In this work, a commentary on Genesis 6–7, the discussion is divided into successive stages modelled after the growth of a tree. 'Within this essential structure, a number of excursive topics are developed from a phrase or word of the rubric; these may bring in other linked texts. Basically the structure is that of a concordance, or *catena*, in which the parts are associated by key-words, each of which pulls other texts and sayings with it' (Carruthers, p. 259). This twelfth-century work is later than the Exeter Book, but it provides a useful parallel to a poetic sequence like that from *The Wanderer* through *The Seafarer*, where certain ideas expressed in one poem give rise to digressions about the nature of God's grace or monastic advice before returning to hitherto undeveloped themes.
[80] Howe, p. 27.
[81] Cicero in *De oratore* discusses memory as one of the five parts of rhetoric, *inventio, dispositio, elocutio, memoria, pronuntiatio* (Yates, *The Art of Memory*, pp. 2, 5).

repeating something from memory, such as laws or lines of verse.[82] By contrast, the other great tradition dealing with *loci*, the topics, were associated with dialectic (philosophical disputes) and hence with logic. The association of the dialectical topic with the organizing of knowledge, which became the basis of the early modern obsession with systematization and hence of the great encyclopaedic endeavours of the sixteenth and seventeenth centuries, was originally only a by-product, yet, I shall argue, one that was inevitable and whose presence can be detected even in medieval encyclopaedias.

The association of topics with dialectic goes back to Aristotle, who calls the discipline he discusses in his *Topics* 'dialectic'. Aristotle never actually explains what a topic is; according to Stump, 'he seems to assume that the meaning of "Topic" as a technical term is familiar'.[83] Aristotle mentions rhetorical and mnemonic topics, but he uses the term mainly in the context of dialectic, where it seems to denote both a strategy of argumentation and a principle of confirming an argument.[84] The method makes use of 'accepted views' or 'plausible standpoints' that are commonly held to be true, but may or may not be.[85] Thus, dialectic is not a science; it cannot prove but only point out what is probable. For this reason, it was later also known as *logica probabilis*, in contrast to the *logica demonstrativa*, which concerned things that could be *shown* (i.e., proved) to be true.[86]

Aristotle's *Topics* were not known at first hand in Western Europe before the twelfth century, and even then they were interpreted through Boethius's works on the subject, in spite of the fact that the latter's conception of Topics is very different from Aristotle's.[87] Boethius's two works on topics, *In Ciceronis Topica* and *De differentiis topicis*, through which the theory was chiefly known during the early Middle Ages, were introduced in the West earlier. Niels Green-Pedersen surmises that the former was known by the year 1000, and that *De differentiis topicis* was certainly read and commented upon well before the middle of the eleventh century.[88] Moreover, there are allusions to both works in Alcuin's *Dialectica*,[89] which means that their contents at least seem to have been familiar during the eighth century, even

---

[82] Cf. Yates, 'The Ciceronian Art of Memory', p. 877.

[83] *De topicis differentiis*, p. 165.

[84] *In Ciceronis topica*, p. 4; see however the discussion in Green-Pedersen, pp. 23–25.

[85] Green-Pedersen, p. 17; *De topicis differentiis*, pp. 18–20.

[86] The *logica probabilis* was supposed to convince through the similarity of the examples used in a specific argument to the original proposition. Cf. Wilhelm Schmidt-Biggemann, 'Was ist eine probable Argumentation? Beobachtungen über Topik', in *Topik und Rhetorik: Ein interdisziplinäres Symposium*, ed. by Thomas Schirren and Gert Ueding, Rhetorik-Forschungen, 13 (Tübingen: Niemeyer, 2000), pp. 243–56 (p. 253): 'Bei einer solchen Argumentation werden allein wahrscheinliche Argumente verwendet. Kein Argument ist schlechterdings schlagend, aber die entfaltete Fülle von imaginierten — und allemal aus semantischer Analogie gewonnenen Vorstellungen begründet am Ende einen Entschluß in überzeugender Weise' ('in this kind of argumentation only probable arguments are used. No single argument is decisive in itself, but the plethora of imagined concepts — that were obtained indeed by semantic analogy — ultimately provides convincing justification of a decision'; my translation).

[87] According to Green-Pedersen, pp. 87 and 342, Aristotle's work was introduced in Western Europe shortly before 1150.

[88] He states as his evidence that Gerbert of Aurillac (*c.* 1000) is reported to have used both works, which he thinks unlikely for *De differentiis topicis* but probable for *In Ciceronis Topica*, and that the three commentaries on *De differentiis topicis* that survive from before 1100 seem to look back on a solid tradition (Green-Pedersen, pp. 123–24). Cicero's *Topica* seems to have been known throughout, but does not seem to have exerted much influence, or at least only in conjunction with Boethius's commentary on it (Green-Pedersen, p. 39). Gneuss (p. 106) lists one manuscript containing both Cicero's *Topica* and Boethius's *In Ciceronis Topica*, which he dates to the ninth or tenth century (MS Oxford, Merton College, 309, fols 114–201).

[89] According to Stump in *In Ciceronis topica*, p. 6. See also Rosamond McKitterick, *The Caroligians and the Written*

if they were not available as complete works.⁹⁰ In fact, the principles of topical arrangement could be learned from existing collections even if the theory behind them was not known.⁹¹ But given that at least one of Boethius's works on the topics seems to have been available by the year 1000, there is some probability that the composition of the Exeter Book, dated conventionally to the last quarter of the tenth century, coincided with an increasing interest in the topical method. If this is correct, then the use of the topical method as a means of organization may be yet another instance of the 'experimentalism and almost pioneering spirit' that Dieter Bitterli detects in the Exeter Book.⁹²

Boethius's discussion of topics is based on Cicero's *Topica*. Cicero's concept of a topic, which he translates as *locus*, is very different from Aristotle's, despite the fact that his *Topica* purports to be a book on Aristotelian topics.⁹³ For Cicero, topics are primarily a method of discovering and assessing arguments. There are two separate steps involved: *inventio* (finding or discovering arguments) and *iudicium* (assessing them). Boethius seems to consider only the *inventio* as topics proper (and it is this part which is also relevant to topical organization), as can be seen in the introductory remarks to *In differentiis topicis*:

> The whole science of discourse (*ratio disserendi*), which the ancient Peripatetics called 'λογική', is divided into two parts: one for discovering, the other for judging. The part which purges and instructs judgment, called 'ἀναλυτική' by them, we name 'analytical.' The part which aids competence (*facultatem*) in discovering, called 'τοπική' by the Greeks, is called 'Topical' (*localis*) by us.⁹⁴

The aim of topics, Boethius explains, is to show in a systematic manner a multitude of plausible arguments. This is achieved by referring to the characteristics of the concept in question. For instance, Boethius claims, in a syllogism mentioned in his *In Ciceronis Topica*, that if 'every animal is either rational or irrational' and that if 'Cicero is rational', then it follows that Cicero must be an animal.⁹⁵ Rationality here is a characteristic shared by Cicero, human beings in general, and some animals: it is divisive of the genus 'animal' (some animals are rational while others are not) but constitutive of the species 'man' (all men are rational).⁹⁶ From the latter

---

Word (Cambridge: Cambridge University Press, 1989), pp. 198–200, who mentions the possibility of an insular influence (via Alcuin and insular monastic foundations such as Fulda) on the Carolingian organization of libraries.

⁹⁰ As Joyce Hill reminds us, there is no simple correlation between works that have been identified as the sources of surviving texts and Anglo-Saxon libraries: even in cases where a text directly refers to a specific work, this work 'may well have been known via some intermediary, such as a compendium or florilegium' (Joyce Hill, 'Leofric of Exeter and the Practical Politics of Book Collecting', in *Imagining the Book*, ed. by Stephen Kelly and John J. Thompson, Medieval Texts and Cultures of Northern Europe, 7 (Turnhout: Brepols, 2005), pp. 77–98 (p. 77)).

⁹¹ This is suggested by McKitterick, who draws attention to the tantalizing possibility that the *Versus Isidori*, a collection of verses on the Bible, a series of church fathers, Christian poets, historians, law codes and medical books, may have played a role 'in disseminating the accepted arrangement of a library' (p. 205). This implies that some degree of cross-fertilization was possible between the arrangement of libraries and that of literary works.

⁹² Bitterli, p. 26.

⁹³ See, however, *De topicis differentiis*, p. 20. For a discussion of the differences between Aristotelian and Ciceronian topics, see *De topicis differentiis*, p. 205.

⁹⁴ Translation from *De topicis differentiis*, p. 29.

⁹⁵ *In Ciceronis topica*, p. 113. The example is confusing because the maximal proposition 'every animal is either rational or irrational' does not preclude that there are irrational or rational things that are not animals. Also, Boethius uses this as an example of the division of genus, although Stump argues that it should be an argument of species rather than genus (*In Ciceronis topica*, pp. 218, endnote 31). I use this example to illustrate the way in which structurally similar arguments can be used to reveal various characteristics of one and the same entity (see below).

⁹⁶ *De topicis differentiis*, p. 239.

proposition, a different argument could be constructed that if Cicero is a man, he must be rational. However, since 'rational' is not the only characteristic of Cicero, one may construct any number of arguments using the same pattern. In another place, for instance, Boethius claims that 'every man is an animal', so if that is accepted it follows that, since Cicero is a man, he must also be an animal.[97]

    The abundance of possible arguments has two implications. First, a variety of good arguments makes a case stronger: even if none of them is able to convince on its own, the sheer number of arguments strengthens the debater's position by making the original claim more probable. Secondly — and this is important in the context of organization — the topical method stresses the multidimensionality and polysemy of a concept by considering its various aspects and associations.[98]

    The topic or *locus*, according to Boethius, is the place from which one draws the argument: 'A topic is the seat of an argument, or that from which one draws an argument appropriate to the question under consideration'.[99] The *locus*, Boethius explains, consists of two elements, a maximal proposition or maxim (*maxima propositio*) and its *differentiae*. A maximal proposition is a statement that is generally accepted as true (it is also sometimes referred to as a 'commonplace') and that cannot be proved by something else. Boethius's standard example of a maximal proposition is: 'If you take equals from equals, the remainders are equal'.[100] The *differentiae* distinguish the maximal propositions from each other, for instance definition, genus, effect or parts of a whole. They can be thought of as the characteristics of the concept that forms the subject of the maximal proposition. The name of the *locus* is identical with that of the *differentia*, e.g. 'from definition', 'from genus' and so on. Since the number of maximal propositions is near infinite but that of their *differentiae* limited, the *loci* are divided and classed according to their *differentiae*.[101] These stand in a generic relation to each other, so that they can be arranged in a kind of tree-diagram, the *arbor porphyriana* or Porphyrian Tree, so-called after its appearance in Porphyry's *Isagoge*, a third-century introduction to Aristotle's *Categories* (fourth century BCE) that was translated into Latin by Boethius and which remained the standard textbook on logic throughout the Middle Ages.[102] Incidentally,

---

[97] *De topicis differentiis*, p. 31.
[98] See Wilhelm Schmidt-Biggemann and Anja Hallacker, 'Topik: Tradition und Erneuerung', in *Topik und Tradition: Prozesse der Neuordnung von Wissensüberlieferungen des 13. bis 17. Jahrhunderts*, ed. by Thomas Frank, Ursula Kocher and Ulrike Tarnow, Berliner Mittelalter- und Frühneuzeitforschung, 1 (Göttingen: V & R unipress, 2007), pp. 15–27 (p. 16) for the connection between polysemy and probability that is so characteristic of topical argumentation: 'It is because arguments are polysemous and hence ambiguous that they prove flexible enough to be arranged in argument structures without becoming sclerotic.' (My translation) 'Argumente erweisen sich als vielseitig und damit uneindeutig, gerade deshalb sind sie elastisch genug, um sich in Argumentationsstrukturen gliedern zu lassen, ohne dabei sklerotisch zu werden.' See also Helmut Zedelmaier, *Bibliotheca Universalis und Bibliotheca Selecta: Das Problem der Ordnung des gelehrten Wissens in der frühen Neuzeit*, Beihefte zum Archiv für Kulturgeschichte, 33 (Köln: Böhlau Verlag, 1992), p. 67.
[99] Translation from *De topicis differentiis*, p. 30.
[100] Green-Pedersen, p. 42.
[101] Green-Pedersen, p. 63.
[102] The categories (substance, quantity, relation, quality, doing, undergoing, place where, time when, position, having; see *De topicis differentiis*, p. 237) were also known during the early Middle Ages from the anonymous, fourth-century *Categoriae Decem*, a work incorrectly attributed to St. Augustine, an attribution that enhanced both the work's and the categories' popularity (John Marenbon, *From the Circle of Alcuin to the School of Auxerre: Logic, Theology, and Philosophy in the Early Middle Ages*, Cambridge Studies in Medieval Life and Thought, 3rd series, 15 (Cambridge: Cambridge University Press, 1981), p. 16). Boethius's translation of Porphyry's *Isagoge* and the *Categoriæ decem* are likewise attested in Anglo-Saxon England since the ninth century (Gneuss, p. 119).

Porphyry's *Isagoge* is mentioned in Leofric's donation list, which also refers to the *mycel englisc boc* thought to be the Exeter Book, a point I will return to later on.

The method of constructing arguments from *loci* is thus based on a system of categories that ultimately goes back to Aristotle's *Categories*. The categories are arranged in a web or tree of systematic interrelations that is best visualized spatially, like the mnemonic items above, hence the use of the same term, *locus*. The similarity is obvious: As Eleonore Stump points out, 'A mnemonic Topic is literally a place that can be used over and over again to "store" and "retrieve" what one wants to remember; it is a place from which things to be remembered are recalled. A dialectical or rhetorical Topic is figuratively a place that can be used again to produce a variety of arguments.'[103] The two kinds of *locus* were consequently seen as analogous, but while the former used associative principles, the latter was based on a categorical system.

The systematic division of arguments or properties obviously lends itself to the division of disciplines or subjects. Tables accompanying early modern encyclopaedias, such as the one prefixed to Conrad Gessner's *Partitiones theologicae, pandectarum universalium liber ultimus* (1549) bear a striking resemblance to diagrams depicting the Porphyrian Tree.[104] According to Wilhelm Schmidt-Biggemann, the development of late-humanist systematic classification took shape through a re-interpretation of *iudicium* as *dispositio*, that is, the disposability of knowledge.[105] Rather than assess the information already gathered, as *iudicium* had done, *dispositio* was to ensure that a field of knowledge was comprehensively covered. These two main tasks of topics, the generation of rhetorical abundance and of systematic classification, separated and developed independently from the late sixteenth century onward.

Schmidt-Biggemann is certainly right in arguing that systematic classification with claims to exhaustiveness was a development of humanism and is not to be looked for in medieval encyclopaedias.[106] Yet as Schmidt-Biggemann himself points out, this humanist project has its origin in the practice of categorizing arguments, excerpts or other items according to more general properties or *loci communes* that goes back to antiquity and is based on topical principles. Peter Ramus (1515–72) has often been credited with introducing dialectical analysis to mnemonics and hence with the introduction of the principle of dialectical order to the organization of encyclopaedias. Yet it is obvious that memory is elemental in keeping available the rhetorical abundance generated by the *inventio* and that the issue of memorizing is thus already present in Ciceronian topics.[107] Frances Yates points out that the arrangement of matter 'in an order descending from "generals" to "specials"' is also implicit in Lullism and that the schematic presentation of texts propagated by the Ramists can already be observed in medieval manuscripts.[108] Indeed, the practice of arranging subjects into a system of categories, which characterizes the early modern encyclopaedias with which the theory of topics is now chiefly associated, can already be seen in the classical and medieval encyclopaedias discussed earlier. The distribution of individual subjects necessitates a prior analysis, an analysis which, in a way, operates like a reversal of the *inventio*: instead of using a list of criteria from which one constructs arguments, one deduces common criteria from

---

[103] *De topicis differentiis*, p. 16.
[104] See the facsimile in Zedelmaier, p. 78.
[105] Schmidt-Biggemann, p. 44.
[106] Schmidt-Biggemann, 'Sinnfülle', pp. 44–45.
[107] Schmidt-Biggemann, 'Sinnfülle', pp. 35, 36–38.
[108] Yates, *The Art of Memory*, pp. 232–238.

the characteristics of the various subjects in order to create a system that holds all of them. Topical analysis can thus be seen as the foundation of systematic order.[109]

One of the defining characteristics of topical order is that it is based on an interrelationship of subjects; that is, the resulting order is based on the material and not on any prefabricated system. Although catalogues of categories were set up in order to facilitate learning and memorizing the method, like the hexameter formula '*quis, quid, ubi, quibus auxiliis, cur, quomodo, quando*',[110] these were never seen as comprehensive or closed: in fact, Aristotle criticizes the Sophists for their method of teaching their pupils sets of examples and compares this practice to that of an artisan who does not teach his apprentice the method of his trade but gives him the finished product. Rather than give the learner a pre-fabricated set of arguments or categories, Aristotle wishes to teach the method itself.[111] Once the method is understood, it is possible to create a system that satisfies the individual needs of each practitioner.[112] What is more, this system can be modified to fit the specific material and the use it is set to — different subject-matter calls for different treatment. As Helmut Zedelmaier observes with regard to Conrad Gesner's mid-sixteenth-century *Bibliotheca universalis*, 'It is the material, or, rather, its treatment, that constitutes the order or system, not the other way round.'[113]

While medieval compilers of encyclopaedic collections did not explicitly theorize their method(s), the division of the material according to categories or *loci communes* that can be observed in many of these works seems likewise to have been determined by material already selected, rather than the choice of material to have been influenced by an already existing grid or system; the more so since medieval collections do not seem to aspire to the same level of completeness as early modern encyclopaedias that usually purport to present the sum total of available knowledge.[114]

Leofric's donation list provides a good example — one that is temporally and spatially close to the production of the Exeter Book — of how the material may shape a document's form. The document, which survives in two copies originally bound into gospel books, lists the lands, ornaments and books that Leofric acquired for the minster at Exeter. These items are divided into categories: alienated lands that Leofric restored, new lands he added, treasures and ornaments he procured for the minster (candlesticks, spoons, cups, chests), and, finally, books. As Richard Gameson observes, the books themselves — a total of fifty-nine volumes in fifty entries — are divided into three separate parts. This division, Gameson suggests, reflects 'the category of the texts' and 'perhaps also [...] differences in their physical location',

---

[109] Cf. Zedelmaier, pp. 52, 60. Wilhelm Schmidt-Biggemann and Anja Hallacker define topics as a method of managing 'the abundance of knowledge in a way that makes it employable for argumentative means' (Schmidt-Biggemann and Hallacker, p. 17: 'Topik verwaltet Wissensfülle, um sie argumentativ anwendbar zu machen'; my translation). A concise but very illuminating summary of the connection between the two topical functions of argumentation and management of knowledge can be found on pages 17–18 of their article.

[110] The verse is ascribed to Matthew of Vendôme (Matthaeus Vindocinensis, †1286), see Zedelmaier, p. 6.

[111] Cf. Sorabji, p. 29: 'The *topos* is a general pattern of argument, rather than an argument, because it is supposed to apply not merely to certainty and uncertainty, but to black and white, good and evil, and any pair of contraries.'

[112] Cf. Zedelmaier, p. 69; *De topicis differentiis*, pp. 174–178. This does not apply to the list of *differentiae* or the Aristotelian categories themselves, which were regarded as all-inclusive. Both could, however, be divided into an infinite number of subcategories. Cf. Green-Pedersen, p. 54 and Stump's discussion in *De topicis differentiis*, p. 237.

[113] Zedelmaier, p. 54 (my translation). 'Das Material bzw. die Praxis des Umgangs mit ihm konstituiert die Ordnung, das System, nicht umgekehrt.'

[114] As Irvine points out, 'The main principle of *compilatio* was the selection of materials from the cultural library so that the resulting collection forms an *interpretive* arrangement of texts and discourse' (p. 193).

thereby hinting at the possible use of topical categories in the ordering of libraries, which encyclopaedic collections sometimes seem to reflect.[115] The first group, consisting only of two volumes — *ii mycele Cristesbec gebonede* 'two large, ornamented gospel books' — is not actually listed with the other books but rather among the treasures. The second group of books, separated from these first two volumes by further items of treasure, includes massbooks, psalters, and other items 'essential for the liturgy and the regular life'.[116] According to Gameson, the two groups together 'comprise the literary *sine qua non* of ecclesiastical life'.[117] However, the second group also includes Alfred's translation of Boethius's *De consolatione philosophiae* and the *mycel englisc boc* thought to be the Exeter Book. These two items appear to bear little relation to the others in this group — in fact, the Old English version of the *Consolatio* would seem to fit much better with the more diverse third group of books, which also includes the Latin *Consolatio*, as well as individual biblical books, more general religious works such as Gregory the Great's *Regula Pastoralis*, Orosius's *Historiae adversus paganos libri septem*, Asser's *Vita Alfredi* and Porphyry's *Isagoge*. An explanation for the inclusion of the Old English *Consolatio* and the *mycel englisc boc* in the second group is provided by Joyce Hill, who has drawn attention to the fact that several items within this group are marked as being written in English, while the third group is introduced as *leden boca he beget inn to þam mynstre* ('Latin books that he [Leofric] acquired for the minster').[118] As in the case of the two ornamented gospel books, listed amongst treasures rather than books, the inclusion of these two Old English volumes in the second group suggests that several principles of ordering are at work here: gospel books, especially when lavishly produced and ornamented, can be classed both as ecclesiastical books and as treasures; book lists can be structured both according to contents and according to language.

An awareness of the multiple ways in which one and the same item can be categorized is already inherent in the topical method of systemizing subjects. We have seen above how any number of arguments can be constructed around any one subject, or, to put it differently, that any subject can be characterized in a variety of ways. Green-Pedersen draws attention to a passage in Boethius's *In Categorias Aristotelis Libri Quattuor* where it is said 'that we may consider Socrates in various ways: either as the individual person, Socrates; or as a substance; or as a father or a son, i.e. as belonging to the category of relation; and there are further possible comprehensions of him.'[119] As Green-Pedersen points out, this passage is a good illustration of the procedure expounded in *In Ciceronis Topica*. Transferred to the method of topical systematization, this means that it can never be possible to unequivocally assign an item to any one category, because there are always multiple ways of considering the subject. It is thus not only the heterogeneity of the material but also the various options available for

---

[115] Gameson, p. 143. Evidence for topical methods in the arrangement of Carolingian libraries is provided by McKitterick (pp. 165–210), who observes that the items in library catalogues and book lists from several important Frankish monasteries are divided into a descending hierarchy of categories, from complete Bibles through individual biblical books (arranged in the customary order of the Old and New Testaments) to patristic writings (usually arranged by author in the chronological order of life dates) and other subjects such as history, law, medicine and grammar, the latter often in conjunction with works by classical authors.

[116] Hill, 'Leofric', p. 85.

[117] Gameson, p. 143.

[118] Hill, 'Leofric', p. 85.

[119] Green-Pedersen, p. 74. *In Categorias Aristotelis* is preserved together with Boethius's translation of *De interpretatione* in a manuscript from the second half of the tenth-century now in Lichfield Cathedral Library, Gneuss p. 57.

ordering it that may at times have prompted compilers to abandon one principle of order mid-way through, if they felt that the material called for different treatment.

The fact that the third group of books in Leofric's list includes Porphyry's *Isagoge* is all the more telling as most of the other items mentioned in the list, as well as the works known to have been copied at Exeter during or shortly after Leofric's time, suggest that Exeter's was a very basic book collection that only just fulfilled the requirements of a new foundation.[120] The presence of the *Isagoge*, a text that can be seen to expound the very principles according to which the list is structured, thus suggests an interest in principles of structuring and categorizing items that, while it cannot explain the organization of the Exeter Book, which was compiled about three generations earlier, at least provides a hint that its structure may have been appreciated by Leofric and his contemporaries, even if the precise reasons why it was acquired remain elusive.[121]

Categories and associative linking in the Exeter Book

As noted above, the Exeter Book is no encyclopaedia, but it does share with this text type a preoccupation with the transmission of knowledge as well as some structural principles. As in the works mentioned above, the contents of the Exeter Book are arranged in categories derived from the material's various characteristics. To recapitulate: the collection opens with a sequence of partly biographical poems with strong hortatory undertones that set up a chain of role models for modes of Christian living,[122] arranged in order of descending cosmological importance, starting with Christ and his relationship to men (*Christ I–III*) and moving on to poems about saints and Old Testament righteous (*Guthlac A* and *B*, *Canticles of the Three Youths*, *The Passion of Saint Juliana*) and, finally, to the homiletic exemplum of the anonymous Christian everyman in *The Wanderer* and *The Seafarer*. These latter two poems are divided and succeeded by a string of poems more generally concerned with wisdom and the transmission of knowledge, many of them using the catalogue as their primary structural principle. The majority of these, too, address ethical or moral questions by discussing the extent to which man's life is predetermined by external forces or more generally God's involvement with the world (*God's Gifts to Humankind*, *The Fates of Mortals*, *The Order of the World*, *Physiologus*) or by presenting advice in the forms of precepts, maxims or proverbs (*Precepts*, *Vainglory*, *Maxims I*).[123] In a similar fashion, the *Physiologus*-poems purport to transmit knowledge of the natural world, with the allegorical interpretations of animal behaviour serving hortatory interests. The riddles present a more playful engagement with knowledge, with an additional connection to the *Physiologus*-poems being provided by a shared interest in natural phenomena and a concern with hidden wisdom and the hermeneutic principles of unravelling it (the bestiary presenting 'nature decoded'), as well as the binary structure of description and explication that is common to both genres. These

---

[120] Gameson, pp. 147, 151.
[121] One further item in the list that likewise attests to an interest in structuring knowledge is Isidore's *Etymologiae*, although this is more of a standard text.
[122] See Muir's introduction in *The Exeter Anthology*, I, p. 23.
[123] The obvious thematic exception is *Widsith* with its more or less unsystematic list of peoples and rulers, yet the poem's form and its instructional potential firmly link it to the other poems in this category.

shared characteristics might also explain the relative vicinity of bestiaries and riddles to be found not only in the Exeter Book.[124]

Yet if the above summary of the Exeter Book poems looks like a neat division into categories, it does so only because it glosses over a number of poems that do not quite fit the scheme, as a glance at the table of poems in the introduction will reveal. For instance, as I have mentioned above, the sequence of unambiguously hagiographical poems (*Guthlac A* and *B*, *Canticles*, *The Passion of Saint Juliana*) is broken up by *The Phoenix*, a bestiary allegory. And why are the obviously didactic and predominantly moral 'wisdom' poems following *The Wanderer* interspersed with so-called 'elegies', first-person accounts of suffering usually resolved by the philosophical acceptance of fate and an embracing of the Christian hope of heavenly reward (*The Seafarer*, *The Riming Poem*, *Deor*)? And why, indeed, are these latter poems not transmitted in sequence?

One possible explanation can be found in what appears to be the compiler's practice of sequencing poems according to associative principles, discussed earlier. Viewed in this light, *God's Gifts* appears like a direct continuation of *The Wanderer*, elaborating the latter poem's closing invocation of grace by pointing out how God's grace can already be observed in the various 'gifts' — talents, skills, good fortune — distributed among mankind. Similarly, *Vainglory* takes up *The Seafarer*'s opposition of the ascetic life of the seafarer and the worldly pleasures experienced by the city-dweller. *The Phoenix* not only echoes the trial-by-fire scenes of the preceding *Canticles* and the following *Passion*,[125] but explicitly draws a parallel between its allegorical interpretation of the phoenix and the role-model aspect of Christ, the saints, and the Christian everyman, the respective subjects of the surrounding poems. Conversely, *Soul and Body II* discusses the consequences of not making one's choice between the ways of God and the ways of the devil, arguably the combined theme of the three preceding *Physiologus*-poems, whose animal-imagery it also shares. The sequence of poems separating the two riddle collections (*The Wife's Lament* through *The Ruin*), while exhibiting a strong interest in penitential and paschal themes, includes a number of texts that resemble the riddles in their enigmatic quality — most obviously *Riddles* 30b and 60, but also *Pharaoh* with its dialogic question-answer structure, as well as *The Wife's Lament* and *The Husband's Message*, both of which poems seem to deliberately veil their speakers' identities and invite the reader to reconstruct the respective speakers' situation and story, the latter even including a runic puzzle, an element present also in a number of the Exeter Book riddles.[126]

One might thus argue that the associative links observable between many of the Exeter Book poems at times work against the systematic order of the categories. Indeed, the interaction — and at times tension — between associative and systematic principles results in

---

[124] Versions of the *Physiologus* and collections of riddles are often transmitted side by side in medieval manuscripts. This is for instance the case in Bern Cod. 611, which also includes the Exeter Book *Physiologus*'s sequence of *panther–cetus–perdix* (panther, sea-monster/whale, partridge).

[125] *The Guthlac Poems*, p. 50.

[126] See *The Exeter Anthology*, pp. 17–18 with regard to *Riddle* 60, *The Husband's Message* and *The Ruin*. *The Wife's Lament* and *The Husband's Message* are discussed by John D. Niles alongside a number of other Old English enigmatic texts that also include several of the Exeter riddles (John D. Niles, *Old English Enigmatic Poems and the Play of the Texts*, Studies in the Early Middle Ages, 13 (Turnhout: Brepols, 2006)). Anderson goes as far as to classify all of the remaining Exeter Book following the three *Physiologus*-poems as riddles by reading the *The Soul's Adress*, *Deor* and *Wulf and Eadwacer* as a riddlic sequence on the wasted life (*Two Literary Riddles*, p. 3, 'Riddle 1') and the poems from *The Wife's Lament* through *The Ruin* as another riddle sequence on the Easter Wake ('the Easter Riddle'). See also *The Old English Elegies: A Critical Edition and Genre Study*, ed. by Anne Lingard Klinck (Montreal: McGill-Queen's University Press, 1992), pp. 47, 57 and Rafał Borysławski, *The*

a highly original and individual arrangement that characterizes the whole collection. But the problem is partly inherent in the topical method of systemizing subjects itself. Leofric's list has provided an example of how items can be characterized and hence sorted in a variety of ways: decorated gospel books can be classed as 'books' or as 'treasures', an English translation of Boethius's *De Consolatione philosophiae* can be categorized according to content or according to language. In the same way, 'elegies' such as *The Wanderer* or *The Seafarer* can be classed as 'spiritual biographies' — that is, as homiletic exempla demonstrating how to deal with misfortune in a way that is pleasing to God — and hence can be sorted with the hagiographical poems preceding *The Wanderer*, or they can be classed as 'wisdom poems' that pass on ethical knowledge through a wise narrator figure. As Tom Shippey observes, to stress the similarities between certain poems means to disregard their differences and, consequently, the potential similarities individual ones might have to poems not included in this group. 'It is only by a process of elimination that our modern ascriptions to either genre have been made possible.'[127]

In the discussion above I have counted *The Wanderer* and *The Seafarer* as homiletic exempla participating in the sequence of 'spiritual biographies' preceding *The Wanderer*, but also pointed out their strong formal and thematic links to the following 'wisdom poems'. Scholars have usually decided in favour of either one or the other of these two categories, the vast majority choosing the former, although Dunning and Bliss have argued, perhaps not wholly convincingly, that 'in many respects, *The Wanderer* is more closely related to *Precepts* and *The Gifts of Men* than it is to *The Seafarer*'.[128] Yet Shippey, observing links in both directions, takes an integrative approach, arguing that '[*The Wanderer* and *The Seafarer*] occupy as it were a 'hinge' position between the long-accepted set of "elegies" and the more recently seen and larger category of "wisdom poems" or "Ancient Sage" poems.'[129] *The Wanderer* and *The Seafarer* can thus be read as both: spiritual exempla and wisdom poems. The difficulty of placing the poems in definite categories is thus not primarily because they do not fit a specific category, but because they fit more than one, depending on what feature or characteristic one prefers to stress.[130]

Shippey's suggestion of a "hinge" position between genres or categories is important for the larger structure of the collection, since *The Wanderer* and *The Seafarer* are placed at the very nexus between the sequence of poems associated with Christian exempla and the more diverse category of didactic and wisdom poems. Their affinity with both categories makes them ideal for achieving the transition from one category to the next. At this point, we thus witness a different kind of concatenation, not between individual poems but between whole categories. This concatenation is made possible through the polysemy of the texts, a polysemy that the topical method draws attention to, resulting in a potential openness of categories that allows for links in different directions that can be exploited for catenulate linking: it is here that the two 'topical' methods meet.

Old English Riddles and the Riddlic Elements of Old English Poetry, Studies in English Medieval Language and Literature, 9 (Frankfurt am Main: Lang, 2004), pp. 202–3.

[127] Shippey, 'The Wanderer', p. 156.
[128] Dunning and Bliss, p. 4.
[129] Shippey, 'The Wanderer', p. 146.
[130] A very good illustration of how many of the Exeter Book poems can be placed in more than one category is Table 5.1 in Drout's discussion of generic features and ambiguities (Drout, *Tradition and Influence*, p. 139). Of course, even these attributions of genre (whether medieval or modern) are only arrived at by ignoring the differences between individual poems within the categories, as are my own in Table 1.

Shippey's argument can be extended to other poems. *Deor* is an obvious case in that it combines, even more obviously than *The Wanderer* and *The Seafarer*, an autobiographical tale of sorrow and hardship with more general pieces of knowledge, in this case historical 'facts' arranged in a catalogue made up of successive stanzas. *Deor* has often been seen, along with the two poems mentioned before, as the archetypal elegy in which personal experience, along with the contemplation of more general truths of life, leads to eventual consolation. (Although in this case, the consolation is somewhat tongue-in-cheek since the poem seems to suggest that one's sorrow cannot last longer than one's life.) But were it not for the last stanza, in which the narrator suddenly steps forward as a character in his own right and tells his story, *Deor* would be nothing but a catalogue of historical exempla illustrating the eventual termination of hardship and sorrow (and thus in many respects not dissimilar to *Widsith* and its list of historical rulers and peoples). *Deor*'s exempla are drawn from Germanic heroic legend and constitute no more than brief allusions which become opaque if the story they refer to is not known. The third stanza is a good example of this technique:

> We þæt Mæðhilde monge gefrugnon —
> wurdon grundlease Geates frige,
> þæt him seo sorglufu slæp ealle binom.
> Þæs ofereode, þisses swa mæg. (*Deor*, lines 14–17)[131]

Scholars have found it unusually hard to interpret this stanza, not least because it has not been possible to identify the legend it refers to.[132] A variety of translations have therefore been suggested, most of which, however, rely to a greater or lesser extent on emendations.[133] The following is from S. A. J. Bradley's anthology of Old English poetry:

> About Maethhild many of us have heard tell that the affections of the Geat grew fathomless so that this tragic love reft them of all sleep. That passed away: so may this.[134]

The fact that the stories are not told in full but only alluded to is wholly in keeping with the principles of the historical exemplum; as von Moos notes, allusion to historical events or persons ('like Nero') is sufficient to generate the necessary context in the mind of the

---

[131] Muir reads the first two lines as 'We þæt Mæðhilde monge frugnon — wurdon grundlease Geatas frige'. I have given the manuscript's forms *gefrugnon* and *Geates* (with added capitalization), as do most other editions of the poem. Muir's emendation *Geatas* suggests a plural form, 'Geats', which is not reflected in the translations given here.

[132] Anderson suggests that this stanza refers to a legend told by Saxo Grammaticus of the Heodenings, in which the Jutish princess Hild each night revives both her father and her lover together with their armies so that they continue to fight over her into all eternity (*Two Literary Riddles*, p. 30). He accordingly translates (*Two Literary Riddles*, p. 69): 'We many have heard of the harvest of Hild. The yeomen of Geat came loose from the ground, so this sorrowful love robbed them all of their sleep. That was moved on; this can be, too.' Anderson interprets the manuscript's *mæð hilde* not as a single personal name, but as two different words, 'harvest' and the personal name 'Hild'.

[133] In fact, the text of Muir's edition, quoted above with the changes mentioned in footnote 129, includes a number of emendations, mostly concerning the spelling of compounds, which in the manuscript frequently appear in two words. In some cases, the manuscript's spelling may give rise to ambiguities that allow for alternative interpretations, as can be observed in Anderson's translation of the stanza in footnote 132. In the case of riddlic texts like *Deor*, I suggest such ambiguities form part of the 'play of the text'.

[134] *Anglo-Saxon Poetry: An Anthology of Old English Poems in Prose Translation with Introduction and Headnotes*, ed. and trans. by S. A. J. Bradley (London: Everyman, 1982), p. 364. Compare this translation with Anderson's in footnote 132 above and with Kevin Crossley-Holland's: 'Many of us have learned that Geat's love for Mæthild grew too great for human frame, his sad passion stopped him from sleeping. That passed away, this also may' (*The Anglo-Saxon World: An Anthology*, ed. by Kevin Crossley-Holland (Oxford: Oxford University Press, 1999), p. 7).

recipient.¹³⁵ But the way in which the allusions are presented — the text almost teasingly withholding information ('þæt him seo sorglufu slæp ealle binom') — lends *Deor* a riddlic quality. In fact, some of the allusions are so vague that an identification of the specific legend has not been possible. While most scholars have attributed this to the sparsity with which medieval heroic legend has survived into modern times, Andrew James Johnston argues that *Deor* is deliberately vague in the identification of its examples. He cites the fifth stanza, which observes merely that 'Theodric owned the Mæring castle for thirty winters — that was known to many' ('Ðeodric ahte þritig wintra | Mæringa burg — þæt wæs monegum cuþ', lines 18– 19).¹³⁶ The fact that there were, on the one hand, at least three bearers of the name *Theodric* known to the Anglo-Saxons and, on the other, that the best-known of these, Theoderic the Great, was associated with at least two completely different traditions — a 'historical' one, in which he featured as the tyrant who put Boethius to death, and a 'legendary' one, in which he was exiled by his uncle and rival Ermanaric — shows that unequivocal identification would not have been possible even to a contemporary audience. The question which of at least three different Theodrics known from Germanic legend is meant turns the stanza into a riddle, in keeping with the generally enigmatic tone of the whole poem.¹³⁷

Deor, then, has affinities not only with spiritual biographies and 'wisdom' poems (even constituting a short catalogue in its own right), but also with the riddles, and it is in fact followed by that most enigmatic of all Anglo-Saxon poems, *Wulf and Eadwacer*, which was regarded by several early editors as the first in the series of riddles that immediately follows it (and is thus another instance of a poem where an unequivocal assignation to a category is impossible).¹³⁸ The Exeter Book thus consciously employs multidimensionality as a means of structuring. The texts' multiple readings participate in the larger arrangement of the collection in that they provide the starting point for digressions or new sequences, thematic or otherwise. The fact that the poems I have just discussed are placed at the intersection of categories, with

---

¹³⁵ Von Moos, p. 61.

¹³⁶ Andrew James Johnston, 'The Riddle of *Deor* and the Performance of Fiction', in *Language and Text: Current Perspectives on English and Germanic Historical Linguistics and Philology*, ed. by Andrew James Johnston, Ferdinand von Mengden and Stefan Thim, Anglistische Forschungen, 359 (Heidelberg: Winter, 2006), pp. 133–50. Anderson notes that *Mæringa burg* may be a kenning, the literal meaning 'a castle of basil' standing for exile in the wilderness (*Two Literary Riddles*, p. 28).

¹³⁷ Johnston, p. 141.

¹³⁸ There are other poems in this section that exhibit affinities to the riddles. Niles refers to the enigmatic quality of *The Seafarer* and other lyric poems from the Exeter Book (*Wulf and Eadwacer*, *The Wife's Lament* and *The Husband's Message*): 'just as with all fifty Exeter Book riddles that are put into the first person singular voice, there is an implied challenge for the reader to discover who the speaker is and to fill out his or her story' (Niles, p. 213). The same applies to the *Riming Poem*, whose narrator, like those of the *Wanderer* and *The Seafarer*, explains how a life of misfortunes has taught him Christian humility. However, unlike the other protagonists, the speaker does not offer any further intimation of what his misfortunes actually were or indeed of his own identity. The few hints given in the text seem to suggest a personified natural force rather than a human being (Lehmann, p. 444). Thus the speaker seems to imply that he received life at the world's creation and also remains after the passing of mankind, for whom he is to dig a grave. Nonetheless, he himself seems to be on the verge of dying. Ruth Lehman has drawn attention to the poem's riddlic quality and tentatively suggested 'the will of God' as a possible solution (Lehmann, p. 444). Against this one might hold that God's will does not die and that it existed before Creation. A better solution would be 'nature' personified or indeed 'Creation' itself (not as act but as result) since these, too, must die once the things created cease to exist. The solution 'Creation' is a felicitous one, not least because *gesceaft godes*, 'God's Creation' is the main theme of the preceding poem, *The Order of the World*, resulting in another catenulate link. It is worth noting that all of these poems, with the exception of *The Seafarer*, are placed in close vicinity to the Exeter Book riddles, many of which are presented as first-person accounts detailing the often tragic life-stories of personified objects — and thus both formally and emotionally very similar to the elegies.

affinities in both directions, suggests a deliberate arrangement, one that reflects and exploits the ambiguities of topical classification.

It is perhaps no coincidence that the poems occupying such hinge positions belong to the class of so-called 'elegies', a modern and decidedly vague category whose defining characteristics involve personal stories of loss and misfortune, often combined with a more general reflection of worldly transience.[139] The fact that these poems were placed at the intersections of homiletic exempla, catalogues of ethical and worldly wisdom, and riddles suggests that they were not necessarily regarded as strictly belonging to the same textual category; rather, their presentation as instructive first-person accounts whose didactic message is based on personal observation or experience opens up the possibility of linking them to poems from a variety of categories.[140] Through these poems we witness an overlap, a concomitance of various categories that may seem unsettling from a modern perspective but is wholly natural from a pre-modern one. Indeed, as we have seen earlier, resistance to a single, clear-cut system of categories is inherent in topical thinking, which stresses the multidimensionality of its objects. It is also characteristic of medieval exegetical thinking with its different *sententiae* or layers of Scriptural meaning, all at work simultaneously and not restricted to the interpretation of the Bible but also applicable to secular texts and the world in general, due to a pansemiotic interpretation of nature evident, for instance, in the allegorical explanations given in the Exeter Book bestiary poems. From the perspective of classical and medieval hermeneutics, the world is inherently multidimensional and polysemous.[141] The Exeter Book uses this multidimensionality as a structural principle: a principle of concatenation, not only between individual poems, but between whole categories.

Ambiguity and multidimensionality

Arranging subjects according to topical principles affords a much more intuitive order than alphabetical organization,[142] hence even modern compendia sometimes adopt it, at least to some extent. The multi-volume *Handbook of the Mammals of the World*, for instance, organizes the various species systematically, i.e. according to biological order (e.g. *Primates, Rodents, Insectivores*) and, within the orders, family (e.g. *Lemuridae, Lorisidae, Hominidae*).[143] This system is supposed to reflect the genetic relationship between the species.[144] Historically, however, this structure is based on a system of shared physical characteristics (analogies) first established by Linnæus in the eighteenth century. Linnæus,

---

[139] This has not precluded the inclusion of non-personal poems like *The Ruin*, as Klinck's choice of texts shows. Klinck comments, 'calling these nine poems [i.e., *The Wanderer, The Seafarer, The Riming Poem, Deor, Wulf and Eadwacer, The Wife's Lament, Resignation, 'Ic wæs be sonde'/Riddle 60, The Husband's Message* and *The Ruin*] elegies is a retrospective classification which relates them to a universal mode' (*The Old English elegies*, p. 223).

[140] This observation resonates with Irvine's point that '[t]he distinguishing feature of the encyclopaedia is its organization by discursive field rather than by work or genre' (Irvine, p. 195).

[141] For the argument that an appreciation of plenitude and diversity as a way of looking at the world is inherent in the encyclopaedic tradition, see Howe, p. 17.

[142] Howe argues that the encyclopaedic tradition began to lose its intellectual seriousness and hence its reputation with the introduction of alphabetization (Howe, p. 11). Cf. also his scathing judgement that, 'while few subjects resist alphabetization, still fewer benefit from it' (Howe, p. 9).

[143] *Handbook of the Mammals of the World*, ed. by Don E. Wilson and Russell A. Mittermeier, 8 vols (Barcelona, 2009–).

[144] Recent research has, however, shown that a clear-cut genealogical tree does not in actuality reflect genetic relationships since there is a much larger amount of cross-breeding, even between supposed species, than has

of course, was using as his framework the principles of topical order still current during his life-time. Another instance of non-alphabetical order in modern compendia would be handbooks of history, which are often arranged chronologically or by geographical area. Electronic encyclopaedias like *Wikipedia* dispense with linear order altogether, using instead a complex network of internal links, which allows them to develop a multi-dimensional system of organization.[145] But while topical organization is certainly not random, it is somewhat unpredictable in a book or manuscript context — which is, by necessity, two-dimensional (that is, linear) — unless it is founded on convention or made explicit, for instance through an introductory note, a table of contents, annotations or cross-references.[146] The same reservation applies, as we have seen, to the assignment of the individual subjects to the various categories. Given the material's multiple characteristics, there are always various ways of categorizing which may lead to conflicting claims of assignment.[147]

In his essay 'The Analytical Language of John Wilkins', Jorge Luis Borges discusses the ambiguities and redundancies inherent in all category-based systems by quoting from *The Celestial Emporium of Benevolent Knowledge*, a fictitious Chinese encyclopaedia, which is said to divide all animals into the following fourteen categories:

> (a) those that belong to the Emperor, (b) embalmed ones, (c) those that are trained, (d) suckling pigs, (e) mermaids, (f) fabulous ones, (g) stray dogs, (h) those that are included in this classification, (i) those that tremble as if they were mad, (j) innumerable ones, (k) those drawn with a very fine camel's hair brush, (l) others, (m) those that have just broken a flower vase, (n) those that resemble flies from a distance.[148]

While many of the categories are in themselves hilarious, their weakness as a system lies of course in the absence of a stable relation between content and category. As Michel Foucault points out in his famous discussion of the passage:

> hitherto been assumed. There is consequently some discussion among evolutionary biologists about replacing the Linnæan system with a multi-dimensional, phylogenetic one, which is supposed to more adequately represent actual genetic relationships. For more information on this issue, see Roger Harris, 'Attacks on Taxonomy', *American Scientist*, 93 (2005), http://www.americanscientist.org/issues/pub/attacks-on-taxonomy [accessed 6 August 2014], and Philip D. Cantino and Kevin de Queiroz, 'PhyloCode: International Code of Phylogenetic Nomenclature' (2010), http://www.ohio.edu/phylocode/PhyloCode4c.pdf [accessed 6 August 2014].

[145] It is surely no coincidence that Bernard Cerquiglini, whose *Éloge de la variante* is often regarded as the defining moment of the so-called 'new philology', argues that electronic editions with their possibilities of multi-dimensional layering are best suited to present the complex interplay of textual variants in medieval textual transmission (Cerquiglini, pp. 78–82, especially at 79). See also Martin K. Foys, *Virtually Anglo-Saxon: Old Media, New Media, and Early Medieval Studies in the Late Age of Print* (Gainesville, FL: University Press of Florida, 2007), who argues not only that 'the medieval and the digital (or pre- and post-print) have much in common that the print medium does not share' (p. xiv) but also that the limitations of print technology have to some extent pre-determined the way Anglo-Saxon literature has been perceived by scholars, suggesting that the possibilities of electronic media can open up new perspectives on Anglo-Saxon sources, including sculpture, textiles, and other works of art.

[146] With regard to the Exeter Book, whose opening pages are missing, Pope notes that 'separate title-pages were not customary and tables of contents are rare' in this period (Pope, p. 31, footnote 21).

[147] Cf. the discussion above. Howe discusses the extent to which classical encyclopaedias reflected a fixed and thus 'proper' order and notes that catalogues such as the one employed by Isidore to list the various winds teach 'a double lesson: the chief facts and terms of a subject as well as the structural order necessary to contain them' (Howe, p. 26). Cf. Carruthers' observation about stocking one's memory with structural models (Carruthers, p. 221), quoted earlier.

[148] Jorge Luis Borges, 'The Analytical Language of John Wilkins', trans. by Ruth L. C. Simms, in Jorge Luis Borges, *Other Inquisitions 1937–1952* (London: Souvenir Press, 1973), pp. 101–105 (p. 103).

> The central category of animals 'included in the present classification', with its explicit reference to paradoxes we are familiar with, is indication enough that we shall never succeed in defining a stable relation of contained to container between each of these categories and that which includes them all: if all the animals divided up here can be placed without exception in one of the divisions of this list, then aren't all the other divisions to be found in that one division too?[149]

It is not possible to divide the animals in such a way that they fit exactly one category; in fact, most animals would fit equally well into almost any of them: an animal that belongs to the emperor might also be trained or look like a fly from a distance; an animal that has just broken a flower vase might also tremble as if it were mad and so on. The assignation to a specific category becomes arbitrary.

Although he quotes *The Celestial Emporium of Benevolent Knowledge* as an extreme example, Borges shows, by referring to other examples like the Bibliographic Institute of Brussels and various 'analytical' or 'general' languages, that the vagueness and contradictions involved in the assignation of topics is an inherent feature of all classification: 'obviously there is no classification of the universe that is not arbitrary and conjectural'.[150] Foucault agrees:

> Order is, at one and the same time, that which is given in things as their inner law, the hidden network that determines the way they confront one another, and also that which has no existence except in the grid created by a glance, an examination, a language; and it is only in the blank spaces of this grid that the order manifests itself in depth as though already there, waiting in silence for the moment of its expression.[151]

This arbitrariness can be countered by taking recourse to tradition or convention, like the cosmological hierarchies chosen by Wilkins or, to return to (late) antiquity, the encyclopaedias of Pliny, Varro or Isidore of Seville. But the ambiguity remains. In contrast to said encyclopaedists, who chose a hierarchical order based on convention to counter the ambiguity of categorization, the Exeter Book draws attention to the multidimensionality and polysemy of its contents, and consequently to the ambiguity of all categories. While promoting topical systematization as a principle of organization the collection thus simultaneously exploits and, one is tempted to say, criticizes its inherent ambiguity.

Conclusion

In many ways, one could argue, most if not all poems in the Exeter Book are concerned with the transmission of knowledge, whether ethical knowledge taught through exempla and homiletic exhortation or in the form of proverbs and sayings, natural and cultural knowledge presented in lists and catalogues, or a more playful engagement with knowledge in the riddles.

---

[149] Michel Foucault, *The Order of Things: An Archaeology of the Human Sciences* (London: Routledge, 2004 [first publ. London: Tavistock, 1970]), p. xviii [first publ. *Les mots et les choses: une archéologie des sciences humaines* (Paris: Gallimard, 1966].

[150] Borges, p. 104. Nevertheless, Borges is much more sympathetic towards human attempts at classification than Foucault: 'the impossibility of penetrating the divine scheme of the universe cannot dissuade us from outlining human schemes, even though we are aware that they are provisional. Wilkins's analytical language is not the least admirable of those schemes. It is composed of classes and species that are contradictory and vague; its device of using the letters of the words to indicate divisions and subdivisions is, without a doubt, ingenious' (ibid.). As Howe points out, Borges's *Emporium* is as much homage as it is a critique (Howe, p. 11).

[151] Foucault, p. xxi.

Indeed, the cursory nature of the material's presentation, especially in some of the shorter poems, and its often mundane nature suggest that these texts are not primarily interested in the material itself but rather in its presentation, in the various different ways knowledge can be transmitted and passed on. From this perspective, the Exeter Book appears as a collection of various text types exploring and engaging in the presentation of wisdom and knowledge, divided into more or less fluid categories, compiled perhaps for personal use as textual models for the composition of texts, or for didactic or devotional contexts as a means of illustrating certain points to a lay audience. This much has been felt and, to some extent, expressed by various scholars working on the Exeter Book.

    Where the present contribution has gone further than previous scholarship is in demonstrating the extent to which these categories interact, overlap and intersect. By taking recourse to late-antique and medieval mnemonic and topical methods, the paper has attempted to place the Exeter Book within a theoretical frame of contemporary compilatory methods, methods that were generating renewed interest around the time the Exeter Book was compiled, and that are likely to have shaped at least the Exeter Book's early reception, if Leofric's list can be taken as evidence. At a time when interest in topics and methods of organization was gaining currency, the Exeter Book may have provided a playground for probing and testing ways of sequencing, linking and arranging texts.

Reading Scribal Intervention in the Squire-Wife of Bath Link of MS Lansdowne 851

Jeremy DeAngelo

For modern textual criticism, the bare fact of scribal intervention in medieval manuscripts has always been a difficult matter. Its existence creates for commentators the bibliographic equivalent of the Uncertainty Principle: as the primary means of textual transmission in the Middle Ages, scribes were necessary for the preservation of texts, but their participation also altered that which they recorded. Despite their care, scribes inevitably produced errors and were in possession of individual personalities and histories that could influence their work, conditions which frustrate those seeking a work's 'best text' — by which is usually meant the authorial version.[1] Such editors often face an irony in that their intent to seek out, preserve, and celebrate the self-expression and originality of one writer — the author — leads them to deplore the same qualities in another. Yet no matter how hard one may wish to achieve the author's voice unmediated, in the absence of an autograph, to engage a text one must engage its scribe(s).

Yet taking scribal readings into account complicates textual interpretation enormously. Most obviously, it multiplies the number of 'texts' available to the scholar, since, from this perspective, every manuscript offers a unique reading. As D. F. McKenzie has observed, in privileging textual variation, 'each reading is peculiar to its occasion, each can be at least partially recovered from the physical forms of the text, and the differences in readings constitute an informative history'.[2] Instead of winnowing exemplars into an authoritative 'best text', the goal is to proliferate the number of worthwhile readings based on scribes' and other

---

[1] See, for example, Eugène Vinaver, 'Principles of Textual Emendation', in *Studies in French Language and Mediæval Literature Presented to Mildred K. Pope by Pupils, Colleagues and Friends*, ed. by Mildred K. Pope (Freeport: Books for Libraries Press, 1939), pp. 351–69 and Brian Blakely, 'The Scribal Process', in *Medieval Miscellany Presented to Eugène Vinaver by Pupils, Colleagues and Friends*, ed. by F. Whitehead, A. H. Diverres and F. E. Sutcliffe (Manchester: Manchester University Press, 1965), pp. 19–27. Ralph Hanna III looks critically at this editorial philosophy in 'Problems of "Best Text" Editing and the Hengwrt Manuscript of *The Canterbury Tales*', in *Manuscripts and Texts: Editorial Problems in Later Middle English Literature*, ed. by Derek Albert Pearsall (Cambridge: Brewer, 1987), pp. 87–94. See also Leonard E. Boyle, 'Optimist and Recensionist: "Common Errors" or "Common Variations"?' in *Latin Script and Letters, A.D. 400–900: Festschrift Presented to Ludwig Bieler on the Occasion of his 70th Birthday*, ed. by John J. O'Meara and Bernd Naumann (Leiden: Brill, 1976), pp. 264–74 and Anne Hudson, 'Middle English', in *Editing Medieval Texts: English, French and Latin Written in England*, ed. by A. J. Rigg (Toronto: University of Toronto, 1977), pp. 34–57.

[2] D. F. McKenzie, *Bibliography and Sociology of Texts* (Cambridge: Cambridge University Press, 1999), p. 19. For other important examinations of the implications of textual variation, see Paul Zumthor, *Essai de Poétique*

readers' reactions to an author's work through their engagement with (and alteration of) their texts. Additionally, the consideration of scribal work, as Tim William Machan points out, must be sensitive to the particularly medieval ways in which writers and scribes viewed their efforts.[3] Literary interpretation of scribal intervention in a medieval text, therefore, must hold two considerations in mind: the precise conditions of a manuscript's creation so as to pursue scribal intent, and their engagement with an earlier work with a separate context. Just as the copied work of a medieval author can never be encountered unmediated, neither too can a scribe's, since scribal activity is by definition working with another's words. Any work of scribal originality, therefore, is coloured by its reliance on its earlier authority and all the complications this entails.

The extent and importance of textual variation can differ widely. However, the tension between the text a scribe receives and the text he eventually produces provides a space for potential reinterpretation and reinvention. Ralph Hanna III has identified the need for scholars to cultivate an understanding of the 'scribal poetics' that arise in such spaces, if only to better identify the efforts of original authors.[4] Scholars of medieval history writing, in particular, have found a space for a scribal authority separate from and complementary to the *auctoritas* ascribed to authors.[5] As Matthew Fisher notes, scribes were often called upon to perform two contradictory tasks, to reproduce a text faithfully and yet also to correct whatever flaws it may have.[6] In striking the proper balance between these twin demands, the most crucial questions — what constitutes a flaw? What is the necessary remedy? — were in turn subject to a variety of considerations that relied upon the state of their exemplars and the desires of their patrons. This is turn affects the critical approach to their works. As Hanna puts it elsewhere,

> in editorial terms, 'authority' is quite intentionally dispersed in unique ways, most of the time not the property of an individual we identify as the literary workman today: variation does not simply inhere naturally in a literary text *per se* [...] but is also the product of

---

Médiévale Variante (Paris: Éditions du Seuil, 1972), pp. 64–106; Bernard Cerquiglini, *Éloge de la Variante* (Paris: Éditions du Seuil, 1981), pp. 62 and 110–11; Jerome McGann, *A Critique of Modern Textual Criticism* (Chicago: University of Chicago Press, 1983); and the 1990 'New Philology' issue of *Speculum*.

[3] Tim William Machan, *Textual Criticism and the Middle English Text* (Charlottesville: University Press of Virginia, 1994), pp. 168–69. Derek Pearsall is generally more critical in 'Variants vs. Variance', in *Probable Truth: Editing Medieval Texts from Britain in the Twenty-First Century*, ed. by Vincent Gillespie and Anne Hudson (Turnhout: Brepols, 2013), pp. 197–205.

[4] Ralph Hanna III, 'Authorial Versions, Rolling Revision, Scribal Error? Or, The Truth About *Truth*', in *Pursuing History: Middle English Manuscripts and Their Texts* (Stanford: Stanford University Press, 1996), pp. 159–73 (pp. 159–60).

[5] Sigbjørn Olsen Sønnesyn, 'Obedient Creativity and Idiosyncratic Copying: Tradition and Individuality in the Works of William of Malmesbury and John of Salisbury', in *Modes of Authorship in the Middle Ages*, ed. by Slavica Ranković (Toronto: Pontifical Institute of Medieval Studies, 2012), pp. 113–32 (pp. 118–20). For *auctoritas*, see J. A. Burrow, *Medieval Writers and Their Work: Middle English Literature and its Background 1100–1500* (Oxford: Oxford University Press, 1982), pp. 29–30; A. J. Minnis, *Medieval Theory of Authorship: Scholastic Literary Attitudes in the Later Middle Ages*, 2nd edn (Philadelphia: University of Pennsylvania Press, 1988), p. 94; Tim William Machan, 'Middle English Text Production and Modern Textual Criticism', in *Crux and Controversy in Middle English Textual Criticism*, ed. by A. J. Minnis and Charlotte Brewer (Cambridge: Brewer, 1992), pp. 1–18 (pp. 6–7); Jocelyn Wogan-Browne, 'Authorizing Text and Writer', in *The Idea of the Vernacular*, ed. by Jocelyn Wogan-Browne, Nicholas Watson, Andrew Taylor, and Ruth Evans (Philadelphia: University of Pennsylvania Press, 1999), pp. 1–19 (pp. 3–8) and Glending Olson, 'Author, Scribe, and Curse: The Genre of Adam Scriveyn', *The Chaucer Review*, 42 (2008), pp. 284–97 (p. 290).

[6] Matthew Fisher, *Scribal Authorship and the Writing of History in Medieval England* (Columbus: Ohio State University Press, 2012), p. 22.

work done under a specific mode of production, a set of material circumstances, a specific confluence between a piece of writing, a patron, and a variety of manual tasks.[7]

Scribes can be seen in medieval manuscripts struggling with their texts and engaging in a form of creativity that is intimately dependent on others' work as well as others' desires for that work; deriving meaning from that evidence constitutes its own struggle as well on the part of the modern scholar. Focusing on a scribe allows for a greater historical context for a text; yet historical context is precisely what is needed — and so often lacking — to make full sense of a scribe's contribution to his or her text.

All of these considerations can be seen operating in the unique link between the *Squire's Tale* and the *Wife of Bath's Prologue* in the *Canterbury Tales* of British Library MS Lansdowne 851. This manuscript, which is one of the earliest we have of the *Canterbury Tales* (c. 1400×25), is an object whose design and creation were done with deliberation. It was intended as a work of visual art along with its literary contents, for at 250×200 mm with a 240×135 frame, it left ample room in the vertical margins for decorations done in blue, mauve, magenta, green, gold, yellow and red. Its script is uniform, too, with a single scribe whose *anglicana formata* hand betrays some northern and western regionalisms but for the most part suggests a professional London scribe.[8] And it was for the gap between the tales of the Wife of Bath and the Squire that this scribe invented a short 11-line interlude that attempts to create a suitable end to the Squire's unfinished tale. This in itself is an act of creation, but what makes the Squire-Wife of Bath link so notable is how it interacts with the original text, and how the scribe's solution to a practical problem creates the opportunity to completely reinterpret the *Squire's Tale*. By leveraging what many modern scholars perceive as flaws in his tale — its excessive *occupatio*, its lack of focus, and the unwieldy size of the story it aims to tell — the Lansdowne scribe creates a swift, fitting end to the work that has the potential as well to revise the portrait of the Squire. Moreover, by appreciating the likely pressures and conditions of scribal work on Lansdowne, and also treating the scribe's contribution with the same seriousness as we would an author's, we can gain a valuable insight into the hybrid task he and other scribes set for themselves when they set out to reconcile their often incomplete exemplars with the expectations placed upon the final product. The result is art that not only relies upon the work it is embedded within, but that interacts with it in startling ways.

Numerous manuscripts of the *Tales* include interpolations,[9] but Lansdowne 851 is particularly notable for this feature. An early representative of Manly and Rickert's group *c*, its exemplar was likely Corpus Christi College Oxford MS 198 or else something very much like it.[10] Manuscripts from this line order the tales differently than the arrangements of either Ellesmere or Hengwrt,[11] and typically contain fewer links between tales such as those

---

[7] Ralph Hanna III, 'Producing Manuscripts and Editions', in *Crux and Controversy in Middle English Textual Criticism*, ed. by A. J. Minnis and Charlotte Brewer (Cambridge: Brewer, 1992), pp. 109–30 (p. 122). See also Daniel Wakelin, 'Writing the Words', in *The Production of Books in England 1350–1500*, ed. by Alexandra Gillespie and Daniel Wakelin (Cambridge: Cambridge University Press, 2011), pp. 34–58 (pp. 49–50).

[8] John M. Manly and Edith Rickert, *The Text of the Canterbury Tales, Studied on the Basis of All Known Manuscripts*, 8 vols (Chicago: University of Chicago Press, 1940), I 304–8 and M. C. Seymour, *A Catalogue of Chaucer Manuscripts*, 2 vols (Aldershot: Scolar Press, 1995–97), II 131–35.

[9] For an account of these, see William McCormick and Janet E. Heseltine, *The Manuscripts of Chaucer's 'Canterbury Tales'* (Oxford: Clarendon Press, 1933), pp. xxv–xxxii and Seymour, *A Catalogue of Chaucer Manuscripts*, II, 21–26.

[10] Norman Blake, *The Textual Tradition of the Canterbury Tales* (London: Arnold, 1985), p. 119.

[11] Their orders, however, are not unusual among the extant manuscripts, and in fact are more numerous if one pairs

of the Cook and *Gamelyn*, the Squire and the Wife of Bath, the Canon's Yeoman and the Physician, and the Pardoner and the Shipman. In the case of Lansdowne, the scribe attempts to smooth over these gaps with several interpolations unique to the manuscript. For some of these points in the text, the solution may have been exceptional but the dilemma was not. The *Cook's Tale* and the *Squire's Tale*, being unfinished, often presented a problem to scribes wishing to record complete versions of the *Tales*. The extant copies can attest to the variety of scribal reactions to this challenge, from leaving space blank to inserting other material to just ignoring it entirely.[12] In the case of the *Cook's Tale*, Lansdowne is one of twenty-five existing manuscripts that uses the *Tale of Gamelyn* to 'fix' the entry, although (as Lansdowne also attests) this does not necessarily obviate the need for a transition.[13] However, compared to the aborted *Cook's Tale*, the *Squire's Tale* was relatively complete, making the insertion of an entirely new story untenable.[14] Moreover, the Lansdowne scribe's exemplar lacked the interruption of the Squire by one of the other pilgrims, depriving the scribe of a plausible transition.[15]

His response here, as with the other awkward transitions, was to invent a link. Discarding (or lacking) the two short lines of the 'Tercia Pars' found in other versions,[16] he brings the tale to a swift end:

> Bot I wil here nowe maake a knotte
> To the time it come next to my lotte.
> For here be felawes behinde, an hepe treulye,
> That wolden talke ful besilye
> And have her sporte as wele as I.
> And the daie passeth fast, certanly.
> Therfore, Hooste, taketh nowe goode heede
> Who schall next tell, and late him speede.[17]

After this the text proclaims: 'explicit fabula Armigeri incipit prologus Uxoris de Bath' ('the Squire's Tale ends; the Wife of Bath's Prologue begins'), and the Wife of Bath takes over with four more invented lines to complete the transition:[18]

> Than schortly ansewarde the Wife of Bathe
> And swore a wonder grete hathe,

---

group *c* with the closely related group *d*. See Seymour, *A Catalogue of Chaucer Manuscripts*, II, 2–9.

[12] See Stephen Partridge, 'Minding the Gaps: Interpreting the Manuscript Evidence of the Cook's Tale and the Squire's Tale', in *The English Medieval Book: Studies in Memory of Jeremy Griffiths*, ed. by A. S. G. Edwards, Vincent Gillespie, and Ralph Hanna (London: British Library, 2000), pp. 51–85.

[13] Partridge, 'Minding the Gaps', p. 55.

[14] The one exception to this is in Christ Church Oxford MS 152, where a later hand added a work by Hoccleve to the gap left by the original scribe. Even here, however, the tale is meant to be the Plowman's, not the Squire's. Partridge, 'Minding the Gaps', p. 61.

[15] Seymour, *A Catalogue of Chaucer Manuscripts*, II, 4–5. For how the *Squire's Tale* came to occupy a place between the *Man of Law's Tale* and *The Wife of Bath's Prologue* in Lansdowne, and why it lacks a natural link, see the discussion of the Corpus Christi College Oxford MS 198 — which was a likely precursor to Lansdowne — in Blake, *The Textual Tradition of the Canterbury Tales*, pp. 97–98.

[16] It is common among the extant manuscripts for the two-line 'Tercia Pars' of the *Squire's Tale* to be omitted. See Partridge, 'Minding the Gaps', p. 62.

[17] 'Spurious Links', in *The Canterbury Tales: Fifteenth-Century Continuations and Additions*, ed. by John M. Bowers (Kalamazoo: Medieval Institute Publications, 1992), pp. 41–53 (pp. 43–44). These lines can be found on folio 87r of the manuscript.

[18] 'Spurious Links', p. 44.

Jeremy DeAngelo

> 'Be Goddes bones, I wil tel next!
> 'I will nouht glose, bot saye the text'

It is possible that the links of the *Canterbury Tales* contain variations that reflect Chaucer's editing, just as the tales do;[19] even so, it would be quite a remarkable circumstance if Lansdowne 851 alone preserved Chaucer's words here. Yet consider the achievement of these eight lines as the product of an anonymous scribe. In his effort to bridge the gap between the *Squire's Tale* and the *Prologue* of the Wife of Bath, he makes alterations to the text that, as we shall see, reconfigure the possible interpretations of the work. He does so effectively, however, only by carefully reading and comprehending the text that he copies, as this interpolation also attests. The reception of the *Squire's Tale* has varied greatly over the centuries as tastes have changed and different aspects of the work have been emphasized. It was highly valued in the Renaissance by Spenser and Milton for its rhetoric and subject,[20] though much of the current assessment of the *Squire's Tale* is less straightforwardly admiring. The general consensus is that the Squire, as written, is overmatched by his material. He has no apparent feel for pacing or plot, is prone to go off on tangents, and may very well have committed a serious social gaffe when he embarks upon a story of Canacee after the Man of Law has expressly condemned her tale. Just when it looks as if the story may come to an ignominious but merciful conclusion, the Squire declares his ambition to tell a story with seemingly no end.[21] Seth Lerer argues that the youth's failure is particularly acute in that he is purposefully attempting to match his father's performance,[22] and a comparison between the two is especially easy to make in Lansdowne, since like most Chaucer manuscripts it places the *Squire's Tale* relatively close to the *Knight's* (it immediately follows the Man of Law, which makes the Squire's invocation of Canacee seem even more impolitic). One fifteenth-century reader's reaction highlights the contrast between the father and son storytellers. Jean d'Orléans, comte d'Angoulême, a hostage held in England from 1412 to 1445, owned and marked a copy of the *Canterbury Tales*, known today as the Paris MS. While he considers the *Knight's Tale* 'valde bona' ('quite good'), he had his scribe cease copying the *Squire's Tale* after only a few dozen lines and explains in a marginal note that 'ista fabula est valde absurda in terminis et ideo' ('this story is extremely ridiculous in its conclusion and its theme').[23]

The Comte's rejection is but an opinion of one; moreover, the absurd quality that Jean d'Orléans identifies in the work may very well have been intentional. That the Squire's contribution is poorly executed and overlong makes necessary the interruption of the Franklin

---

[19] Norman Blake, 'The Links in the Canterbury Tales', in *New Perspectives on Middle English Texts: A Festschrift for R. A. Waldron*, ed. by Susan Powell and Jeremy J. Smith (Cambridge: Brewer, 2000), pp. 107–18 (p. 109).

[20] Gardiner Stillwell, 'Chaucer in Tartary', *Review of English Studies*, 24 (1948), 177–88 (pp. 177–78) and David Lawton, *Chaucer's Narrators* (Cambridge: Brewer, 1985), pp. 107–8.

[21] Chaucer, *SqT*, lines 661–70. Important commentaries on the *Squire's Tale* include Stillwell, 'Chaucer in Tartary', pp. 177–88; D. A. Pearsall, 'The Squire as Story-Teller', *University of Toronto Quarterly*, 34 (1964), 82–92; Robert S. Haller, 'Chaucer's *Squire's Tale* and the Uses of Rhetoric', *Modern Philology*, 62 (1965), 285–95; John P. McCall, 'The Squire in Wonderland', *The Chaucer Review*, 1 (1966), 103–9; Stanley J. Kahrl, 'Chaucer's *Squire's Tale* and the Decline of Chivalry', *The Chaucer Review*, 7 (1973), 194–209; and Lawton, *Chaucer's Narrators*, pp. 106–29. For a thorough analysis of the significance of Canacee, see Elizabeth Scala, 'Canacee and the Chaucer Canon: Incest and Other Unnarratables', *The Chaucer Review*, 30 (1995), 15–39.

[22] Seth Lerer, *Chaucer and his Readers: Imagining the Author in Late-Medieval England* (Princeton: Princeton University Press, 1993), p. 57; also Kahrl, 'Chaucer's *Squire's Tale* and the Decline of Chivalry', pp. 207–9.

[23] Paul Strohm, 'Jean of Angoulême: A Fifteenth-Century Reader of Chaucer', *Neuphilologische Mitteilungen*, 72 (1971), 69–76 (p. 72). *Terminis* is difficult to translate. It could indicate either the parameters of the story or else its word choices.

or Merchant in the manuscripts that preserve these versions.[24] If so, however, then this reading of the Squire is precisely what the Lansdowne scribe contradicts in his interpolation. Consider Chaucer's use of *occupatio* in the *Squire's Tale*. It is one of the rhetorical features for which Chaucer's verse has often been praised, and the *Squire's Tale* contains many examples. Multiple scholars, however, have argued that its frequency here is not to the piece's benefit, as *occupatio* proves deadly in the hands of the Squire.[25] Here he attempts to employ the form to move his story along:

> The knotte why that every tale is toold,
> If it be taried til that lust be coold
> Of hem that han it after herkned yoore,
> The savour passeth ever lenger the moore,
> For fulsomnesse of his prolixitee;
> And by the same resoun, thynketh me,
> I sholde to the knotte condescende,
> And maken of hir walkyng soone an ende.[26]

The passage is an illustrative example of the Squire's self-defeating tendency as a storyteller. Perceiving that he is lagging, he attempts to swiftly summarize the current episode and move on to the next. However, he is so self-conscious of his need to make a 'knotte' and move on that he cannot resist commenting on it, stretching what should be a simple transition into a laborious metatextual explanation of a matter that requires none. By trying to shorten his story he effectively lengthens it in a way that explicitly calls attention to his failure.

The Lansdowne scribe recalls this tendency when he has the Squire once again voice his desire to make a 'knotte' in his work. The repetition of a tale's key words or ideas seems to have been the scribe's preferred strategy when composing new lines to link various passages. He does the same later in the same link when he has Alisoun say 'glose' and again when he has the Host repeat terms and imagery from the *Canon's Yeoman's Tale* in the spurious transition between that story and that of the Physician.[27] In this case, however, his choice of reference calls back not only to Chaucer's voice but to the particular failings of his narrator. This is important, as the scribe's addition has the effect — intended or not — of rehabilitating the Squire. The Squire is criticized by modern critics for a great many perceived shortcomings, but the final straw for many has been his stated ambitions at the end of his 'Secunda Pars' ('second part'), when he breaks off in his story of Canacee and the falcon — with the promise to return to it later — to 'speken of aventures and of batailles':[28]

> First wol I telle yow of Cambyuskan,
> That in his tyme many a citee wan;
> And after wol I speke of Algarsif,

---

[24] As Marjorie Curry Woods points out, medieval audiences were familiar with the use of rhetoric for parodic purposes. 'In a Nutshell: *Verba* and *Sententia* and Matter and Form in Medieval Composition Theory', in *The Uses of Manuscripts in Literary Studies: Essays in Memory of Judson Boyce Allen*, ed. by Charlotte Cook Morse, Penelope Reed Doob, and Marjorie Curry Woods (Kalamazoo: Medieval Institute Publications, 1992), pp. 19–39 (p. 32).

[25] For a discussion of the Squire's *occupatio*, see Haller, 'Chaucer's *Squire's Tale* and the Uses of Rhetoric', p. 288; Kahrl, 'Chaucer's *Squire's Tale* and the Decline of Chivalry', pp. 201–2; and Lawton, *Chaucer's Narrators*, pp. 118–23.

[26] Chaucer, *SqT*, lines 401–8.

[27] 'Spurious Links', p. 44.

[28] Chaucer, *SqT*, lines 651–60.

> How that he wan Theodora to his wif,
> For whom ful ofte in greet peril he was,
> Ne hadde he ben holpen by the steede of bras;
> And after wol I speke of Cambalo,
> That faught in lystes with the bretheren two
> For Canacee er that he myghte hire wynne.
> And ther I lefte I wol ayeyn begynne.[29]

Suddenly this already rambling work has ballooned into something wholly unmanageable, especially for a narrator as prone to long-windedness and tangential *occupatio* as the Squire. As Derek Pearsall says ominously, 'the tale is growing, as romances tend to do, almost of their own will, into a monstrous oriental saga, and the Squire is no longer in control'.[30] However, the Lansdowne scribe places the Squire firmly back in charge of his runaway narrative. And he is only able to do so by being an attentive, perceptive reader of the *Canterbury Tales*.

William Kamowski has a more sympathetic reading of the *Squire's Tale*, particularly of the moment above where the Squire declares his ambitions. He sees it as a part of many rhetorical devices employed by Chaucer to slow the story down, hint at intriguing details but decline to indulge, and therefore build anticipation as well as encourage readers to fill in the gaps of the narrative with their own imaginings. Ultimately, the abortive ending to the tale is the last and most dramatic of these tricks.[31] Of course, whether this is a virtue or a fault of the poem depends on one's taste, and on the tale's execution; as Kamowski acknowledges, this may not be true for the *Squire's Tale*.[32] Yet the disappointment of the unfulfilled promise of the Squire is precisely what the scribe of Lansdowne appears to be combating directly in his intervention in the text, and he uses the withholding tendency of the Squire that Kamowski identifies to do it. As we see, immediately after his promise to 'ayeyn begynne' in the Lansdowne manuscript, the Squire expressly declines to do so, instead here declaring his intention to 'maake a knotte'. However, he follows right after with the assurance that the story will continue at 'the time it come next to my lotte'.[33] Here the Lansdowne scribe invokes the structure of the entire *Canterbury Tales* to excuse the unfinished nature of the *Squire's Tale*. As Harry Bailly declares in the *General Prologue*, each pilgrim is to tell four stories apiece — two on the way to Canterbury, and two on the return.[34] This, obviously, is not the form in which the *Canterbury Tales* ultimately appeared. Several characters (the Five Guildsmen, the Plowman, the Knight's Yeoman, and the Nun's other two priests) introduced in the *General Prologue* do not even get one tale to tell, and none, save Chaucer, get a second. Yet the Lansdowne scribe recalled the initial ambitions of the work and had the Squire not only invoke them but use them to his storytelling advantage. In stating his synopsis for the remainder of his tale, the Squire divides it into three parts: that concerning Cambyuskan, that of Algarsif, and that of Cambalo (one assumes that the conclusion to Canacee's encounter with the falcon will occur during the Cambalo episode as the Squire seems to imply[35]). While Pearsall is right in that the Squire's intentions are far too ambitious for one of the *Tales*, they may do if spread around,

---

[29] Chaucer, *SqT*, lines 661–70.
[30] Pearsall, 'The Squire as Story-Teller', p. 90.
[31] William Kamowski, 'Trading the "Knotte" for Loose Ends: The *Squire's Tale* and the Poetics of Chaucerian Fragments', *Style*, 31 (1997), 391–412 (pp. 392–95).
[32] Kamowski, 'Trading the "Knotte" for Loose Ends', pp. 394–95.
[33] 'Spurious Links', p. 43.
[34] Chaucer, *GP*, lines 788–809.
[35] Chaucer, *SqT*, lines 652–57.

and with his story roughly one-quarter over and three turns ahead of him, the Squire is now well-positioned to conclude his yarn. Moreover, by transforming his final words into a 'teaser', as it were, the Lansdowne scribe removes the suspicion that the Squire has taken on a project he has no hope in completing and instead uses this portion of the story to stimulate interest in its later instalments. This new ending becomes yet another device in heightening the readers' anticipation, just as the rest of the poem has primed them throughout. Of course, in suggesting a second turn for the Squire the Lansdowne scribe is promoting a fantasy, and on these grounds Partridge criticizes the Lansdowne scribe for promising something he cannot provide.[36] Yet as Charles A. Owen, Jr. notes of the various Chaucer manuscripts, 'the text of the *Canterbury Tales* nowhere supports the theory [...] that Chaucer abandoned the homeward journey'.[37] If scribes had only their collection of exemplars as their guide, rather than the whole of the extant *Canterbury Tales* corpus, they might very well have expected a more complete version of the collection to exist somewhere. When they encountered a lacuna in their text, not all could say with confidence, as Adam Pynkhurst does in one instance in Hengwrt, 'Of This Cokes Tale Maked Chaucer Namoore'. What's more, a scribe's full degree of access to alternative exemplars can never fully be known. Those with access to Ellesmere or its descendants, for example, would have a quote from the Host revising the parameters of the pilgrims' game ('ech of yow moot tellen atte leste/ A tale or two, or breken his behest'[38]). Yet if the Lansdowne scribe had access to these lines he would have had no need to create his own link between the *Squire's Tale* and the next, and so he improvised using the information he had at hand. Experience also likely led scribes to expect incomplete exemplars to exist elsewhere in fuller forms. Chaucer's *Tales*, like other medieval texts, circulated in numerous versions, together and in fragments. Poor-quality, incomplete, or disordered exemplars were not necessarily unusual, but they typically left more of the responsibility in the scribes' hands of how to order and present the text.[39] The existence of gaps and blank folios in the manuscripts attests to the expectation (or hope) on the part of scribes that a more complete exemplar existed and may fall into their hands some day. Fifteenth-century extensions of the *Canterbury Tales* such as Lydgate's opening to the *Siege of Thebes* and the *Canterbury Interlude* before the *Tale of Beryn* also reveal an audience that was able to entertain the notion of — if it did not just simply expect — a return journey for the pilgrims, and more chances at a story.[40] After all, the *General Prologue* retains the promise of the *Tales*' original structure as well, so its persistence elsewhere perhaps should not occasion comment.

The Lansdowne scribe is therefore manipulating his material to change the characterization of his copy of the *Canterbury Tales* through the insertion of original material. Yet this is a provisional originality, dependent on his exemplar's author, Chaucer: Chaucer's words, his poetic forms, and the content of the *General Prologue* are all manipulated to create the product of the Lansdowne scribe. This is different from Chaucer's own acknowledgement of sources because of scribes' usual practice of camouflaging their contributions. Chaucer states

---

[36] Partridge, 'Minding the Gaps', pp. 55–56.
[37] Charles A. Owen, Jr., 'The Alternative Reading of *The Canterbury Tales*: Chaucer's Text and the Early Manuscripts', *PMLA*, 97 (1982), 237–50 (p. 247).
[38] Chaucer, *SqT*, lines 697–98.
[39] N. F. Blake, 'Geoffrey Chaucer: Textual Transmission and Editing', in *Crux and Controversy in Middle English Textual Criticism*, ed. by A. J. Minnis and Charlotte Brewer (Cambridge: Brewer, 1992), pp. 19–38 (p. 21).
[40] John M. Bowers, '*The Tale of Beryn* and *The Seige of Thebes*: Alternative Ideas of the *Canterbury Tales*', *Studies in the Age of Chaucer*, 7 (1985), 23–50 (pp. 26–37).

frankly that he is taking others' work in several of his adaptations of earlier material.[41] Yet just as his discussion of the scribe's role serves to distinguish him as the creator of the work, by acknowledging his sources Chaucer asserts ownership of the material since the product — which in truth differs greatly from its antecedents — is his. Moreover, even as he names authorities Chaucer also neglects to mention many of his closest sources, which obscures those with the greatest claims of influence over his work and increases the impression of his own originality. In contrast, scribes do not attach their names to texts and ascribe them wholly to their *auctores*, no matter what the scribal contribution. In comparing authorial and scribal poetics, therefore, the desire for self-effacement — and the mimicry it inspires — is a crucial distinction.

The usual scribal impulse to remain in the background also makes it difficult to determine scribes' intent. Of course, this is a tricky matter with known authors as well, but what goes for a named writer such as Chaucer would seem to go double for a scribe.[42] Fisher has made an effort towards addressing this challenge, but he illustrates its difficulty by choosing scribes — Thomas Hoccleve, the Harley Scribe, and Ranulf Higden — who are unlike the typical scribe in the extent that their biographies or writing practices are known.[43] Yet Hoccleve, who reveals so much about himself in his poetry, calls no attention to himself when acting as a scribe, and most of his professional brethren were the same. Just as most scribal changes are not intended to call attention to themselves, they are also not designed to say anything about the person holding the pen, nor their editorial decisions.[44] Scribes are also usually silent on the state of their materials, which frustrates efforts to learn more about the text. It is possible, for example, though unlikely, that the Lansdowne links are from a lost exemplar, making their composer even more of a mystery. What could ever be known about his intentions with the physical copy of his text lost?[45] Does the scribe reflect his own desires or a patron's in his efforts?[46] Such questions come to bear when assessing a scribe's contribution to a text, but are very difficult to determine in most cases. For Lansdowne, it cannot be said definitively that the Lansdowne scribe meant to rehabilitate the Squire in the process of forging a link between his tale and the next. It may just be an unintentional side effect. Yet why did he invent the links at all? The answers likely depend on unknowns — the origin of the manuscript, its patron (if any), and his or her preferences.

Tentative conclusions can be proposed, however. In recent years, palaeography and codicology have become increasingly important in textual interpretation, and in many cases they have advanced our knowledge not only of the contents of manuscripts but also of their scribes. Most prominent is the 2006 identification of the scribe of Hengwrt and Ellesmere,

---

[41] Chaucer, *Troilus and Criseyde*, lines 1.394 and 5.1653; *Anelida and Arcite*, line 21; *ClPro*, lines 21–56 and *PhysT*, line 1.

[42] Hanna, 'Producing Manuscripts and Editions', p. 125.

[43] Matthew Fisher, 'When Variants Aren't: Authors as Scribes in Some English Manuscripts', in *Probable Truth: Editing Medieval Texts from Britain in the Twenty-First Century*, ed. by Vincent Gillespie and Anne Hudson (Turnhout: Brepols, 2013), pp. 207–22.

[44] As Anne Hudson says about a hypothetical *Piers Plowman* scribe, 'it would require heroic patience to discover what any individual medieval scribe made of the poem'. This statement can be extended to most of his compatriots. Hudson, 'Middle English', p. 43. See also Hanna, 'Problems of "Best Text" Editing', pp. 89–90.

[45] A. I. Doyle, 'Retrospect and Prospect', in *Manuscripts and Readers in Fifteenth-Century England: The Literary Implications of Manuscript Study*, ed. by Derek Pearsall (Cambridge: Brewer, 1983), pp. 142–46 (p. 145).

[46] Machan, *Textual Criticism and the Middle English Text*, p. 171 and Hanna, 'Producing Manuscripts and Editions', p. 75.

which almost immediately impacted the debate over the primacy of either manuscript.[47] A consideration of Lansdowne's physical features will not reveal the name of its scribe, but may give some indication of his working conditions, which in turn may give some insight into his reasoning. Specifically, by connecting the importance of Lansdowne as an art object to the prevailing tastes of the time, it is possible to make a tentative argument for the presence of its unique links in the manuscript.

The scribe of Lansdowne 851 likely had a patron. As already noted, it was designed to create a pleasing visual presentation, and is heavily ornamented, with a famous portrait of Chaucer in its first historiated initial.[48] This was, in other words, a deluxe copy, produced for a patron for their own private enjoyment or to display to 'call attention to their own status as patrons of letters'.[49] Those commissioning such works in the early fifteenth century represented a new market for Chaucer's poetry, one which intended to demonstrate its newfound wealth and sophistication through such luxury objects. Pearsall characterizes the shift in patronage as moving from 'court poetry', where the intended recipients for Chaucer's verse were members of the king's court, to 'courtly poetry', where the audience was broader and unaristocratic.[50] The merchant class became the primary audience for Chaucer's work, and in their adoption of his verse they sought to copy the tastes and trappings of court. Yet in their own ideas of what constituted courtly culture, these new patrons were ultimately more conservative than the actual lords and ladies from Chaucer's generation. Innovations in form and social impropriety were unpopular with this new group, and some of Chaucer's verse fell out of favour as a result.[51] In other cases, the material was edited to conform to expectations, a process that Seth Lerer, borrowing from Lee Patterson, describes as 'disambiguating' — obscuring or excising original material so as to avoid the troublesome implications of challenging themes.[52]

Scholars have drawn a connection between the tastes of early fifteenth-century patrons and the physical appearance of their books. Just as society had to be properly ordered, so too must its texts. The *Canterbury Tales*, then, which existed in several fragments and in several orders, with several tales which could easily be considered subversive, would find it particularly difficult to conform to this preference. Many of the 'worst' tales, from this point of view, were both disorganized and disrespectful. The *Cook's Tale* is an obvious example. Daniel J. Pinti draws its form and content together expressly, seeing both Perkyn Revelour and his story as 'unfinished', the implication being that if one allows one's books to be disorderly, one may

---

[47] Linne R. Mooney, 'Chaucer's Scribe', *Speculum*, 81 (2006), pp. 97–138. Critical responses to that article and assessments of its impact on the Hengwrt/Ellesmere question include Estelle Stubbs, ' "Here's One I Prepared Earlier": The Work of Scribe D on Oxford, Corpus Christi College, MS 198', *The Review of English Studies*, 58 (2007), 133–53; Alexandra Gillespie, 'Reading Chaucer's Words to Adam', *The Chaucer Review*, 42 (2008), 269–83; Simon Horobin, 'Adam Pinkhurst, Geoffrey Chaucer, and the Hengwrt Manuscript of the *Canterbury Tales*', *The Chaucer Review*, 44 (2010), 351–67; and Jordi Sánchez-Martí, 'Adam Pynkhurst's "Necglygence and Rape", Reassessed', *English Studies*, 92 (2011), 360–74.

[48] Seymour, *A Catalogue of Chaucer Manuscripts*, II, 131 and 134. See also Manly and Rickert, *The Text of the Canterbury Tales*, I, 304–8.

[49] Lerer, *Chaucer and his Readers*, p. 17.

[50] Derek Pearsall, *Old English and Middle English Poetry* (Boston: Routledge & Kegan Paul, 1977), pp. 212–13.

[51] Paul Strohm, 'Chaucer's Fifteenth-Century Audience and the Narrowing of the "Chaucer Tradition" ', *Studies in the Age of Chaucer*, 4 (1982), 3–32 (pp. 18–21) and Glending Olson, 'The Misreadings of the Beryn Prologue', *Medaevalia*, 17 (1991), 201–19 (p. 204).

[52] Seth Lerer, 'Rewriting Chaucer: Two Fifteenth-Century Readings of the *Canterbury Tales*', *Viator*, 19 (1988), 311–26 (p. 322). Also Lee Patterson, 'Ambiguity and Interpretation: A Fifteenth-Century Reading of *Troilus and Criseyde*', *Speculum*, 54 (1979), 297–330 (pp. 297–300).

countenance a similar state for society. In V. A. Kolve's reading of what there is of the tale, the Cook swiftly sketches out a conflict between the artisan class and their unruly apprentices.[53] Those from such rising classes who commissioned lavish manuscripts such as Lansdowne (and Bodley 686, Pinti's focus), were liable to have to deal with their own rebellious underlings and were invested in the status quo; therefore, in Pinti's construction, degenerates such as Perkyn and deficient texts such as Chaucer's *Cook's Tale* must be 'mastered'.[54] The insertion of the *Tale of Gamelyn* in many of the manuscripts both reversed the moral trajectory of the story and obscured the tale's unfinished state; in Lansdowne, the scribe once again takes it upon himself to add an additional few lines to smooth the transition:

> Fye, therone, it is so foule! I wil nowe tell no forthere
> For schame of the harlotrie that seweth after.
> A velany it were thareof more to spell,
> Bot of a knighte and his sonnes, my tale I wil forthe tell.[55]

In Chaucer's version of the *Cook's Tale*, whether by design or by chance, the provocations of Perkyn and his friends stand unanswered. By having the Cook denounce his own tale, the Lansdowne scribe serves a swift (if abrupt) corrective, then transitions into the more conciliatory *Gamelyn*. Bodley 686, in contrast, lacks *Gamelyn*, and so resorts to more extreme measures. It heavily edits the *Cook's Tale* to make sure that Perkyn and his friend meet unhappy ends for their misbehaviour. The wife, for her part, is saved from prostitution by the stroke of the scribe's pen — she now 'pleyed' rather than 'swyved' for her sustenance.[56]

Lansdowne conforms quite well to this interpretation of luxury manuscripts and their contents. The quality of its production is high, and its invented links speak to the same impulse to rectify perceived shortcomings in the text. One can see this carried out at an even finer level in Lansdowne than in Pinti's Bodley 686 example, for whereas the Bodley scribe actively altered Chaucer's wording in his revision, the Lansdowne scribe, as we have seen, instead repeated key terms from Chaucer so as to make his transitions even more seamless. Moreover, the Lansdowne scribe's final product speaks to the priority he gave to completeness, both actual and illusory. Lansdowne is the only manuscript from group *c* that contains Chaucer's *Retraction*, for example, giving the work a definitive end.[57] As we have seen, it also completely integrates *Gamelyn* into its structure whereas other manuscripts show hesitation on the part of their scribes as to how to proceed.[58] Lansdowne, in short, is notable for the absolute regularization of its visual form, as well as its uninterrupted flow from one tale into the other.[59] The scribe's goal was physical and narrative completeness, at the expense of

---

[53] V. A. Kolve, *Chaucer and the Imagery of Narrative: The First Five Canterbury Tales* (Stanford: Stanford University Press, 1984), pp. 267–75.

[54] Daniel J. Pinti, 'Governing the *Cook's Tale* in Bodley 686', *The Chaucer Review*, 30 (1996), 379–88 (p. 384). See also Partridge, 'Minding the Gaps', pp. 63–64.

[55] 'Spurious Links', p. 43. In Lansdowne, these lines are found on fol. 54r–54v.

[56] 'The Cook's Tale', in *The Canterbury Tales: Fifteenth-Century Continuations and Additions*, ed. by John M. Bowers (Kalamazoo: Medieval Institute Publications, 1992), pp. 33–39 (p. 37). For a reading of 'pleyed' vs. 'swyved' and the redeeming of Perkyn's wife, see David Lorenzo Boyd, 'Social Texts: Bodley 686 and the Politics of the Cook's Tale', *Huntington Library Quarterly*, 58 (1995), pp. 93–95.

[57] Stephen Partridge, ' "The Makere of this Boke": Chaucer's *Retraction* and the Author as Scribe and Compiler', in *Author, Reader, Book: Medieval Authorship in Theory and Practice*, ed. by Stephen Partridge and Eric Kwakkel (Toronto: University of Toronto Press, 2012), pp. 106–53 (p. 117).

[58] N. F. Blake, 'Chaucer, Gamelyn and the Cook's Tale', in *The Medieval Book and a Modern Collector: Essays in Honour of Toshiyuki Takamiya*, ed. by Takami Matsuda, Richard A. Linenthal, and John Scahill (Cambridge: Brewer, 2004), pp. 87–98 (p. 94).

[59] Partridge, 'Minding the Gaps', p. 55.

fidelity to his exemplar and without the hope that supplemental materials might come his way. That he made his changes to create an attractive object for his patron is a plausible explanation for his actions.

It should be noted, however, how conjectural this conclusion is. Nothing is known in fact about the scribe of Lansdowne or his patron; the circumstances of the manuscript's commission may not conform to the expectations of such a lavish work, and whoever commissioned it may not fit the stereotype of the new fifteenth-century reader. With Lansdowne, too, we are dealing with a relatively clear instance of scribal intervention. In other cases, it is far harder to determine just what is scribal invention and what is authorial revision. On issues where there is a difference of opinion — whether the *Canon Yeoman's Tale* is authentic,[60] or if the expansions to the *Wife of Bath's Prologue* are authorial[61] — the interpretation of the text hinges upon one's decision over what is or is not Chaucerian. And, as many have noted, in the hardest cases such decisions can only be subjective.[62] The surviving *Canterbury Tales* corpus is also not ideal for making clear delineations between Chaucer's work and others'. It exists in fragments and in various orders, and there is no extant autograph to guide modern commentators. In addition, as Ralph Hanna III has noted, of what we can perceive of Chaucer's writing process, he rarely made major, systematic revisions to his work such as those which produced the discrete versions of *Piers Plowman*. Instead he practiced 'rolling revision', making small changes here and there in ways that are very similar to scribal activity.[63] In such circumstances it is often difficult to say with any certainty what is authorial in a manuscript and what isn't.

The Squire-Wife of Bath link in Lansdowne 851 represents, therefore, not only the potential for innovative scribal art that plays upon the contents of the text and the desires of a patron, but also how those pressures shaped the manuscripts that ultimately resulted. Hanna describes 'scribal poetics' as 'a much shabbier thing' than the words of the author: 'the series of disruptive and degenerative choices that could be associated inductively with the activity of scribes'.[64] The implication of this definition is that scribes, unlike authors, operated under constraints — primarily the requirement that they copy a text faithfully. These constraints either discouraged or undermined originality, leading, inevitably, to a degeneration of the work. Yet, as Chaucer understood, the scribe's position gave him an enormous amount of power over a text. Scribal effect is diffuse, but obscured, making the scribe fit for a number

---

[60] Norman Blake, 'Editing the *Canterbury Tales*: An Overview', in *The 'Canterbury Tales' Project Occasional Papers, vol. 1*, ed. by Norman Blake and Peter Robinson (London: Office for Humanities Communication, 1993), pp. 5–18 (p. 8) and Blake, 'Chaucer, Gamelyn and the Cook's Tale', pp. 97–98.

[61] Beverly Kennedy, 'Contradictory Responses to the Wife of Bath as Evidenced by Fifteenth-Century Manuscript Variants', in *The 'Canterbury Tales' Project Occasional Papers, vol. 2*, ed. by Norman Blake and Peter Robinson (London: Office for Humanities Communication, 1997), pp. 23–39 (pp. 27–32).

[62] See Blake, *The Textual Tradition of the Canterbury Tales*, pp. 46–48; Blake, 'Editing *The Canterbury Tales*', p. 7; Helen Cooper, 'The Order of the Tales in the Ellesmere Manuscript', in *Ellesmere Chaucer: Essays in Interpretation*, ed. by Martin Stevens and Daniel Woodward (San Marino: Huntington Library, 1995), pp. 245–61 (p. 246); and Simon Horobin, 'Editorial Assumptions and the Manuscripts of *The Canterbury Tales*', in *The 'Canterbury Tales' Project Occasional Papers, vol. 2*, ed. by Norman Blake and Peter Robinson (London: Office for Humanities Communication, 1997), pp. 15–21 (pp. 19–20).

[63] Hanna, 'Authorial Versions, Rolling Revision, Scribal Error?', pp. 160–61.

[64] Hanna, 'Authorial Versions, Rolling Revision, Scribal Error?', p. 159.

of behind-the-scenes roles — critic,[65] editor,[66] censor[67] — or, even, ultimately, author.[68] This is the result of the great variability of their task and to the variety of effects their actions could have on a manuscript. The dynamism in the work of writing in this period makes the study of scribal contribution difficult yet necessary, as the fluidity between the roles scribes might take and the tension that existed between the demands placed on them produced such unique products as the Squire-Wife of Bath link in Lansdowne 851.

---

[65] B. A. Windeatt, 'The Scribes as Chaucer's Early Critics', *Studies in the Age of Chaucer* 1 (1979), 119–41.

[66] Celia Millward, 'The Medieval Scribe as Editor: The Case of *La Estoire del Evangelie*', *Manuscripta*, 41 (1997), pp. 155–70.

[67] Boyd, 'Social Texts', pp. 81–97; Pinti, 'Governing the *Cook's Tale* in Bodley 686', pp. 379–88 and Kennedy, 'Contradictory Responses to the Wife of Bath as evidenced by Fifteenth-Century Manuscript Variants', pp. 23–39.

[68] Patricia Stoop, 'The Writing Sisters of Jericho: Authors or Copyists?', in *Constructing the Medieval Sermon*, ed. by Roger Andersson (Turnhout: Brepols, 2007), pp. 275–308; Aidan Conti, 'Scribes as Authors, Transmission as Composition: Towards a Science of Copying', in *Modes of Authorship in the Middle Ages*, ed. by Slavica Ranković (Toronto: Pontifical Institute of Medieval Studies, 2012), pp. 267–88; and Fisher, *Scribal Authorship*.

'Do not Give that which is Holy to Dogs': Noble Hunting, the *Curée* Ritual, and the Eucharist

Andrew Pattison

Introduction

The importance of hunting in the late-medieval period cannot be overemphasized. From its origins of protecting society from wild animals and providing sustenance, hunting transformed during the Middle Ages into a privileged sport of the nobility, a 'passion for kings and lords', and, importantly, a way to underscore noble preeminence in society.[1] The right to hunt the king's deer was amongst the most sought-after privileges in the Middle Ages. In late-medieval England, hunting was indeed a very royal affair. After the Conquest of 1066 the Norman kings had transformed the best woodlands of England into veritable hunting preserves in which the king alone reserved the prerogative to hunt.[2] With this in mind, hunting in the late-medieval era should be viewed as a performance of sorts, as a symbolic flaunting of social rank and power and affinity to royalty.[3] Status and privilege were intrinsically linked in the medieval world, and both played important roles in maintaining order in society.[4] In general terms, the social order of late-medieval England was underwritten by the understanding that each estate, indeed every person, even the humblest peasant, was owed certain privileges in return for certain duties — the terms of which were effectively the mortar that bound society together.[5] Though the framework for such a system remained static as a matter of course,

---

[1] This theme has long interested historians and as such is oft articulated. See, for example, Roland Bechmann, *Trees and Man: The Forest in the Middle Ages* (New York: Paragon Press, 1990), pp. 27–36; Susan Crane, *Animal Encounters: Contacts and Concepts in Medieval Britain* (Philadelphia: University of Philadelphia Press, 2013), pp. 101–19; Ryan Judkins, 'The Game of the Courtly Hunt: Chasing and Breaking Deer in Late Medieval English Literature', *Journal of English and Germanic Philology*, 112 (2013), 70–92.

[2] For a discussion of the Norman influence on royal forests and hunting in England, see Richard Almond, *Medieval Hunting* (Stroud: Sutton Publishing, 2003), pp. 13–18; Emma Griffin, *Blood Sport: Hunting in Britain since 1066* (New Haven: Yale University Press, 2007), pp. 11–24 and 36–41.

[3] These themes are developed by Almond, pp. 28–29, and Griffin, pp. 30–32.

[4] See, for example, Robert Fossier, *The Axe and the Oath: Ordinary Life in the Middle Ages* (Princeton: Princeton University Press, 2000), pp. 252–85. See also Peter Cross, 'An Age of Deference', in *A Social History of England: 1200–1500*, ed. by Rosemary Horrox and W. Mark Ormrod (London: Cambridge University Press, 2006); Richard Kaeuper, 'Social Ideals and Social Disruption', in *The Cambridge Companion to Medieval English Culture*, ed. by Andrew Galloway (Cambridge: Cambridge University Press, 2011), pp. 87–106.

[5] Fossier, pp. 117–27, offers an overview of this notion; Phillipp Schofield, *Peasant and Community in Medieval*

medieval society was marked by an elemental state of contestation in which the prevailing social hierarchy need eternally be reaffirmed, lest it sunder and be recast anew.

In this context hunting takes on unique importance, a poignant social gesture in 'the age of gesture'.[6] Alexander Pluskowski could refer to hunting as part of a seigneurial semiotic system predicated on appropriated animal bodies — 'a visual language expressing and negotiating power relations'.[7] As a point of departure, this article will examine the prominent hunting ritual known as the *curée* in which the hounds are feasted upon freshly killed venison in a highly ritualized rite. In line with previous research, hunting ritual is examined as a projection of noble dominance over society. The paper deviates, however, from existing research in not seeking to understand the message of the noble hunt or what it communicated, but rather on examining *the resonance* of the message and thus on how, and to what end, ritual was used to present ideological messages. Although a number of researchers have posited a link between the rituals of the hunt and religious rites, the theme has not been explored exhaustively.[8] This paper focuses on the *curée* as a unique ritual of the hunt that has not received due attention. Aside from a notable but brief foray by William Perry Marvin, the *curée* has been largely overlooked by researchers in their search for socially meaningful rituals in the hunt. This is presumably because it would seem to lack any clear link to social gesture, serving only as part of the 'blood spectacle that commits the act to memory', as Marvin puts it.[9] Essentially, it has been seen as more 'practical' than ritual.[10] This notwithstanding, the paper builds on the observation that the *curée* bears a marked resemblance to the liturgical rituals of the Catholic mass and therefore may have played an important role in the post-kill hunting rituals. I will argue that the *curée* is in fact closely intertwined with liturgical ritual in terms of form and idiom, and that the *curée* is the product of a unique historical context and temporal ideological needs. Through close contextualization and comparative reading, this paper examines how the interpellative thrust of the ideology inherent in noble hunting rituals was constructed and received in late-medieval England, and thereby suggests a nuanced conceptualization of non-sacred rituals as objects of historical research.

The article unfolds in four sections. First, the rituals of the noble hunt and the *curée* in particular are described and then examined against the backdrop of previous research and ritual theory. The next section further explores the *curée* ritual and aims to understand its ritual form as well as how it resonates with the Catholic liturgy. The third section will examine the rituals of the liturgy in as much as they pertain to the *curée* with the aim of better disclosing the ideology and dispositions inherent in their analogues in the *curée*, and will touch on the issue of reception. The final section will briefly trace the historical trajectory of the *curée* as a ritual within its cultural and social context, and will offer a few final observations. Together, the

---

England: 1200–1500, (Basingstoke: Palgrave Macmillan, 2003), pursues the subject in more detail in an English setting.

[6] Fossier, p. 54.

[7] Alexander Pluskowski, 'Communicating through Skin and Bone: Appropriating Animal Bodies in Medieval Western European Seigneurial Culture', in *Breaking and Shaping Beastly Bodies: Animals as Material Culture in the Middle Ages*, ed. by Alexander Pluskowski (Oxford: Oxbow Books, 2007), pp. 32–51 (pp. 46–47).

[8] Typically these are relegated to broad pronouncements. Spearing, for example, referred to the hunt as 'a sacrament, a ritual by which violent energies are at once expressed and contained', but took the theme no further. A. C. Spearing, *The Gawain-Poet* (London: Cambridge University Press, 1970), pp. 9–10.

[9] William Perry Marvin, *Hunting Law and Ritual in Medieval Literature* (Cambridge: Brewer, 2006), pp. 134–141. John Cummins, *The Hound and the Hawk: The Art of Medieval Hunting* (London: Weidenfeld & Nicolson, 1988), pp. 41–42, briefly commented on the religious nature of the *curée* as well.

[10] See Marvin, p. 118; Almond, pp. 77–78; Cummins, pp. 40–41, 44.

various points of concord between the two traditions (hunting and liturgy) are used to elucidate their mutual resonance and associability and, thereby, the ideological messages inherent in the noble hunt.

The *curée* and hunting 'by strength'

Hunting 'by strength' was the most esteemed version of the noble hunt and the style of hunting that features most prominently in late-medieval England. Hunting by strength referred to the practice whereby a large hunting party, sometimes hundreds of people, would single out one animal, usually a male red deer, and chase it with relays of hounds and hunters on horseback. Groups of attendants would be stationed at predetermined intervals to ensure that the quarry advanced along the desired course. After the deer had been chased to near exhaustion, the entire hunting party (including the hounds) would approach for a view of the kill. After dispatching the creature, an intricate butchering of the carcass would ensue, and the hounds would then be rewarded in a ritual known as the *curée*. As it represented a central feature of hunting by strength, the rites of the *curée* are described in detail in most Middle English medieval hunting treatises, but occur in finest detail in Edward of Norwich's *Master of Game*.[11] There the blood of the deer is carefully collected and then mixed with bread and offal on the hide. Next, the hide is rearranged — the mixture hidden within — to give the package a semblance of the creature's natural form. For the climax, the head of the deer, already severed from its body, was then raised aloft by the ranking nobleman and then placed back in its natural position at the neck-end of the hide; the hounds were made to bay and the 'package' was opened, revealing the hounds' reward. Afterwards, the head of the deer (aloft again) was taken back to the nobleman's manor, with the entire hunting party following in procession. Specified parties would be allotted certain cuts of meat, according to tradition and hierarchy. The aim of the entire endeavor was to take one prized deer, in great spectacle.

In one form or another, the *curée* appears in all late-medieval Middle English hunting manuals and is commonly featured in the imaginative literature of the era. Although the totality of these sources will be considered in this paper, the focus will be on the *curée* as it occurs in *Master of Game*. The work represents the zenith of the hunting treatise genre in England. *Master of Game* is preserved in 27 medieval manuscripts and two modern editions; I follow the most recent edition, edited by James I. McNelis III.[12] With respect to historical context, the hunting treatises examined here are understood to generally describe English noble hunting practices of the thirteenth–early-fifteenth century. The treatises are not concerned with utilitarian issues but rather those features of the medieval hunt that made it courtly.[13] *Master of Game* itself is dedicated to Henry of Monmouth, later Henry V, and

---

[11] James I. McNelis III, 'The Uncollated Manuscripts of "The Master of Game": Towards a New Edition' (unpublished Ph.D. dissertation, University of Washington, 1996). Largely a translation of Gaston de Phebus' late-fourteenth-century *Livre de Chasse*, Edward's work nevertheless contains much original writing about English circumstances including a chapter on hunting by strength that details the *curée*. *Livre de Chasse, Gaston Phébus*, ed. by Gunnar Tilander (Karlshamn: Almqvist & Wiksells, 1971).

[12] For a discussion of the manuscripts and editions, see McNelis, pp. 63–126. I also draw on William A. Baillie-Grohman's 1909 edition, *Master of Game: The Oldest English Book on Hunting* (Milton Keynes: Lightning Source UK, 2010) [first publ. 1909].

[13] Anne Rooney, *Tretyse off Huntyng* (Brussels: OMIREL, 1987), pp. 38–39.

Edward compiled the work while he held the title of master of game in Henry IV's court.[14] *Master of Game* thus represents the epitome of courtly hunting.

A salient point about the hunting rituals described in the treatises is that, however superfluous and impracticable they may seem, they reflect actual hunting practices of the era. Recent archaeological findings imply that the ritual butchering and division of the carcass described in the treatises was in fact fairly common during the era.[15] Given this, we can comfortably assume that the *curée* ritual was similarly prevalent. That the *curée* commonly features in imaginative literature would support this assumption.[16] Although hunting by strength in the elaborate form depicted in *Master of Game* was practiced essentially by royalty and the high nobility, its features were surely known throughout society by virtue of multiple repetition and through the its performative nature.[17] In this sense, the hunting practices described in the treatises would likely have been viewed by a wide spectrum of society, and therefore were socially meaningful. Whether as active participants or passive spectators, all classes of society were involved in the hunt by strength, including peasants recruited to aid in the hunt. Thus, despite its noble tenor and focus, hunting by strength was in essence a performance that involved a wider audience. The practice seems to have developed before the thirteenth century and achieves a somewhat standardized form in the treatises by the early fourteenth century.[18] Within the manuscript context of *Master of Game* the rituals of the noble hunt would have been widely familiar to medieval society.

That hunting was an important prerogative of the elite in the medieval era is not in question. Researchers have long noted the significance of hunting as a highly meaningful social gesture.[19] A more recent research trend, however, has focused on the rituals of the hunt, generally interpreting them as indicative of the social and ideological complexion of medieval society. Ryan Judkins, for example, has argued that far from being an innocuous hobby, the noble hunt entailed acute social consequences: whereas a successful hunt projected a message of social cohesion and therefore reinforced existing hierarchies, an unsuccessful hunt communicated the opposite, a ritual failure.[20] Susan Crane for her part has argued convincingly that the rituals of the hunt involved an interpellative effect: working along the lines of

---

[14] McNelis, pp. 9–12.

[15] Naomi J. Sykes, 'The Impact of Normans on Hunting Practices in England', in *Food in Medieval England: Diet and Nutrition*, ed. by C. M. Woolgar, D. Serjeantson, and T. Waldron (Oxford: Oxford University Press, 2006), pp. 162–75 (pp. 170–75); Naomi J. Sykes, 'Animal Bones and Animal Parks', in *The Medieval Park: New Perspectives*, ed. by Robert Liddiard (Macclesfield: Windgather Press, 2007), pp. 49–62 (p. 155); Jean Birrell, 'Procuring, Preparing and Serving Venison in Late Medieval England', in *Food in Medieval England: Diet and Nutrition*, ed. by C. M. Woolgar, D. Serjeantson, and T. Waldron (Oxford: Oxford University Press, 2006), pp. 176–88. Sykes and Birrell espouse this view while Richard Thomas cautiously embraces it in 'Chasing the Ideal? Ritualism, Pragmatism and the Late Medieval Hunt', in *Breaking and Shaping Beastly Bodies*, ed. by Alexander Pluskowski (Oxford: Oxbow Books, 2007), pp. 125–48.

[16] The *curée* appears prominently in *Gawain and the Green Knight* and *Sir Tristan*, for example. See *Gawain and the Green Knight*, in *The Norton Anthology of English Literature*, vol. I, ed. by M. H. Abrams (New York: Norton, 2000), ll. 1319–64, and Gottfried von Strassburg, *Tristan, with the 'Tristan' of Thomas*, trans. by A. T. Hatto (St Ives: Penguin Classics, 2004), pp. 78–82.

[17] Such diffusion would have been aided by the fact that, during the era under inspection, king and nobleman alike would have spent much of their time in itinerary, travelling from manor to manor, often hunting whenever conditions permitted. See Christopher Woolgar, *The Great Household in Late Medieval England* (New Haven: Yale University Press, 1999), pp. 1–9.

[18] Judkins, pp. 72–74.

[19] Spearing, pp. 9–10, is an early example.

[20] Judkins, *passim*.

performativity theory, Crane posits that in presenting a message of aristocratic preeminence over society the noble hunt was ideologically coercive.[21] The upshot of this research trend has been the drawing of a clear link between hunting ritual and social implication. Nevertheless, this research trend tends to hinge on a somewhat cursory employment of ritual theory, one that is partially at odds with classical definitions. That is to say, this line of research has tended to focus on social affect without always fully theorizing or contextualizing its ritual underpinnings.

An example from Susan Crane's essay 'The Noble Hunt as a Ritual Practice' is indicative of this phenomenon. Crane notes, quite correctly, that 'ritual' is commonly used in the scholarly discourse on hunting but 'typically receives little elaboration'.[22] To address this shortcoming, she duly parses the classical interpretation of rituals, associated with Van Gennep and Victor Turner, and notes that the classical definitions would not seem to suit the practices of the noble hunt. There is no Gennepian liminal change, no inflection of roles as in Victor Turner, and, importantly, there is no invocation of the supernatural.[23] Crane nevertheless then turns to the notion of 'secular ritual' and switches to ritual as performance and interpellation, employing the work of Clifford Geertz and Eve Sedgwick. Thus, (classical) ritual is made to dovetail with (ideological) performativity, which she then uses to examine the interpellation of the noble hunt.[24] The concept she ultimately settles on is *mimetic ritual*, concluding that: 'the hunt à force is a mimetic ritual designed to celebrate and perpetuate noble authority'.[25] This and similar lines of argumentation betray a very simple fact: as a research subject, ritual is very tempting to use but utterly difficult to pin down.[26] The benefit of Crane's approach, however, is that it elucidates the wider potential of marrying ritual theory and performativity theory. While the nuance of her employment of ritual theory may be questioned, her instincts are correct and her work offers a refreshing take on medieval hunting ritual. This paper does not seek to question the recent shift toward interpellation and social indexing as critical components of the noble hunt, nor does it seek to argue that hunting rituals were of scant significance. Nevertheless, rituals occur in specific contexts, and as Catherine Bell notes, ritual acts must be considered 'within the semantic framework whereby the significance of an action is dependent upon its place and relationship within a context of all other ways of acting'.[27] Similarly, the limitations of ritual as an ideological tool should be noted: 'ritual alone cannot control communities' although it can 'ground arbitrary or necessary ideas in an understanding of the hegemonic order'.[28] Historians by and large have had a tendency to neglect the nuance of ritual.[29] Where this paper seeks to differentiate itself from the previous literature is in focusing not so much on discerning ideological messages but on examining the mode of messaging, on examining

---

[21] Crane, pp. 101–19.
[22] Crane, pp. 105–6.
[23] On these classical interpretations of ritual, see Van Gennep, *The Rites of Passage* (Chicago: University of Chicago Press, 1992) and Victor Turner, *The Ritual Process: Structure and Anti-Structure* (New Brunswick: Aldine Transaction, 2008).
[24] Crane, pp. 103–5.
[25] Crane, p. 107.
[26] For a discussion, see Philippe Buc, *The Dangers of Ritual: Between Early Modern Texts and Social Scientific Theory* (Princeton: Princeton University Press, 2001), pp. 1–12.
[27] Catherine Bell, *Ritual Theory, Ritual Practice* (Oxford: Oxford University Press, 2009), p. 220.
[28] Bell, p. 222.
[29] Buc was highly critical on this point. See Buc, pp. 1–4.

the ritual of the medieval hunt in terms of 'what it echoes, what it inverts, what it alludes to, what it denies' in an attempt to better disclose its constitution.[30]

In this line of thinking, a fruitful approach to ritual (and performance theory) is to be found in the work of anthropologist Stanley Tambiah. As a researcher, Tambiah is unusual in how he situates ritual within the framework of the cultural and the social. Tambiah sees in ritual a duality that entails two simultaneous thrusts: semantically, with respect to cultural pre-suppositions and cultural understandings, and pragmatically with respect to the social and interpersonal context of ritual action.[31] Ritual, according to Tambiah, does not intentionally communicate but instead aims to instill a 'permanent attitude'; it offers certain realities or dispositions against which others can be judged.[32] Tambiah notes that the messages of ritual are linked to the status claims and interests of the participants, and therefore are open to contextual meanings. These contextual meanings represent 'variable components' around the solid core of ritual, but are nonetheless highly reliant on pre-existing ritual forms.[33] Tambiah highlights that in order for ritual to 'perform anything' a marriage of context and form is essential. Ritual is strongly constrained by prevailing ritual forms, as it 'rides on the already existing grids of symbolic and indexical meanings' but may also embrace 'new resonances'.[34] Tambiah also emphasizes that cosmological understandings and social indexing are both critically involved in ritual performances, and indeed in ritual's dynamics of cultural pre-suppositions and social indexing he sees a primary social mode of action. In terms of performativity theory, Tambiah understands ritual as performative in three ways:

in the Austinian sense of performative, wherein saying something is also doing something as a conventional act; in the quite different sense of a staged performance that uses multiple media by which the participants experience the event intensively; and in the sense of indexical values [...] being attached to and inferred by actors during the performance.[35]

The theoretical point of departure in the present paper understands that ritual is inherently performative and involves instilling dispositions in the participant/spectator. Thus: 1) ritual can instill beliefs, that is, certain realities or dispositions against which others can be judged, 2) ritual involves interpellation through presenting ideological, socially indexing claims, and 3) ritual forms are strongly contingent on prevailing ritual forms, and are characteristically multimodal in drawing on multiple experiential channels.

---

[30] Bell, p. 226.
[31] Stanley Tambiah, *Culture, Thought and Social Action* (Cambridge: Harvard University Press, 1985), p. 156: 'important parts of a ritual enactment have a symbolic or iconic meaning associated with the cosmological plan of content, and at the same time how those same parts are existentially or indexically related to participants in the ritual, creating, affirming, or legitimating their social positions and powers'. The duality of ritual has two simultaneous thrusts: semantically, with respect to cultural pre-suppositions and cultural understandings, *and* pragmatically with respect to social and interpersonal context of ritual action, the lineup of the participants and the process by which they establish and infer meanings. Thus sacred and social are of equal importance.
[32] Tambiah, p. 134. To explain how these are inferred, Tambiah (pp. 156–57) cites Grice's formulation of conversational implicature: 'by saying or enacting something a certain meaning is *implicated*, which can be readily understood [...] or is capable of being "worked out" [...] given certain contextual features and certain communicational understandings'.
[33] Tambiah, p. 125.
[34] Tambiah, pp. 129, 161.
[35] Tambiah, p. 128.

Andrew Pattison

The resonance of the *curée* as ritual

As mentioned, the recent scholarly discourse has tended to see the rituals of the noble hunt as a message about the desired social order. In this research trend the focus has clearly been on the ritual butchering and division of the deer's carcass as well as the attendant social-ideological meanings involved (social indexing, social cohesion, noble preeminence in society/over nature).[36] The logic undergirding such arguments is that the interpellation of the noble hunt draws its potency from ritual. This is of course logical. The post-kill ceremony employs much imagery from the standard toolkit of ritual; the ritual forms of procession, elevation, revelation, ritual division and sacred space are all well-represented in the 'by strength' hunt. To this, we might add that themes of a more overtly supernatural nature are present as well: ritual sacrifice, sacred transformation and ritual feasting all appear in forms that have fairly recognizable analogues in the late-medieval Catholic liturgy.[37] These aspects of the post-kill ceremony pertain most directly to the *curée* and have generally been overlooked, perhaps because they would seem to have little relevance to the social-ideological messages that have attracted recent scholars.[38] See Marvin 2006, pp. 134–141. The religious significance of the *curée* has thus eluded the gaze of most scholars. The deeper import of the liturgical resonances of the *curée* is fully appreciated when once recalls that ritual is traditionally understood to entwine the twin axes of the sacred and the mundane, and that any ritual indexing of society need involve cosmological considerations as a matter of course. Thus any similarities between the *curée* and the liturgy would have implications for the social/supernatural nexus of ritual and would be meaningful with respect to the ideological messages and interpellation that have been claimed to underlie the noble hunt as a practice.

The wider issue of associability is in fact critical: similarly to how the intended messages must be capable of being inferred or worked out by the onlooker, in order for the interpellation purported to be at the heart of noble hunting rituals to be effective they must be recognizable as rituals. The effectiveness of ritual requires not only scrutable contextual features and messages but also fidelity to recognizable ritual forms.[39] Thus, any similarities between the *curée* and the Catholic liturgy would only have been as meaningful as they were resonant.

Meticulousness and sacred goods

In itself, the *curée* as described in the manuals was an extraordinary event. It took place only in the context of the hunt by strength and *Tretyse off Huntyng* associates the *curée* with the hart in particular.[40] In this sense, the undue level of care that is afforded to the hart's carcass should come as no surprise but is telling nonetheless. The post-kill rituals appear in sharp relief in comparison with the fairly unceremonious killing of the hart, which is not described

---

[36] Cummins, pp. 32–46; Marvin, pp. 118–40, Crane, *passim*, Judkins, *passim*.
[37] For a detailed consideration of the forms of the late-medieval Catholic mass, see James Monti, *A Sense of the Sacred: Roman Catholic Worship in the Middle Ages* (San Francisco: Ignatius Press, 2012), pp. 26–104.
[38] However, Marvin did note a pseudo-spiritual aspect of the hunt in the breaking, though he sees only a 'tenuous' link to the spiritual realm in the noble hunt.
[39] Tambiah, pp. 156–57.
[40] 'How many venesonez bene þer? I answer, þe hert, þe boor, þe har […] How many in quyrry? þe hert'. *Tretyse off Huntyng*, ed. by Anne Rooney (Brussels: OMIREL, 1987) ll. 171–72. On the hunting by strength, Cummins, pp 32–46; Judkins, *passim*.

in great detail in the manuals.[41] Commenting on Gottfried von Strassburg's *Tristan*, Anne Rooney notes that there 'is a religious meticulousness in the precision with which Tristan breaks the deer' and finds significance in the fact that Tristan insists that the deer be brought into court in an order 'preserving the shape of a hart'.[42] Tristan's emphasis on instructing King Mark's huntsmen on the particulars of the breaking is as telling as his shock at the specter of them undoing the hart improperly.[43] Baillie-Grohman also took especial note of the care dedicated to the breaking of the hart, noting that the hunter who undid the deer took pride in 'doing it according to laws of woodmanscraft' and in 'performing everything so daintily that their garments should show no bloodstains; nobles, and princes themselves, made it a point of honour to be well versed in this art'.[44] It is notable that *Master of Game* clarifies that the hart is only broken (or 'undone') thus for a *curée*; this level of meticulousness only applies when the lord decides that a *curée* is merited. In other cases, a simpler reward for the hounds is prepared and a less fastidious breaking applies.[45] Additionally, whereas Edward does not delve to explain the undoing process ('I passe ouere lyghtly, for þer nys no wodman ne good hunter in Englonde þat þei ne can do it wel inow, and wele bettir þan I can tech hem'), he does go to the trouble of detailing how to choreograph the *curée*:[46]

> neuerthelesse, when so is þat þe paunche is taken oute clene and hole, and þe smale guttes, one of þe gromes chacechiens shuld take þe paunch and go to þe next water withalle, and slytte it, and cast oute þe fylth, and wassh it clene þat no fylth abyde þerynne, and þan bring it agein and kutte it in smale gobettes in þe blood that shuld be kept in þe skynne, and þe longes withall (if þei be hote, and ells noght), and alle the smale guttes withall, and brede broke therynne, aftir that the houndes ben few or many; and alle this turned and mengled togyddres among þe blood tille it be wele enbrowed in the blood.[47]

In this passage several parallels emerge with respect to the Eucharist. As noted, the absolute precision of the breaking was accompanied by the social dictate that no drop of blood be spilled or stain the hunter's clothes. This would appear to parallel the dictates from medieval missals about how no crumb of the host nor drop of wine be lost during the consecration.[48] Although *Master of Game* only mentions 'þe blood that shuld be kept in þe skynne [...] wyth as moche blood as may be saued', *Boke of St Albans* clarifies the need to preserve the blood: 'withal the blode that ye may gete and wyn'.[49] The undoing was also marked by the prominent role of wine in the ceremony. Again, presumably because Edward assumes his reader is familiar with the undoing, *Master of Game* is silent on the point; however, *Boke of Saint Albans* notes that immediately before dissecting the carcass: 'and then shall ye goo | at

---

[41] A typical example comes from *Master of Game*, which emphasizes the authority of the bidder rather than the specifics of the act itself: 'þan shuld whoso were moste maistir þere bydde som of þe hunters go spay hym, euen byhynde þe shulder forthewards to þe hert' ll. 2740–41.

[42] Anne Rooney, *Hunting in Middle English Literature* (Cambridge: The Boydell Press, 1993), pp. 87–93.

[43] *Tristan, with the 'Tristan' of Thomas*, pp. 78–82.

[44] William A. Baillie-Grohman, *Master of Game: The Oldest English Book on Hunting* (Milton Keynes: Lightning Source UK, 2010) [first publ. 1909], pp. 208–9. Though Gottfried has Tristan roll up his sleeves during the breaking. *Tristan, with the 'Tristan' of Thomas*, pp. 79–80.

[45] For the *curée* treatment, see *Master of Game*, ll. 2787–840; for the simple treatment, ll. 2779–87.

[46] *Master of Game*, ll. 2794–96.

[47] *Master of Game*, ll. 2796–804.

[48] On the treatment of the Eucharist goods, see Miri Rubin, *Corpus Christi: The Eucharist in Late Medieval Culture* (Cambridge: Cambridge University Press 2004), p. 43.

[49] *Master of Game* l. 2806; *Boke of Saint Albans*, ed. by William Blades (London: Elliot Stock, 1901), fiiiii.

chaulis: to begynne assone as ye may'.[50] Aside from the passage's resonance with the theme of communion,[51] 'goo at chaulis' refers to the custom whereby before the hart is undone the huntsman must first drink 'a good harty draught' of red wine or else the deer's flesh would putrefy.[52] In itself this enological invocation is conspicuous in its resonance with the themes of sacrifice, ritual feasting, incorrupted flesh and the Eucharist, and the presence of wine at the *curée* is further evidenced in *Master of Game*: 'and whanne he cometh home he cometh ioyfullich, for his lord haþ gyue him to drynke of his gode wyne at kirre'.[53] In the *curée* there may thus be echoes of the communal partaking of the Eucharistic goods after the ritual of the consecration.

The *curée* involves another possible echo of the Eucharist which touches on the other constituent of the Catholic secretory rite. Edward stipulates that to the hounds' reward should be added: 'brede broke therynne, aftir that the houndes ben few or many; and alle this turned and mengled togyddres among þe blood tille it be wele enbrowed'.[54] The theme of broken bread 'mengled togydders among þe blood' broadly recalls the commixture (the mixing of the consecrated host and wine).[55] Although the commixture would not have been visible to the parishioner during the liturgy (it being obscured by the rood screen), presumably the trope of body and blood, bread and wine mixing would familiar to the medieval audience. The carcass of the slain hart itself may have involved religious symbolism. The theme of Christ as a hunted stag is indeed well known in imaginative literature in the late-medieval period, and the image of the stag has long been associated with religious symbolism in the Christian tradition.[56] The conceit of the dead hart as a metaphor for the Crucified Christ may not have been fanciful or even difficult to make, and may have been readily recognizable to late-medieval audiences.[57] This question will be considered in more detail below but first a closer examination of the handling of the carcass and the preparation of the *curée* will examine further points of concord between the two ritual sets.

Visibility, gaze and sacred space

In being aimed at a wider spectatorship, the *curée* was clearly a performative act. And although *Master of Game* encourages 'euery man draweth þidder',[58] the kill itself was unceremoniously located wherever it chanced to occur. Presumably, the entire body of the hunt would not have been present. Conversely, in the *curée* the role of the audience could be better accommodated, and catering to the needs of the spectator is explicitly mentioned in the manuals. Edward notes

[50] *Boke of Saint Albans*, fiii.
[51] See *OED*, s.v. 'chalice'.
[52] Quoted in Baillie-Grohman, p. 209.
[53] *Master of Game*, ll. 225–27.
[54] *Master of Game*, ll. 2802–2804. Although Edward mentions that the intestines and sometimes the lungs are also to be included in the *curée* reward, the blood and bread were presumably the main constituents.
[55] The bread and blood are, of course, also mentioned in other treatises; they also feature in *Sir Gawain and the Green Knight*. See *Livre de Chasse, Gaston Phébus*, ed. by Gunnar Tilander (Karlshamn: Almqvist & Wiksells, 1971), pp. 182, 220; *Boke of St Albans*, fiii; and *Gawain and the Green Knight*, l. 1361.
[56] An Smets and Baudouin van den Abeele, 'Medieval Hunting', in *A Cultural History of Animals in the Medieval Age*, ed. by Brigitte Resl (Oxford: Berg, 2011), p. 75; Rooney, *Hunting in Middle English Literature*, pp. 102–39; Cummins, pp. 71–74.
[57] Matt Cartmill referred to the hunted hart's carcass as 'emblem of the crucified Christ'. Matt Cartmill, *A View to Death in the Morning: Hunting and Nature through History* (Cambridge: Harvard University Press, 1996), p. 69.
[58] *Master of Game*, ll. 2721–22.

that the *curée* should be in an open, well-known place to attain maximum visibility, or 'þe place there as þe quirrees at huntynges haue been accustumed to be'.[59] In being affixed to a specific locus, embedded in a certain type of landscape, the *curée* is attuned to the necessities of ritual space. In the preparation for a larger hunt, the countryside would have been informed beforehand and presumably informed of the locale of the *curée*.[60] It is interesting to note that the performance of the *curée* is not fixed to the location of the kill. Edward specifies that whereas the undoing occurs on the spot of the kill, once the hounds' reward is prepared the entire 'package' is removed to a suitable spot where the *curée* will be enacted: 'and þan look where a smothe plot of grene is, and þidder bere all þis vpon þe skynne, wyth as moche blood as may be saued, and þere lay it, and sprede þe skynne þere vpon þe here syde vpwarde'.[61] While the practice of gathering at a sacred space in which something extraordinary habitually takes place is a standard in the playbook of ritual, the wider significance of the performative locus of the *curée* is better appreciated upon noticing the visual resonances with the Eucharist that such a novel space affords. The presentation of the *curée*, and specifically how hunter, hound and hart are situated, is revealing. After the hounds' reward has been readied and moved to the requisite locale:

And þen the lorde shuld take vp þe hertes hede by the right side [...] and þe maistir of þe game the left syde in the same wyse, and holde þe hede vpright, and þat the nose touche þe erth. And þan euery man þat is there [...] shuld stonde afronte in eythir syde þe hede with roddes, that none houndes com aboute, noþir on þe sydes, but þat all stonde afore. And when this is redy, the maistir of þe game or the sergeaunt shuld bydde þe berners bring forth here houndes, and stonde stille aforne hem a small coytes cast fro thennes, as the abay is ordeyned.[62]

The point of gaze and treatment of the hart's head during and after the *curée* is noteworthy, with the severed head acting as the focal point of the line of hunters and drawing the audience's gaze. And, although the manuals are unclear as to how high the head is in fact raised, the 'taking up' of the severed head of the hart broadly recalls the Elevation of the Host.[63] The line of hunters also brings to mind the obscuring of the rituals of the consecration, with the Host visible to the parishioner only at the moment of Elevation.[64] Here, the hunters themselves — each armed with a *fayre small rodde in his honde*, with the lord grasping the hart by one antler, the master of game by the other, broadly recalling the latticework of a rood screen — act as the barrier separating the realms of the sacred and the mundane, just as the rood screen 'separated the realms of the clergy and the laity'.[65] The sense of sacred space is further evident in *Master of Game*: the hounds are kept away from the carcass while it is reassembled and only come to see the 'reanimated' hart at the *curée*.[66] At a larger hunt with multiple quarry,

---

[59] *Master of Game*, ll. 2998–99.
[60] Edward mentions that the forester should 'warne þe shyrref of þe shyre' when the king will hunt. *Master of Game*, l. 2996.
[61] *Master of Game*, ll. 2804–6.
[62] *Master of Game*, ll. 2815–22.
[63] *Tretyse off Huntyng* is equally vague on the point of elevation: 'þan shall we take vp þe hede' (l. 112). However, Edward's summation of the *curée* implies elevation: 'and a faire þing is þe kirree, and faire þing is to vndo him wel, and for to reise þe rightes wel; and fair þing and good is þe venisoun'. *Master of Game*, ll. 520–21.
[64] Daniel Thiery, *Polluting the Sacred: Violence, Faith and the 'Civilizing' of Parishioners in Late Medieval England* (Leiden: Brill, 2011), p. 64. *Sarum Missal* instructs the priest to elevate the host 'so that it can be seen by the people'. This is notable for in no other place is the issue of visibility or gaze mentioned in the missal. *The Sarum Missal, vol. I*, ed. by Frederick E. Warren (London: De La More Press, 1911), p. 45.
[65] Thiery, p. 64.
[66] *Master of Game*, ll. 2815–22.

the hunters as well are excluded from the space of the *curée*. Edward writes that the servants 'shuld kepe þat no man come withynne þe quire till þe kyng come, saue þe maistir of þe game'.[67]

At this point the bay was 'ordeyned', or prepared: the hounds were organized a short distance from the *curée* space, presumably formed into a line, and then signaled to bay at the hart's head, with the hunters sounding their horns in encouragement.[68] Medieval writers were apt to describe the baying of the hounds in terms of churchly 'music', and the cacophony of the hunt could be likened to the sacred music of the mass.[69] The metaphor is best evidenced in the foxhunt in *Gawain and the Green Knight*: 'Hit watz þe myriest mute þat euer men herde, | Þe rich rurd þat þer watz raysed for Renaude saule', which Ad Putter interprets as a requiem mass for the dead fox.[70] Broadly, this aural mode of the *curée* could be interpreted as an analogue for churchly music.[71] When the lord feels that the bay has lasted long enough, the head is skirted away, the package opened, and the hounds allowed to rush to their reward. When the meal is finished, the lord blows a final horn to signal the end of the *curée*. Here Edward specifies that the lord 'shuld strake in his wyse, þat is to say: blow iiii. moot; and stynt noght half ane Ave Marie while; and blow othir foure moot, a litill lengere þan the fyrst foure moot. And þus should no wight strake but when the hert is sleyne with stregthe'.[72] The pause of 'half ane Ave Marie while' is interesting. The effect of using a prayer as a measure of time may have been to prompt the participant to contemplate the *curée* in religious terms, or even recite the prayer when reading the treatise.[73] That this injunction is to take place only when the hart is taken 'by strength' underscores its uniqueness as well as the uniqueness of the *curée*. (Other rewards have different protocols.) At this, the hunting party departs with the hart's head at the fore of a procession. Although *Master of Game* is silent on this point, *The Art of Hunting* mentions that after a *curée*: 'þo hed schalle be born hom before þo lord'.[74] As we have seen, the romance *Tristan* implies that the broken deer was brought into court in an order 'preserving the shape of a hart'.[75] Presumably the body of the hunting party was hierarchically ordered in a similar fashion. Taken together the affair evokes the highly orchestrated *Corpus Christi* procession, with the hart's head primarily positioned in the place of the venerated Host.[76]

Thus, in terms of treatment of the body of the hart, demarcation of sacred space, and similar tropes, there is a degree of resonance at the level of metaphor between the ritual set

---

[67] *Master of Game*, ll. 3095–97.
[68] Master of Game, ll. 2822, 2824.
[69] Ad Putter, 'The Ways and Words of the Hunt: Notes on *Sir Gawain and the Green Knight, The Master of Game, Sir Tristrem, Pearl*, and *Saint Erkenwald*', *The Chaucer Review*, 40 (2006), 375–79.
[70] Putter, p. 376.
[71] The ringing of the sacring bell attendant to the consecration comes to mind as a close parallel, or alternatively, chorale music.
[72] *Master of Game*, ll. 2836–40.
[73] The prayer itself notably condenses the notions of birth, death, sin, salvation and Jesus. To this writer's knowledge, the only other example of using a prayer as a measure of time in late-medieval literature is the 'paternoster-while' of *Piers Plowman*, ed. by J. A. W. Bennett (Oxford: Clarendon Press, 1972), *passus* v, l. 348. The passage uses the word to underscore the irreligiousness of Gluttony's uncouth behavior. The evidence for common prayers as standards of time measurement would imply that such prayers functioned as invocations, for example in recipes. See, for example, E.P. Thompson, 'Time, Work-Discipline and Industrial Capitalism', *Past and Present*, 38 (1967), 56–98.
[74] *The Middle English Text of 'The Art of Hunting' by William Twiti*, ed. by David Scott-Macnab (Heidelberg: Winter, 2009), p. 11, ll. 113–14.
[75] Rooney, *Hunting in Middle English Literature*, p. 89.
[76] On the Corpus Christi procession, see Miri Rubin, pp. 243–71, *passim*.

of the *curée* and the Eucharist. The rituals attendant to the *curée* direct viewer and participant alike towards roles and perspectives analogous to those familiar from the Catholic mass. The overall effect may therefore have been to incline the hunting party to interpret the spectacle of the *curée* in terms of the liturgy. Explaining why this was the case, and to what end, will be addressed below. Before doing that, however, a closer look as the rituals of the liturgy is in order.

The dispositions and inculcations of the liturgy

According to the theory of interpellation, to gaze is tantamount to accepting a message.[77] Although securing the salvation of man was the doctrinal aim of the mass, to the parishioner the central point of the Catholic mass, particularly after acceptance of the theory of transubstantiation in the thirteenth century, was the real presence of Christ in the form of the Eucharistic goods coupled with the priest's ability to effect this. One went to 'hear mass' but went to see the actual body of Christ.[78] Fossier has noted that the Christian faith uniquely made this concrete dimension of truth a necessary and a requisite 'line of spiritual conduct'.[79] At its heart, then, the late-medieval mass was a visual ritual that encapsulated the concrete link between the natural and supernatural world. Its rites represented the perfect archetypes of late-medieval ritual, the condensed points of reference against which any ritual metaphor must be considered.[80] As the Elevation was the culmination of the mass, the moment when God's body was manifested to the laity, this moment in particular was pregnant with interpellative potential.

To further contextualize the messages embedded in the mass, the *Lay Folks Mass Book* is of aid. Popular amongst the literate during the late-medieval era as a type of layperson's guide to interpreting the mass, *Lay Folks Mass Book* can be used to disclose the concerns of the church with respect to its messaging. *Lay Folks Mass Book* makes clear that during the Elevation the parishioner was meant to consider the significance of the real presence of Christ, and the churchgoer is instructed to gaze upon the Host in reverence: 'and so þo leuacioun þou be-halde, | for þat is he þat iudas salde'.[81]

Added to this, the laity is also prompted to meditate on the promise of resurrection and salvation:

> And sithen was scourged & don on rode,
> and for mankind þere shad his blode
> and dyed & ros & went to heuen,
> and ȝit shal come to deme vs euen.[82]

It is clear that the Elevation was meant to condition spectators to meditate on the significance of the moment, thus any parallel forms in the *curée* would have similarly encouraged the spectator to consider it as something revelatory and spiritually meaningful. The above excerpts

---

[77] For a brief discussion of interpellation, see Crane, pp. 104–5.
[78] For a discussion, see Monti, pp. 23–36.
[79] Fossier, p. 368–69.
[80] Burkert called the crucifixion the 'perfect sacrifice'. Quoted in Amity Reading, ' "The Ende of Alle Kynez Flesch": Ritual Sacrifice and Feasting in *Cleanness*', *Exemplaria*, 21 (2009), 274–95 (p. 279).
[81] *Lay Folks Mass Book, or The Hearing of Mass*, ed. by Thomas Frederick Simmons, Early English Text Society, o. s. 71 (London: Early English Text Society, 1879), p. 38.
[82] *Lay Folks Mass Book*, p. 38.

also highlight the visceral realism of the crucifixion tradition, which itself is a notable point of reference and informs the wider context of the liturgical rite. Widely depicted in religious settings, the imagery of the crucifixion adds a layer of associability with which the parishioner can frame his/her interpretation of the mass as a condensed rite. *Lay Folks Mass Book* enjoins the churchgoer to fixate on the violence of Jesus' death, in tones of darkness and light:

> A knight smat him to þe hert, he had no mercy;
> þe sone be-gane to wax myrk qwen iesu gon dy.
> lord out of þi syd ran a ful fayre flude
> As clere as well water our rannson bi þi blode.[83]

With respect to the *curée*, the Eucharist's focus on the violent death of Jesus as well as on his sacred blood as the promise of salvation is relevant, particularly when considered against the blood/wine dyad's pervading the post-kill rituals. That here the knight's piercing of Jesus's side initiates the blood ritual would seem to bring the two traditions into even closer alignment, and the imagery in *Lay Folks Mass Book* recalls Edward's instructions for dispatching the cornered hart: a hunter should 'go spay hym, euen byhynde þe shulder forthewards to þe hert'.[84] In terms of visual mode, the visceral violence of the hunt would have had an analogue in the wider crucifixion tradition as well. Through visual and literary depictions, and also through countless reenactments of the mystery plays, the visual minutiae of the crucifixion would have been well conditioned in the viewer. The violent images of the Passion represented a vocabulary that could be drawn on to 'trigger certain feelings and reactions'.[85] This is all the more true of the mystery plays, which were explicitly realistic.[86]

With respect to terminology, the two traditions also share a peculiar collocation of terms. For example, the term 'flay', which is prominent in religious texts on the crucifixion and *arma Christi*, is also a technical term of the noble hunt.[87] Which quarry are flayed and which are stripped is a point of great distinction in the treatises, with 'flay' emerging as the term that applies specifically to the hart.[88] The association of terms may have added a layer of resonance between the crucifixion tradition and the rituals of the hunt. In similar vein, the term 'scourge' evidences an interesting link between the traditions in that it shares a common etymology with *curée*.[89] It is even possible that during the Middle English period the words

---

[83] *Lay Folks Mass Book*, p. 86.

[84] *Master of Game*, ll. 2740–41.

[85] Mary Poellinger ' "The Rosselde Spere to His Herte Rynnes": Religious Violence in the Alliterative *Morte Arthure* and the Lincoln Thornton Manuscript', in *Robert Thornton and His Books: Essays on the Lincoln and London Thornton Manuscripts*, ed. by Susanna Fein and Michael Johnson (York: York Medieval Press, 2014), p. 170.

[86] It has been intimated, for example, that real blood and guts were used in the reenactments to emphasize the suffering of Jesus. See, Hans-Jürgen Diller, *The Middle English Mystery Plays: A Study in Dramatic Speech and Form* (Cambridge: Cambridge University Press, 2005), pp. 233–34.

[87] Aside from *LFMB*, examples are seen in *Lay Folks Catechism*, (ed. by Thomas Frederick Simmons and Henery Edward Nollath (London: Early English Text Society, 1901): 'beten with skourges that no skyn held' (p. 28); *The Pearl*, ed. by Sarah Stanbury (Kalamazoo: Medieval Institute Publications, 2001): 'wyth boffetes was Hys face flayn' (ll. 809); and the *York Play of Crucifixion*, ed. by Clifford Davidson (Kalamazoo: Medieval Institute Publications, 2011): 'For alle his fare he schalle be flaied | That one assaie sone schalle ye see' (*Crucifixio Christi*, ll. 43–44).

[88] *Boke of St Albans* (eiii) for example lists 'wiche beestes shall be flayne & wich stripte', and *Art of Hunting* offers a similar list (p. 17). *Boke of St Albans* clarifies that the hart is flayed: 'than cut of the coddis the bely euen froo | Or ye begynne hym to flee' (fii); *Master of Game* concurs: 'and þan shuld þe huntere flene doune þe skynne, as fer as he may', ll. 2752–53; as does *Tretyse of Huntyng*: '& þen be we aboute to opyn hym & fley hym' (l. 108).

[89] The terms derive from the Latin *excoriare*, which led to *curée* in French and *excoriaten* > *skourge* in Middle

were near homophonic.⁹⁰ The word *curée* may have evoked the religious register of 'scourge' and therefore the scourging of Jesus as well. A focus on terminology is indeed reasonable when considering the two traditions. It should be noted that the hunting treatises, which are fairly useless as practical guides to hunting, focus instead on detailing the proper comportment of the hunt but also heavily emphasize the proper terms of the hunt.⁹¹ Mastery of terms appears as a crucial aim of the manuals and the granular attention afforded to terminology indicates that it served as a type of sacred language of the hunt.⁹² The terminology of the noble hunt is closely linked to French, which occurs as somewhat of a sacred language akin to how Latin served as the sacred language of Christianity. In the manuscript context of *Master of Game* (late-fourteenth–early fifteenth century) French was of course still the language of prestige in England, and largely would have been as incomprehensible to the populace as the Latin of the mass.⁹³ It is notable that the English literary tradition treats Tristan as the father of the hunt in England and as something of a mythical conduit of hunting terminology.⁹⁴ His words are thus treated as a sacred revelation of sorts, and access to them had relevance in terms of social hierarchy, as Sir Thomas Malory writes:

> all jantyllmen that beryth olde armys ought of rygtht to honore sir Tristams for the goodly tearmys that jantylmen have and use and shall do unto the Day of Dome, that thereby in a manner all men of worshys may discever a jantylman frome a yoman and a yoman frome a vylayne.⁹⁵

The hunting treatises' focus on explaining these terms, on decoding the messages as it were, in fact rather parallels the glossing of the Latin terms and rites of the liturgy that are at the core of the *Lay Folks Mass Book*.⁹⁶

Here it should be noted that the ritual efficacy of a sacred language does not necessarily hinge on intelligibility but rather on its recognition as such.⁹⁷ Nor does the audience of a ritual need to fully understand the allusions of the rites. To quote Walter Burkert, 'the fact of understanding is thus more important than what is understood'.⁹⁸ In addressing 'the collectivity of the faithful' ritual therefore exploits the fact that the familiar spectator is already preconditioned to receive whatever disposition the ritual aims to inculcate by virtue of his very

---

English. On the Anglo-Norman heritage of *excoriate curée*, see Marvin, p. 137. *Scourge* of course had biblical resonances, achieving by the fourteenth century authoritative status as the word used to describe Jesus's suffering at the pillar, replacing the earlier *swingan* of Ælfric. See 'scourge', *OED*.

⁹⁰ The first appearance of the *curée* in the form of 'excoriate' is in Gottfried von Strassburg's *Tristan*, which putatively derives from an Anglo-Norman text (see Marvin, p. 137). Through metathetical shift ME *exoriaten* may well have led to a pronunciations close to the ME manifestations of *scourge*, which would possibly imply near homophonic pronunciation: *excoriaten* > **eskorge* > *skourge* (perhaps with orthographic interference from Latin resulting in the graph ⟨g⟩ representing the allophone [j]. On the various forms of these cognate doublets, cf. *OED*, s.vv. 'excoriate' and 'scourge'.

⁹¹ *Tretyse off Huntyng*, ed. by Anne Rooney (Brussels: OMIREL, 1987), pp. 37–38.

⁹² Spearing noted (p. 10) that hunting 'terminology forms the liturgy of this aristocratic sacrament' but never investigated the link.

⁹³ Charles Barber, *The English Language: A Historical Introduction* (Cambridge: Cambridge University Press, 2003), pp. 140–44.

⁹⁴ Rooney, *Hunting in Middle English Literature*, pp. 9, 14.

⁹⁵ *The Works of Sir Thomas Malory*, ed. by Eugène Vinaver, 2nd edn (Oxford: Clarendon Press, 1967), quoted in Spearing, p. 10. Spearing notably examines the heritage of hunting terms here as well.

⁹⁶ This notwithstanding the treatises' similarities to the bestiary genre. On the parallel, see McNelis, pp. 39–49, and Crane, pp. 101–2.

⁹⁷ Tambiah, pp. 17–34.

⁹⁸ Quoted in Reading, p. 279.

familiarity with ritual forms.⁹⁹ Thus the numerous liturgical echoes and resonances evident in the rituals of the noble hunt together form a common mode of inculcation, communicated via various channels, whose resonance rides upon some of the central-most elements of the Christian religion but without appearing to overtly appropriate them. Multiple modes of communication are indeed seen as essential to effective ritual, as is the simultaneous use of different sensory channels.¹⁰⁰ Together, these are condensed into the single experience against which other experiences can be judged. A picture thus emerges in which the *curée* widely draws on the multimodal channels available in the liturgical tradition to seek its interpellative ends. The particular nature of these ends will be examined next.

Merita missae

What effect might these resonances have had? Aside from the abstract benefit of spiritual salvation, the liturgy tradition makes clear that the mass had many other benefits, often of a more earthly nature. The *merita missae* tradition in particular is helpful in contextualizing the wider functions of the mass. Popular from the thirteenth century on, the *merita missae* tradition (or the merits of the mass) heavily emphasizes the many, and often miraculous, benefits of hearing the mass and seeing the Host. Aside from miracles such as curing the sick, hearing the mass was also said to cause the parishioner to eschew the deadly sins, as well as promote a general piety but also sense of communal brotherhood in the spectators.¹⁰¹ This was particularly true of the rituals attendant on the Eucharist. This brotherhood amongst the parishioners, however, was an ordered one, and the mass involved socially indexing elements. The holy bread rite in particular serves as an example. Most parishioners only rarely communicated, typically once a year at Easter, and holy bread served as a substitute for the actual sacred goods. Blessed by the priest, its distribution after the mass was dictated by social hierarchy and the bread itself was provided by the community according to accepted social norms. A similar function has been seen in the pax blessing, in which social hierarchy determined the order in which the body of the parishioners is blessed with the altar paraphernalia.¹⁰² That both these rites are ostensibly directed at instilling brotherhood but actually enforce hierarchy is notable.

Interesting parallels can be found in the hunting literature. Similar to the *merita missae* tradition, the hunting literary tradition commonly emphasizes that hunting makes a man pure and pious.¹⁰³ This ethos is well espoused in the manuals, most notably in *Master of Game* but also in its source text *Livre de Chasse* in which Gaston de Phebus presents himself as a holy man.¹⁰⁴ Edward, too, has much to say about the spiritual benefits of the hunt, for in the introduction he writes that 'this game causeth ofte a man to eschewe þe vii. dedely synnes' (ll. 110–11). Indeed, *Master of Game* dedicates over 190 lines to delineating the benefits of the hunt (spiritual, social and physical).¹⁰⁵ Underlying such arguments is likely a need to justify

---

⁹⁹ Tambiah, p. 128.
¹⁰⁰ Tambiah, pp. 164–66.
¹⁰¹ On the miracles, see Rubin, pp. 63, 108, 341; for brotherhood, see, *LFMB*, pp. 48–53.
¹⁰² On holy bread and pax, see Rubin, pp. 73–74 and Thiery, pp. 117–18.
¹⁰³ On the spiritual benefits of hunting, see Rooney, *Hunting in Middle English Literature*, pp. 127–30 and Hannele Klemettilä, *Animals and Hunters in the Late Middle Ages: Evidence from the BnF MS fr. 616 of the Livre de chasse by Gaston Fébus* (New York: Routledge, 2015), pp. 187–91.
¹⁰⁴ Klemettilä, pp. 190–191.
¹⁰⁵ *Master of Game*, ll. 107–98.

the excesses of the noble hunt.[106] On the other hand, this may also be linked to the arguments about hunting's wider aims of social cohesion and ordering.

Underlying their socially indexical functions, however, the pax and holy bread rituals also served as contestable elements of the mass and as such offered a mode for contesting the prevailing social hierarchy. The strict order of distribution prescribed by local tradition could be broken or challenged, even during the mass itself.[107] A hierarchy of distribution pervades the noble hunt as well,[108] and alongside it a degree of permissible contestation can be discerned. At a large-scale hunt, with many deer slain, *Master of Game* mentions quarrels regarding the division of the kill (ll. 3138–50) and that the master of the game is required to judge all of the 'striues and discordes þat long to huntyng' (l. 3150). Edward's mention of post-hunt feasting also typifies the social cohesion that underlies the wider endeavor. He relates that the master of game must ensure

> that alle þe hunters soupere be wele ordeyned and that thei drynke none ale, for nothyng but alle wyne that nyght for þe good and grete labour that thei haue hadde for the lordes game and disporte, and for the exploite and makyng of the houndes; and also, þat þai may the more merely and gladly telle what iche of them hath done of all þe day, and whiche houndes haue best ronne, and boldlyast. (ll. 2861–66)

Fractious 'strifes and discords' settled and forgotten, the post-kill feast recapitulates the link between feasting, ritual and social obligation, and serves to cohere the group. Such invoking of unity would seem to imply that while social hierarchies may be threatened and perhaps even slightly altered in the hunt, the primary function is their reinforcement — a theme that runs deep in both the mass and hunting tradition.

As mentioned, there is a broad consensus amongst researchers that social cohesion and ordering lie at the heart of the noble hunt, chiefly with respect to the distributional and communal nature of the hunt.[109] On the other hand, a degree of social looseness has also been discerned. Richard Almond, for example, sees a notable level of egalitarianism in the medieval hunt, an argument seconded by Sykes, who sees hierarchy within an imagined (and open) community.[110] Nevertheless, it is clear that hunting played a role in reinforcing society hierarchy and that game could function as an indicator of social status.[111] With respect to animal carcasses and hunting, Pluskowski has argued that seigneurial groups appropriated animal bodies and used them within a known semiotic system: 'a visual language expressing and negotiating power relations'.[112] In similar vein, Dorothy Yamamoto sees hunting as a discourse 'especially concerned with maintaining boundaries' and notes that animal 'bodies become counters in the game, claimed, manipulated, and marked over by the dominant side'.[113] This line of thought is pertinent because it touches on the bi-directional link between

---

[106] Rooney, *Hunting in Middle English Literature*, p. 197.
[107] On hierarchal distribution and disputes over holy bread and pax, see Thiery, pp. 69–71, 117–18.
[108] *Tretyse off Huntyng* offers the following: 'And also whoso breketh hym shall haue þe chyne, & þe parson þe ryght shulder, & a quarter to pore men, & the parker þe lyfte shulder', ll. 241–43. At a larger hunt, the hunter who fells the deer is allowed a share of the carcass.
[109] Cf. Judkins, *passim*, Crane, pp. 101–19, and Marvin, pp. 133–57.
[110] Almond, 'Crossing the Barriers', *passim*; Sykes, p. 155, also touches on this theme.
[111] Krish Seetah, 'The Middle Ages on the Block: Animals, Guilds and Meat in the Medieval English Period', in *Breaking and Shaping Beastly Bodies: Animals as Material Culture in the Middle Ages*, ed. by Alexander Pluskowski (Oxford: Oxbow Books, 2007), pp. 18–31 (pp. 24–25).
[112] Pluskowski, pp. 46–47.
[113] Dorothy Yamamoto, *The Boundaries of the Human in Medieval English Literature* (Oxford: Oxford University Press, 2000) pp. 99–102.

the social and the ritual: the socially indexical aspects of hunting are linked to ritual as a matter of course. In communicating the cosmos to a community, ritual (such as blood ritual) is forced to formalize itself and thus is forced to be socially ordering by virtue of the issue of access to rites.[114] This, in turn, encourages cohesion amongst the viewers, a reverent deference to the prevailing order. Above all, ritual thus aims to convey a sense of prescribed order which its adherents are meant to accept. However ill-defined or vaguely alluded to, in order to instill beliefs a ritual must involve a supernatural power so as to vouchsafe the belief system. Like the socially indexical rituals of the mass, the rituals of the hunt likewise required an association with the supernatural to achieve their interpellative ends. That both ritual sets involved and even allowed a degree of contestation indicates the tension inherent in rituals of social hierarchy and social indexing. This tension is well exemplified in the late-medieval liturgical tradition and forms a thread that runs throughout the noble hunting tradition as well as English medieval hunting in general, particularly in the form of poaching.

Reception

Any performance is read against its contextual backdrop. Contextual and formal fidelity are essential constituents of the ritual effect. Participants understand ritual in varying measure, according to their lights, interests, and commitment.[115] In addressing the 'collectivity of the faithful', ritual acts as such cannot be deemed false in terms of fidelity or legitimacy, but rather infelicitous or illegitimate.[116] Additionally, some spectators may have been less receptive to the message conveyed in hunting rituals than others. Whereas the archaeological evidence suggests that deer were in fact broken and distributed in the manner described in treatises, this is not true in every social context.[117] The lower classes may have rejected or ignored the rituals of the noble hunt in their own practices. Prominent use of the idiom also invited coopation, and it should not be forgotten that the noble hunting rituals could also be used for socially disruptive purposes or to mock authorities/institutions.[118] And, although the nobility generally took a leading role, it is worth noting that poaching, and thus contestation, occurred across the social spectrum. In this sense poaching should be read in terms of contested social hierarchy, and appropriated hunting rituals as salient semiotic tools. This highlights that the rituals of the hunt could be used by different agents for different effects, ranging from contestation/reinforcement of hierarchies to subversion/buttressing of institutions. Miri Rubin has touched on a similar vein in the Eucharistic tradition, which was similarly open to contestation and appropriation by various actors.[119]

While the benefits of hunting were invariably lauded by the nobility, the noble hunt was criticized by some for its excesses but also on religious grounds. Criticism of the irreligious nature of hunting was a prominent theme in the literature of era and such critiques stand in contrast to *Master of Game*'s defense of hunting.[120] Hunting was commonly criticized as a vain, worldly pursuit but may also have drawn the ire of critics due to its socially disruptive

---

[114] Tambiah, pp. 155–56.
[115] Tambiah, p. 166.
[116] Tambiah, pp. 60–86, esp. 77–84.
[117] Sykes, pp. 51–57.
[118] See Barbara Hanawalt, 'Men's Games, King's Deer: Poaching in Medieval England', in *Journal of Medieval and Renaissance Studies*, 18 (1988), 133–53.
[119] Rubin, pp. 334–46.
[120] Rooney, *Hunting in Middle English Literature*, pp. 118–33.

potential or its vaguely sacrilegious undertones. Using ritual forms associable with those of the liturgy invited their being mocked as such. Erasmus' well-known critique of the rites of the noble hunt is a fitting example:

> bareheaded, on bended knee, with a special sword for the purpose (it would be sacrilege to use any other), with ritual gestures in a ritual order he cuts the ritual number of pieces in due solemnity, while the crowd stands round in silence and admires the spectacle it has witnessed a thousand times and more as if it was some new rite. And then if anyone's lucky enough to get a taste of the creature, he fancies he's stepped up a bit in the world. All they achieve by this incessant hunting and eating wild game is their own degeneration.[121]

The link Erasmus draws between eating venison and social betterment (or degeneration) is interesting in its own right but the sarcasm of the passage acquires its biting edge when read against the background of the *merita missae* tradition and the benefits of communicating.[122]

The proposition of an associative link between the noble hunting rituals and the Eucharist indeed raises the issue of sacrilege in general and the hounds' role in particular. While shocking at first glance, the notion that in the *curée* the hounds are partaking of a 'mass' may not have been so very shocking to the medieval onlooker. As the numerous pronouncements against the practice make clear, dogs were commonly brought to church in the era and in many ways were even elevated to the human legal plane at times.[123] Much has been made of the fact that dogs appear next to man in medieval Bestiaries and were even worshipped as saints occasionally.[124] Furthermore, the role of animals as mediators of the cosmic order was an accepted one in the medieval period.[125] It should not go without note that *Master of Game* includes two miracle fables about the preternaturally noble nature of hounds, underscoring the ambiguous place of hounds in terms of social hierarchy.[126] In this sense, the presence of the hounds at the *curée* may have been fairly unremarkable.

To this must be added that the Church's stance on hunting, which was one of general approval. And despite the countless denunciations in the historical record, churchmen often hunted, high church officials especially, and even popes.[127] Putter's example of an Anglo-Norman cleric-poet arguing that there is no good reason for churchmen to refrain from hunting is probably indicative of the general attitude.[128] And as with all traditions, there may have been a fundamental unwillingness to confront the inertia of custom and consider the full

---

[121] *The Praise of Folly*, trans. by Betty Radice, quoted in Julián Jiménez Hefferman, *Shakespeare's Extremes: Wild Man, Monster, Beast* (Basingstoke: Palmgrave Macmillan, 2015), p. 191.

[122] The rather free translation by Hamilton, Adams & Co (London, 1887) further emphasizes the themes of mock Eucharist and social hierarchy: 'And he that can but dip his finger, and taste of the blood, shall think his own bettered by it' (p. 87). See also discussion of Roger B. Manning, *Hunters and Poachers: A Cultural and Social History of Unlawful Hunting in England 1485–1640* (Oxford: Clarendon Press, 1993), pp. 39–40; and Frederika Bain, 'Dismemberment and Identity-Formation in the Medieval and Early-Modern English Imaginary' (unpublished Ph.D. dissertation, University of Hawaii, 2014).

[123] Fossier, pp. 197–98.

[124] Crane, p., 68; Brigitte Resl, *A Cultural History of Animals in the Medieval Age*, p. 22.

[125] For a discussion of the place man and beast in Christian philosophy, see Sophie Page, 'Good Creation and Demonic Illusions: The Medieval Universe of Creatures', in *A Cultural History of Animals in the Medieval Age*, pp. 30–47; Crane, pp. 11–41.

[126] *Master of Game*, ll. 1198–374. In both anecdotes the hounds transcend their animal nature and comport with noble esteem.

[127] Cummins, p. 10; Smets and van den Abeele, pp. 73–75. Nicholas Orme, 'Medieval Hunting: Fact and Fancy', in *Chaucer's England: Literature in Historical Context*, ed. by Barbara Hanawalt (Minneapolis: University of Minnesota Press, 1992), 133–53 (pp. 134–35), also touches on the theme of hunting icons in churchly settings.

[128] Putter, pp. 377–78.

implications of an association between hunting ritual and church ritual. That the noble hunt's aim of reinforcing the prevailing social hierarchy was seen as generally beneficial to society may have helped to quiet any counterarguments. Additionally, throughout the era, churchmen remained noblemen *de facto*, a central tension in the social-religious fabric of the medieval era, and one that would have complicated any attempts to condemn the practices of the hunt. Indeed, with respect to the relation between ritual and social, a social order can be as essential to a society's cosmology as the society's gods.[129]

As we have seen, the interpellation of the *curée*, underscoring acceptance of the social order, hinges on the associability of the form of the rite with respect to the rituals of the Catholic Eucharist tradition. In terms of gaze, fastidious treatment, modes of inculcation and social prerogative, several parallels between the liturgical rituals and hunting rituals have been noted as priorities of form. Liturgical ritual appears as a point of reference for the post-kill rituals, informing the numerous parallels and points of concord pertaining thereto. As such, a general resonance can be posited between the two ritual sets. In similar vein, the tensions inherently involved in social indexing were seen to be alleviated by a ritual emphasis on brotherhood and unity under the gaze of the sacred. That the *curée* should emerge as the central ritual of the noble hunt in the same age that the real presence of Christ is embraced in medieval culture is notable and will serve as the focus of the next section, which considers the historical context and evolution of the post-kill hunting rituals in general and the *curée* in particular.

Blood sacrifice to Corpus Christi

There is, of course, a common heritage that binds the rituals of the hunt and the Christian ritual. The historical ritual forms of sacrifice and feasting widely inform both traditions. Walter Burkert even went so far as to deem hunting and blood sacrifice as central to the evolution of society and religion.[130] In this sense a certain degree of concord is to be expected. The long inheritance of the late-medieval English hunting rituals is evidenced by the fact that they include many antecedent, presumably pagan forms. One such example is the casting of the corbin's bone — a piece of inedible gristle offered to the ravens — which Marvin interpreted as 'hunting occult' and possibly 'a talisman for success in the next hunt', and likely of great antiquity.[131] This propitiatory rite mirrors the chalice of wine that prevents the deer's carcass from putrefying and evidences that an element of superstition was embedded in the post-kill rituals. As mentioned above, ritual is strongly constrained by prevailing ritual forms, by 'existing grids of meaning', but also by the inertia of custom: together, these dictate the stable core around which the variable components of ritual may be arranged. Nevertheless, rituals always are performed in specific historical junctures and contexts, and 'participants understand ritual in varying measure, according to their lights, interests, and commitment'. In this they are open to 'opposite turnings and new resonances in light of shifts in conditions or contexts'.[132]

Within the wider manuscript context of *Master of Game* and other late-medieval English hunting manuals a number of social and cultural shifts are pertinent. Foremost, the social reordering that accompanied the Black Death of 1348 and Peasant's Rebellion of 1381, in

---

[129] Tambiah, p. 130.
[130] Walter Burkert, *Homo Necans* (Berkeley: University of California Press, 1983), pp. 1–48.
[131] Marvin, pp. 125–26.
[132] Tambiah, pp. 161–66.

which the rebels notably demanded the freedom to hunt,[133] but also the attendant Game Law of 1389, which further curtailed the peasant's right to hunt.[134] If the *curée* could be seen to reach its apogee as a reinforcer of noble preeminence in society in *Master of Game*, then this development should be read within the context of the social turbulence of the fourteenth century and aristocratic anxiety pertaining thereto.[135] Turbulent times would seem to necessitate a re-articulation of recognized social hierarchies. That the semiotic system of the noble hunt as an expression of power relations becomes 'increasingly elaborate' starting in the late-fourteenth century would seem to underscore this point.[136] In addition, the archaeological record attests to a shift in finds during the thirteenth–fourteenth century, implying that the rituals later codified in the manuals were increasingly being taken into use in actual hunting settings.[137] Conversely, there is also a religious shift in the historical context as regards the evolution of the *curée*. Any examination of the noble hunting rituals as liturgy must take note of the rise of the real presence in Eucharist in the late-medieval era. According to Jacques le Goff, 'by the thirteenth century, the rich univocal power nexus and symbolic system of the Church was "running out of steam"', and the innovation of the real presence of Christ was in part a reflection of this problem.[138] As the Eucharist becomes the central gesture of the mass in the late-medieval era, the doctrine of transubstantiation brings with it changes in the ritual formulae and points of inflection of the liturgy in terms of gaze, handling of Host, spiritual purity, magical properties, and so on.[139] The rise of the *curée* as the central rite of the post-kill rituals is contemporaneous with the rise of the doctrine of the real presence and could be interpreted as partly inspired by it. This shift takes place at the same time as the Continent sees increased aristocratic interest in the cult of St. Hubert and St. Eustace, saints whose legends are linked to hunting, as well as the advent of the practice of using deer heads as amuletic trophies and occasionally devotional artifacts, a practice evidenced in England as well.[140] As we have seen, the metaphoric links between religion and hunting were strong in the late-medieval era, and the theme of Christ as the hunted stag must have added a layer of association to the post-kill rituals and the *curée* in particular.

Dispositions such as those associated with hunting ritual are inherently precarious because they have to be inculcated, preferably repeatedly.[141] For the ritual to be effective requires a certain fidelity to convention, yet not at the expense of over-dissemination or redundancy. Although dissemination and repetition are central to the ritual effect, the overexposure of a rite can risk the ruination of its transfixing effect. Here Judkin's argument for a deliberate shift away from describing the butchering process in manuals is interesting. He interprets the shift as an effort to prevent overexposure of the rites, primarily their dissemination to

---

[133] Charles Oman, *The Great Revolt of 1389* (London: Oxford University Press, 1969), p. 95.
[134] See, for example, Griffin, pp. 61–62.
[135] It should not pass without note that it was Edward's cousin, Richard II, that confronted the peasants during the rebellion.
[136] Pluskowski, pp. 46–47.
[137] Thomas, pp. 144–45.
[138] Quoted in Barbara R. Walters, Vincent Corrigan and Peter T. Ricketts, *The Feast of Corpus Christi* (University Park: University of Pennsylvania, 2006), p. xvi.
[139] Rubin, pp. 13–82.
[140] See Pluskowski, pp. 40–42, 44–46. Nicholas Orme also discusses how hunting trophies and emblems permeated church life in late-medieval England (pp. 146–49).
[141] Pierre Bourdieu, *Distinction: A Social Critique of the Judgement of Taste* (London: Routledge and Kegan Paul, 1984), p. 71.

lower strata of society, hinting perhaps at the readership of the manuals.[142] This echoes Miri Rubin's findings about a concern amongst churchmen regarding the over-dissemination of Eucharistic practices, and indicates that the fading efficacy of rituals was well understood by the illuminati.[143] A shift away from emphasis on the overexposed rituals of the hunt towards novel adaptations like the *curée* could be interpreted as an attempt to keep the rituals of the hunt sharp and fresh, but also elite. It may be that the increasing popularity of the rituals (and manuals) seen in the thirteenth–fourteenth century helped to instigate the deinstitutionalization of the breaking ritual as the apex of the hunt, and thus spurred a rupture in the genre evidenced by *Master of Game*'s novel, extended treatment of the *curée*. Unexceptional and diffused, the earlier post-kill rituals may have lost their impact and were accordingly supplanted by more transfixing counterparts. The *curée* as the central rite of the post-kill rituals would seem to have evolved as an emergent ritual form in response to this need.

Ritual forms are in fact intrinsically linked to such evolution. To remain significant, any ritual tradition must embrace evolution in order to avoid atrophying into what Tambiah called 'the stagnancy of an exhausted style'.[144] Emergent meanings ride on preexisting forms but also need to display new resonances. These innovations do not interrupt but rather substitute and elaborate, and, over time, emergent meanings may become conventional and ultimately be incorporated into the existing framework of conventions. In Tambiah's words, 'Ritual oscillates in historical time between the poles of ossification and revivalism [...] substance nourishes formalism and conspires to empty it of meaning over time'.[145] The emergence of the *curée* and the Corpus Christi tradition could well be interpreted in this light.

Rituals evolve through the interplay of metaphor and metonymy.[146] It has been argued that the hunting manuals and religious literature of the era freely drew on the same allegories and images.[147] Here it is interesting to note Putter's observation that hunting terminology extends into religious metaphor in imaginative literature. He also touched on the interanimation of hunting metaphors in medieval religious literature, pointing out that such conceits are perhaps more expressive than is readily acknowledged.[148] A similar research trend has also pointed out how medieval romance could draw on the imagery of the Passion for literary effect, and how biblical tropes could be used to condense time, space and subject and thereby make audiences complicit in that which they view.[149] The wide borrowing from the Eucharistic idiom evidenced in the post-kill rituals of *Master of Game* may be indicative of a similar dynamic; it is not implausible that the ritual forms of the liturgy and the hunt work in a similar way, that is, that they interanimate one another. That there is not an explicit association between the two ritual traditions in no wise precludes effective interanimation. Like in any performance, the viewer of a ritual is prompted to take note of 'the abstract similarities' and thus to 'mobilize his past experience and stereotypical thinking'.[150] And while the *curée*

---

[142] Judkins, pp. 91–95.
[143] Rubin, pp. 334–42.
[144] Tambiah, p. 165.
[145] Tambiah, pp. 161–65.
[146] Tambiah, p. 164.
[147] Klemettilä, p. 197.
[148] Putter, pp. 373, 374–80.
[149] See Poellinger, pp. 157–76, and also Daisy Black, ' "Nayles Large and Lang": Masculine Identity and Anachronic Object in the York *Crucifixion Play*', *Medieval Feminist Forum*, 50 (2015), 85–104.
[150] Erving Goffman, *Presentation of Self in Everyday Life* (Harmondsworth: Penguin, 1984), p. 36.

could not have been construed as a true mass, it could nevertheless instill some of the same dispositions as conveyed in the Catholic mass, like respect for a divinely sanctioned social order. This relates to the philosopher of language J.L. Austin's observations on the etoliation of language and language parasitism, that is, that an unserious (or hollow) performative act can nonetheless impart serious effects on its audience.[151] Indeed it has been noted that the etoliating parasite (the hollow performative act) may often play a not insignificant role in constituting that which it parasitizes (the host/serious performative act).[152] Thus, a hollow performative act such as the *curée* which successfully resonates with its serious counterpart (the Catholic liturgy) plays a notable role in constituting that counterpart. Although certainly on unequal terms, through their reciprocal roles as target and source of metaphor they are mutually constitutive.

The *curée* thus is free to resonate with the liturgy without actually having to be anything like it in a salvational or essive sense. Indeed it could be argued that the *curée* served as a constituting element of the liturgical ritual which it parasitizes, interanimating it with novel resonances. Ultimately, the resonance of the *curée* as a meaningful ritual rests on its metaphorical alignment with respect to the rites of the mass. The converse could also be said to be true, albeit to a lesser degree. Given the shared heritage of the two ritual traditions as derivatives of blood sacrifice, it is not implausible to assume that their ritual forms have developed over time in tandem, sometimes drifting apart, sometimes lurching towards a closer proximity, but always more or less locked in an orbit of mutual influence. The many points of concord examined in the present article would support this interpretation, as would the historical link between hunting and religion. The observation that the ritual forms of the noble hunt evolved in a nexus of mutual influences that can be examined and described is germane to the wider contextualization of medieval hunting as a practice. That on occasion these ritual sets seem to shift in response to contemporary social expediencies could be read as felicitous happenstance, or alternatively as deliberate ideological manipulation, but is noteworthy nonetheless.

---

[151] J. L. Austin, *How To Do Things with Words* (Oxford: Oxford University Press, 1988), pp. 21–22. For a discussion, also see James Loxley, *Performativity* (London: Routledge, 2007), p. 13.

[152] As Derrida points out, any attempt to judge one over the other is to take part in a dogmatic judgment whereby the corollary of the derivative that exists in the host is denied in the parasite. For a discussion, see Loxley, pp. 73–75.

Sexual Sin and 'Anxieties of Outreach' in Thirteenth-Century England: Two Manuals for Penitents and their Adaptations

Krista A. Murchison

Introduction

Scholars of medieval history and literature have long recognized that medieval manuals that were designed to guide confessors through the confessional interrogation express significant unease about describing sexual activity, and with good cause. Medieval confessors were, as Pierre Payer relates in his study focused on manuals for priests, deeply concerned with the question of how to probe a penitent's conscience without inadvertently introducing new sins, or reminding penitents of old ones.[1] The *Summa de casibus poenitentiae* (c. 1225), Raymond de Pennaforte's remarkably influential guide for priests, warns confessors against this specific danger: 'Nevertheless, I advise [the confessor] that in his questions he not descend to special circumstances and special sins; for many fall severely after such an interrogation who otherwise would never have dreamt of it.'[2] Since sexual sins could be committed in private, knowledge of them could be guarded — in theory, at least. So significant was a concern over teaching new sexual sins that, according to Payer, trepidations surrounding confessional interrogation 'are virtually always about sexual offenses'.[3] These sins are, therefore, particularly important for understanding medieval tensions surrounding confessional practices.

While much has been written about how anxieties surrounding sexual sin are manifested in manuals for confessors, there has been relatively little about how these are manifested in the educational outreach material that was written for penitents, both lay and clerical, about

---

[1] Pierre Payer, *Sex and the New Medieval Literature of Confession, 1150–1300* (Toronto: Pontifical Institute of Mediaeval Studies, 2009), p. 59.

[2] Translated in Thomas N. Tentler, *Sin and Confession on the Eve of the Reformation* (Princeton: Princeton University Press, 1977), p. 115.

[3] Payer, p. 60. Similarly, Tentler suggests, while discussing fears of introducing new sins in Raymond de Pennaforte's *Summa de casibus poenitentiae*, that these were generally centered on sexual sins: 'it is difficult to believe that Raymond had anything in mind except sexual sins when he advised against descending into detail' (p. 115). The same view is expressed by Peter Biller in 'Confession in the Middle Ages: Introduction', in *Handling Sin: Confession in the Middle Ages*, ed. by Peter Biller and A. J. Minnis (Woodbridge: York Medieval, 1998), pp. 1–42 (p. 13).

how to prepare for confession.[4] These texts, termed 'manuals for penitents' by Lee Patterson, proliferated in the late medieval period, especially after the Fourth Lateran Council of 1215, which mandated annual confession for all believers who had reached the age of majority.[5] The proliferation of these texts, which could be used with the help of a confessor or on one's own, made it increasingly possible for medieval penitents to learn about sins in a self-directed manner, and to probe their own consciences in new ways. The increasing importance of this type of 'distance education' led to new and significant concerns for the Church — part of the wider 'anxieties of outreach' described by Jocelyn Wogan-Browne that emerged in the wake of the Fourth Lateran Council.[6]

Since these manuals enabled penitents to learn about potential sins on their own, it is to be expected that they would, perhaps even more than manuals for priests, exhibit a marked trepidation about descriptions of sexual sin, which had the potential of giving penitents new ideas. This article is thus aimed at exploring, for the first time, a particular form of the new 'anxieties of outreach' that emerged after the Fourth Lateran Council: the fears that developed about the potential of confessional literature for introducing new sins. In particular, it aims to uncover how — and why — these fears are less pronounced when manuals address clerical penitents rather than more general ones. By elucidating the increased unease around the description of sexual sins in texts aimed at those outside of the cloister — and, in so doing, highlighting the major concerns about sexual discourse that had permeated medieval society in the wake of the Fourth Lateran Council — the findings here contribute to a broader movement of recognizing the multiple, diverse, and sometimes conflicting forms of self-knowledge available to medieval minds.

Two manuals addressed to penitents lie at the center of this investigation: Robert Grosseteste's *Perambulauit Iudas* (c. 1235), which was written in England, and Robert de Sorbon's *Qui vult vere confiteri* (c. 1260–74), which was written in France.[7] Both texts provide insight into views of sexual sins because, as we shall see, both were adapted for new audiences, and, in both cases, this adaptation history contains clues about what medieval authors considered appropriate for different types of readers. Grosseteste's was translated and incorporated into the Anglo-Norman *Compileison* (c. 1254–74), a text which anticipates a wider audience and also contains an expanded translation of the well-known anchoritic guide, *Ancrene Wisse* (c. 1220–30). Robert's was translated into French for a more general audience and, eventually, incorporated into Friar Laurent's widely popular *Somme le roi* (c. 1279).

Of course, determining the audience of a medieval text requires careful consideration. As Ruth Evans notes, a text's audience can be constructed in a variety of different ways, some

---

[4] Allen J. Frantzen considers the depiction of sexual sins in Anglo-Saxon penitentials in *The Literature of Penance in Anglo-Saxon England* (New Brunswick: Rutgers University Press, 1983). But, according to Frantzen, such manuals are primarily written from the perspective of the priest, not that of the penitent (13). The recent and significant *New History of Penance*, edited by Abigail Firey (Leiden: Brill, 2008), dedicates surprisingly little space to medieval understandings of sexual sin.

[5] Lee Patterson, 'The "Parson's Tale" and the Quitting of the "Canterbury Tales" ', *Traditio*, 34 (1978), 331–80.

[6] Jocelyn Wogan-Browne, 'Time to read: Pastoral Care, Vernacular Access and the Case of Angier of St. Frideswide', in *Texts and Traditions of Pastoral Care: Essays in Honour of Bella Millett*, ed. by Cate Gunn and Catherine Innes-Parker (Woodbridge: York Medieval, 2009), pp. 62–77 (p. 77).

[7] For the dating of Grosseteste's work, see Joseph Goering and F. A. C. Mantello, ' "The Perambulauit Iudas..." (*Speculum Confessionis*) Attributed to Robert Grosseteste', *Revue Bénédictine*, 96 (1986), 125–68 (p. 132). For its authorship, see Goering and Mantello, pp. 126–29. For the dating of the latter work and its authorship, see F. N. M. Diekstra, 'Robert de Sorbon's *Qui Vult Vere Confiteri* (c. 1260–74) and its French Versions', *Recherches de théologie et philosophie médiévales*, 60 (1993), 215–72 (p. 216).

implicit and some explicit, and a text's constructed audience is not necessarily the same as its actual one. Evans, drawing on the work of Paul Strohm and others, distinguishes between four audience functions: 1) the 'actual audience', which may or may not be named explicitly in a text, 2) the 'inscribed' audience, which comprises any listeners described within a text (such as Chaucer's pilgrims), 3) the 'intended audience', which Evans describes as those 'sometimes identified by dedications and addresses to patrons' and 4) the 'implied audience', which Evans describes as 'the text's "ideal reader", anticipated or constructed by statements in the text with which he or she is encouraged to agree'. A text may have different audiences in each of these categories, or they might overlap.[8]

Among manuals for penitents, many texts that explicitly address one audience will nevertheless describe some sins that would have no relevance to it; for example, a text addressed to the laity might contain some specifically clerical sins. In other words, the intended and implied audiences of a manual for penitents often differ. Indeed, a tendency toward compendiousness in these manuals means that most contain sins that are applicable to those in a variety of specific circumstances, and most therefore have very broad implied audiences, whereas their intended audiences are generally narrower. Given that in any given text the implied and intended audiences might differ from each other, I consider both of them here.

Robert Grosseteste's *Perambulauit Iudas* (c. 1235) and its adaptation

The earliest of the texts considered here is Grosseteste's *Perambulauit Iudas*. It begins with a preface addressed to an anonymous learned friend who asked for a confessional guide for his own use.[9] The guide that follows is a "form of confession" text. These formulaic texts, which have been studied in depth by Michael Cornett, are brief lists of sins cast in the voice of a confessing penitent.[10] Joseph Goering and F. A. C. Mantello suggest that the descriptions of sins in this first guide, which include, for example, references to the roles of cellarer and prior, have an implied audience of Benedictine monks. From these sins and from the preface, Goering and Mantello suggest that the guide was written for 'a superior in a house of monks or regular cannons'.[11]

The next part of the *Perambulauit Iudas* is addressed explicitly to a group of 'simpler brothers' (*simpliciores fratres*); Goering and Mantello describe this part as a '"mirror of confession" (*speculum confessionis*) concerning all the sins committed both in the cloister and in the world'. This second part begins with an interrogatory — questions that penitents could ask themselves to prepare for confession (sections 26–36), then supplies definitions of sins (sections 37–42). When both parts of the treatise are taken into account, it seems that it was prepared for a group of monks and their spiritual advisor.[12]

---

[8] Ruth Evans, 'Readers/Audiences/Texts', in *The Idea of the Vernacular*, ed. by Jocelyn Wogan-Browne, Nicholas Watson, Andrew Taylor and Ruth Evans (Pennsylvania: Pennsylvania State University Press, 1999), pp. 107–25 (pp. 115–16).

[9] Goering and Mantello, p. 132; Grosseteste writes to his friend, 'me rogasti vt tibi scriberem formam confessionis' ('you have asked me to write a form of confession') and specifies that the friend is intelligent ('intelligenti'): Goering and Mantello (pp. 148, 150).

[10] Michael Cornett, 'The Form of Confession: A Late Medieval Genre for Examining Conscience' (unpublished doctoral dissertation, University of North Carolina, 2011), p. 5.

[11] Goering and Mantello, pp. 132–33; 125.

[12] Goering and Mantello, p. 141.

Sexual Sin and 'Anxieties of Outreach' in Thirteenth-Century England

The *Perambulauit Iudas* exhibits a relative openness about sins that could be committed in privacy. It includes a lengthy discussion of lechery, which includes two 'sins against nature': 'sodomy' and non-procreative ejaculation.[13] In the section on the sin of touch, Grosseteste describes examples of lechery committed through touching others. He clearly considers the subject a delicate one; he advises confessing such sins to a priest or to God alone, for otherwise the 'weak' could be 'scandalized' ('quia infirmi forte talia possint inde scandalizari').[14] Yet his decision to include these sins in his text despite their potential for scandal suggests that he thought the benefit to his audience outweighed any possible risk.

Almost all of the *Perambulauit Iudas* was adapted and incorporated into the Anglo-Norman *Compileison*.[15] Before examining the changes that were made in this process, it is necessary to briefly consider the *Compileison* and its audience. Although best known for containing an adaptation of the well-known religious guide *Ancrene Wisse*, the *Compileison* is in fact much wider in scope; Nicholas Watson and Jocelyn Wogan-Browne describe 'the massive structuring and originality of conception and voicing of this 29,000-line prose work of moral theology.'[16] All parts of *Ancrene Wisse* are incorporated into the *Compileison* save for part 1, on anchoritic devotions. The others have been carefully reordered and substantially extended; W. H. Trethewey, who edited the *Ancrene Wisse* portion of the text, finds that *Ancrene Wisse* material accounts for only about 42 percent of the complete *Compileison*[17] The author's other sources remain somewhat elusive, but parallels have been found in Guilelmus Peraldus' *Summa de vitiis,* his *Summa de virtutibus* (both c. 1236), and Raymond de Pennaforte's *Summa de casibus poenitentiae* (c. 1225).[18] Aside from the translation of Grosseteste's *Perambulauit Iudas* the work includes a translation of the *Peines de Purgatorie*, which is occasionally ascribed to Grosseteste.[19]

---

[13] Grosseteste, p. 164. The passage is given in full below.

[14] Grosseteste, p. 154.

[15] With the exception of the passages translated from Grosseteste's text, I have taken passages from the *Compileison* from the copy in Trinity College Cambridge MS R.14.7, since this is the one W. H. Trethewey uses as a base text for his edition. Abbreviations have been silently expanded. Translations of the *Compileison* are my own.

[16] Nicholas Watson, and Jocelyn Wogan-Browne, 'The French of England: The *Compileison*, *Ancrene Wisse*, and the Idea of Anglo-Norman', *Journal of Romance Studies*, 4 (2004), 35–59 (p. 42).

[17] W. H. Trethewey, 'Introduction', in *The French Text of the Ancrene Riwle: Edited from Trinity College, Cambridge MS. R. 14.7, with Variants from Bibliotheque Nationale MS. F. fr. 6276 and MS. Bodley 90*, ed. by W. H. Trethewey, Early English Text Society, o. s. 240 (London: Oxford University Press, 1958), pp. ix–xxxiii (p. xxiii).

[18] Germaine Dempster, 'The Parson's Tale', in *Sources and Analogues of Chaucer's Canterbury Tales*, ed. by W. F. Bryan and Germaine Dempster (Chicago: University of Chicago Press, 1941), pp. 723–60 (p. 727).

[19] Ruth J. Dean and Maureen B. M. Boulton, *Anglo-Norman Literature: A Guide to Texts and Manuscripts* (London: Anglo-Norman Text Society, 1999), pp. 357, 366. For a study of the translation of the *Perambulauit Iudas*, see Matthias Hessenauer, 'For a Larger Audience: Grosseteste's *Perambulavit Iudas* in Anglo-Norman', in *Robert Grosseteste: His Thought and its Impact*, ed. by Jack Cunningham (Toronto: PIMS, 1964), pp. 259–313. In the copy preserved in Trinity College, Cambridge MS R.14.7 (James no. 883), parts 1–26 of the *Perambulauit Iudas* are translated on fols 67a–70a of the *Compileison*. The *Compileison* then turns to 'de dis commandemenz e de set mor/teus p[e]chez. e lour especes solonc le eseing/nement de seint gregorie' ('the Ten Commandments and the Seven Deadly Sins, and their species, according to the teaching of Saint Gregory', fols 70a–71a). It then returns to the *Perambulauit Iudas*. Parts 27–35 are translated on fols 71a–73b. Only parts 36–43 of Grosseteste's text are omitted. Only two copies of the *Compileison* contain this translation: the Trinity copy and that in Paris, Bibliothèque nationale, Fonds français MS 6276. Oxford, Bodleian Library MS Bodley 90 does not contain the translation of the *Perambulauit Iudas*, as the text cuts off before this section and in the middle of the *Compileison de seinte penance*. For an edition of the *Peines de Purgatorie*, see Robert J. Relihan, 'A Critical Edition of the Anglo-Norman and Latin Versions of "Les Peines de Purgatorie" ' (unpublished doctoral dissertation, University of Iowa, 1978).

The intended audience of the *Compileison* is complex and broad. It addresses 'gent de religion' ('people of religion'), and 'hommes e femmes de religion' ('men and women of religion').[20] These 'gent de religion' are not, as Cate Gunn notes, from one order alone; the address is more generally to those 'living a dedicated religious life.'[21] Yet the author also writes for others outside of a disciplined religious life:

> quoteceo est conquilli en semble. des set pechez morteus. e de lur esspeces. sicome nus les auom troue en seinte escripture pur aprendre les leaument e sanz feintise a tote genz mes especiaument e par deuant tuz autres a hommes e a femmes de religioun.[22]

> This [work] was [*lit.* is] gathered together from the seven deadly sins and their species, as we have found them in sacred scripture, in order to teach them faithfully and without deceit to everyone, but especially — and above all others — to the men and women of religion.

Here, the primary audience is those following a religious life, and the secondary one is anyone else. Occasionally, the text singles out the religious audience in particular. The adaptation of the *Perambulauit Iudas*, introduced by a rubric stating that it is for the 'gent de religion', is one such place: 'Isci comence li primer chapitle de la secunde partie de la tierce partie de confession. ky nus mustre coment genz de religion se deiuent de tute leur uie confesser' ['Here begins the first chapter of the second part of the third part of confession, which shows us how people of religion should confess about all their lives')].[23] The *Compileison*'s broad intended audience is consonant with its implied audience; many of the sins described in the first part of the text are specific to lay life: 'peche homme par auarice [...] par trop elarger ses terres ou ses mesons a tort' ('man commits avarice [...] by enlarging his lands too much, or his houses wrongfully').[24] In general, then, the text has a wider audience than that of the *Perambulauit Iudas*, although sections, including the translation of the *Perambulauit Iudas*, are addressed to a more limited one.

Lechery is discussed at length twice in the *Compileison*: once in the adaptation of the *Perambulauit Iudas* addressed to the 'gent de religion', and once in a passage for which no direct source has been found, addressed to a more general audience. That addressed to a wider audience is markedly less candid about sexual sin than is the *Perambulauit Iudas*. The author includes many of the same species of lechery as Grosseteste does, but the treatment of 'sins against nature' is different and somewhat vague compared to that in Grosseteste's text:

> peche en countre nature est. ky tout a homme tote la reson de la nature. issi ky il nen est pas pae de sa mauueste fere naturement. etuz sen entremet de totes maneres de ordures ky il poet ou par esgarder. ou par tast. ou par manier. ou par bestes. ou par oiseaus contrefere. kar il ne font si come nature les a prent. e li mauueis le fet encountre nature.[25]

> The sin against nature is that which deprives man of natural reason such that he is not satisfied — because of his depravity — to behave naturally, but instead engages in all

---

[20] Fols 125d, 105d. The audience is also addressed under other titles, including "freres e suers en deu" (fol. 106c).
[21] Cate Gunn, 'Reading Edmund of Abingdon's *Speculum* as Pastoral Literature', in *Texts and Traditions of Pastoral Care: Essays in Honour of Bella Millett*, ed. by Cate Gunn and Catherine Innes-Parker (Woodbridge: York Medieval, 2009), pp. 100–14 (p. 105).
[22] Fol. 1b.
[23] Fol. 67a.
[24] Fol. 17b.
[25] Fol. 24a.

kinds of indecencies, whether by looking, by touching, or by imitating animals and birds, since they only do as nature has taught them, but the depraved man [who does the same] does it against nature.

The passage is marked by circumlocution — a practice that medieval rhetoricians considered a method of evading delicate subjects.[26] While Grosseteste's *Perambulauit Iudas* mentions 'sodomy' in its list of sins, the *Compileison* here does not. It does place non-procreative ejaculation among the 'sins against nature', but is vague about what is intended:

> E sachez bien ky entotes les maneres ky homme ou femme par la uolunte en euillante sachant sul par sei ou e autre parcure pollicion de la char. hors de mariage ou en mariage autrement ky nature de homme e de femme demaunde. cest asauer en autre manere ky homme deit enfant engendrer. e femme conceuer; tot est peche mortel. e peche en countre nature.[27]

> And know well that in all the manners in which a man or woman procures by will the pollution of his or her flesh, in watching or awareness, alone by oneself, or accompanied by another, out of marriage or within marriage, differently than nature requires of a man and woman — namely in another manner than man can [*lit.* should] engender a child, and woman conceive — all [this] is mortal sin, and sin against nature.

This passage, like the first, relies on circumlocution to avoid potentially sensitive details. Yet the second discussion of lechery — that addressed more specifically to the 'gent de religion' and adapted from the *Perambulauit Iudas* — gives more detail. As Matthias Hessenauer notes, the translation of Grosseteste's text is remarkably faithful; 'only rarely does [the author of the *Compileison*] make slight changes'.[28] This makes the places where changes were made particularly interesting, and an extended comparison between it and its original provides valuable insight into the approach favoured by the author of the *Compileison*:[29] see Table 1.

Table 1. Comparison of *Perambulauit Iudas* and the *Compileison*: text

Perambulauit Iudas	*Compileison*
DE LUXURIA,	De luxure deit venir avant la enqueste en tiele manere:
Fornicacionem, incestum, adulterium, vicium sodomiticum uel peculiale, uel aliquid simile actu uel uoluntate patrasti, vel aliis consensisti.	Fornicacion, avoterie, incest, pecche encontre nature ou especial pecche ou acune semblance par fet ou par volunte avez fet, ou a ceo consentu;

[26] Matthew Vendôme, for example, suggests that through *periphrasis*, 'sententiae foeditas circuitu evitatur' ('the foulness of an idea may be avoided by a roundabout statement') in 'Ars versificatoria', in *Les Arts poétiques du XIIe et du XIIIe siècle*, ed. by Edmond Faral (Paris: Champion, 1958), pp. 106–93, p. 185; translation in *The Art of Versification*, trans. by Aubrey E. Gaylon (Ames, Iowa: Iowa State University Press, 1980), p. 105. For others who championed *periphrasis* as a means of avoiding delicate subjects, see the discussion in Jan M. Ziolkowski's chapter on 'Obscenity in the Latin Grammatical and Rhetorical Tradition', in *Obscenity: Social Control and Artistic Creation in the European Middle Ages*, ed. by Jan M. Ziolkowski (Leiden: Brill, 1998), 41–60 (pp. 56–57).
[27] Fol. 24a.
[28] Hessenauer, p. 262.
[29] Grosseteste, p. 164; Hessenauer, p. 310.

Perambulauit Iudas	*Compileison*
Virginem deflorasti.	avez virgine despucele de soen pucelage?
Excitasti in te affectus libidinis.	Avez vus esmu en vus le talent de leccherie?
In cogitacione libidinosa delectatus fuisti.	Avez delitee en leccheruse pense?
Pudenda inpudenter tractasti.	Avez vus treite hontousement les hontouses membres ou en vus ou en autres?
Si unquam extra uas ultro fudisti.	Si vus onkes hors du dreit vessel par vostre ein degre espandistes voste semence?
Aliquo modo curam adhibuisti ut libidini satisfaceres.	Avez vus en acune manere mis diligence ke vus assez feissez a leccherie?
Per sompnum pollutus fuisti.	Fuistes onkes soillee par pollucion en songe, e si vus avez este, dites coment?
Quo modo concupisti. Voluisti concupisci et ob hoc te ornasti.	Avez onkes coveite ou voillez estre coveite e puis vus, aurnastes; e si vus avez ceo fet, dites coment!
Quo modo fornicacionibus consensisti, consilium et auxilium impendendo.	Avez consenti a fornicacions en donant conseill ou eide?
In puericia aliquid luxuriosum sinistrum egisti.	Avez fet en vostre enfance acun pecche de luxure?
Aliquam inpudenter tractasti uel te tractari permisisti.	Avez nule femme trete hontousement ou suffert de lui hontousement estre tret?

Comparison of *Perambulauit Iudas* and the *Compileison*: translation

Perambulauit Iudas	*Compileison*
ON LECHERY.	Lechery should be subject to investigation in the following manner:
Fornication, incest, adultery, the vice of sodomy — either in itself, or a similar act — either brought about by free will, or by consenting to others.	fornication, adultery, incest, and sin against nature — either that specific sin or any similar deed — done in act or in intention, or by consent.
You deflowered virgins.	Have you deflowered a virgin?
You roused, from within yourself, lecherous desire.	Did you rouse, from within yourself, a desire for lechery?
You took delight in lustful thought.	Did you delight in lustful thought?
You stroked genitals shamelessly.	Did you very shamefully stroke shameful parts of the body — either your own, or those of others?

Perambulauit Iudas	*Compileison*
If you ever expelled outside of the proper vessel.	If you ever by your own free will expelled your seed outside of the proper vessel?
You have taken care to satisfy your lust in any manner.	Have you taken care to satisfy your lust in any manner?
You have expelled in defilement during sleep.	Were you ever defiled by pollution while sleeping — and if you have been, say how?
If you were, in any way, moved by desire — or wished to be desired — and, for this reason, adorned yourself.	And have you been moved by desire, or wished to be desired, and then adorned yourself? And if you have done this, say how!
If you participated in fornication in any way through counsel and granted aid.	Have you consented to fornication by giving counsel, or aid?
You performed some sinister act of lechery during your childhood.	Did you commit any act of lechery during your childhood?
You stroked someone shamelessly, or let yourself be stroked by someone.	Have you shamefully stroked any woman, or let yourself be shamefully stroked by her?

At first glance, it is hard to say if the *Compileison* is more or less explicit here than the *Perambulauit Iudas*. On one hand, the *Compileison* is more direct, as it describes the spilling of 'semence' ('seed' or 'semen') which is described only implicitly in the source ('Si unquam extra uas ultro fudisti'), and which the *Compileison* describes, as we have seen, more circuitously elsewhere, when addressing a wider audience. On the other hand, the *Compileison* here is less specific about sodomy; where the *Perambulauit Iudas* describes it as 'the sin of sodomy' ('vicium sodomiticum') the *Compileison* describes it in more general terms as 'sin against nature' ('pecche encontre nature'). This is in keeping with the approach to sodomy elsewhere in the text. Overall, then, the *Compileison* is somewhat more guarded in its descriptions of sexual sin than the *Perambulauit Iudas*. The section addressed to a general audience deploys circumlocution to avoid describing it, and that addressed to 'gent de religion' gives some detail, but nevertheless does not mention 'sodomy' by name.

Robert de Sorbon's *Qui vult vere confiteri* (c. 1260–74) and its adaptations

To see whether the increased trepidation that characterizes the depiction of sexual sin in the *Compileison* is typical of manuals for mixed audiences, it is useful to look at Robert de Sorbon's *Qui vult vere confiteri* (c. 1260–74) and its French translation, both of which are 'guides to confession'.[30] Both contain confessional statements in the first person, but unlike the first part of Grosseteste's work, they are not, strictly speaking, forms of confession, because

---
[30] Diekstra, 'Robert de Sorbon', p. 218.

these confessional statements are introduced with third-person narration, such as 'Et debet sic dicere peccator' ('And the sinner should say this').[31] The Latin version was written first and supplied the soruce for the French version according to F. N. M. Diekstra, who edited both versions, although Diekstra notes that 'it is not inconceivable that among the Latin versions there are instances of "backformation", in which the French served as the model rather than the Latin exemplar.'[32]

Given the connection between them, both Latin and French versions printed by Diekstra can help with establishing the relationship between the audience of a manual for penitents and its author's relative willingness to describe private sins. Both imply a mixed audience to some extent;[33] they contain 'worldly' sins, such as, under the heading of 'avarice', disguising meat with the intent to deceive the buyer.[34] Both also list some sins that would have been particular to certain forms of clerical life. So, both include, also under 'avarice', the buying and selling of benefices, a type of avarice which, both versions acknowledge, pertains mostly to the clergy and others living religious lives. That said, the Latin text contains more sins particular to clerical readers than does the French one; in the same section on the sin of avarice, the Latin text gives both the selling of benefices and the selling of sacraments, whereas the French gives only the selling of benefices.[35]

As always, we cannot take the implied audience — either clerical or lay — as the audience in any straightforward way. But in the case of these two versions of *Qui vult vere confiteri,* the one with the fewest clerical sins — the French one — also explicitly addresses a more general audience; it alone ends with a statement that it is for 'all good Christians' ('toute boine gent crestiienne').[36] So, while both texts construct a general audience to some degree, the French one is particularly committed to this audience.

---

[31] Robert de Sorbon, 'Robert de Sorbon's *Qui Vult Vere Confiteri* (c. 1260–74) and its French Versions', ed. by F. N. M. Diekstra, *Recherches de théologie et philosophie médiévales,* 60 (1993), 215–72 (p. 243). Translations from both Latin and French versions are my own.

[32] Diekstra, 'Robert de Sorbon', pp. 231–32.

[33] The only comment that Diekstra makes regarding the audience of these two works is that they were written for 'laymen' ('Robert de Sorbon', p. 218), but it would seem that he means 'those examining their consciences' since this statement occurs in a larger passage stating that the text was designed for penitents (as opposed to priests), and since he does not provide any evidence for why the text is for the laity in particular.

[34] The Latin text gives: 'alia species [apparet] in carnibus; et fit ibi dolositas quando ille qui vendit carnes facit credere de carne suina vel suilla quod sit porcina et [apponit] ibi signum porci; vel [de] carne caprina quod sit arietina; vel simul ponit carnem veterem non habentem bonum odorem cum recenti, [et ita] aliqui decipiuntur' ('another species [of this sin] is found in meat; and in this case when the person who is selling the meat claims that sow's meat [*lit.* the flesh of *suina* or *suilla*] is boar's meat and labels it as such, or that goat's meat is mutton, or, in the same way, disguises meat that is aged and does not have a good odor as new, and so deceives some'; p. 250). The French text gives: 'en char vendre fait on trecherie quant cil ki le vent fait entendre de char de truie ke c'est chars de [marle; et si mest en saegne de marle], u de char de kievre ke c'est chars de mouton; u il mesle le vielle [et ki ne flaire mie souef] avoec le jovene' ('fraud takes place in the selling of meat when the person selling the meat claims that sow's meat is boar's meat, or that goat's meat is mutton; or he mixes the old that has gone off with the fresh meat'; p. 250).

[35] The Latin text has: 'septimus ramus avaricie est symonia, quando venduntur vel emuntur sacramenta vel prebende [vel aliquid] ecclesiasticum vel religionis. Sed tale peccatum pertinet ad clericos et religiosos' ('the seventh branch of avarice is simony, when sacraments, or prebends, or anything ecclesiastical or religious, are sold or bought'; p. 251). The French text has: 'la sisime branche est simonie, quant lais hom vent u achate les benefisses de Sainte Eglise. Cis pechiés monte plus as clers u as gens de religion ke il ne fait as lais' ('the sixth branch is simony, when men sell or buy benefices of Holy Church. This sin is more important to members of the clergy or to people of religion than it is to layfolk'; p. 251).

[36] Robert de Sorbon, p. 259.

Like the *Compileison*, which also constructs a mixed audience, both versions of *Qui vult vere confiteri* exhibit some trepidation around sexual sin. This is especially true of the section on sins against nature. Unlike Grosseteste, Robert, in his Latin text, avoids using the term 'sodomy' altogether, and describes this sin circuitously: 'Sextus ramus luxurie est quando [homo facit] quoddam peccatum contra naturam, de quo legitur Deum fecisse talem vindictam quod quinque civitates destructe [et combuste] sunt igne fetido propter ardorem vel fetorem luxurie' ('The sixth branch of lechery is when man does a kind of sin against nature, of which we read God took [*lit.* made] such vengeance that five cities were destroyed and were burnt in stinking fire, because of the heat and the stench of lechery').[37]

In this same discussion of sins against nature, Robert also describes masturbation in terms that are somewhat vague: 'quando homo facit peccatum per se sicud faceret cum muliere et percipit bene quod est contra naturam; vel quando eciam illicite et [inhoneste] virilia membra sua vel aliorum tenuerit vel palpaverit vel [respexerit]' ('when a man commits a sin by himself as he would do with a woman and perceives well that it is against nature, and when he illicitly and shamefully holds, feels, or touches his own or others' male members'). Robert finally notes that, aside from these ways, sins against nature can be committed 'aliis modis qui non debent dici in aperto, sed omnia in confessione debent manifestari' ('by other ways that should not be said in the open, but all these things should be declared openly in confession').[38] Where Grosseteste, whose text addresses monks and their spiritual director, was willing to list a variety of sins in this category, including sodomy, Robert describes these more circuitously.[39]

Following the tendency to be more watchful when writing for a wider audience, the later, French version, which is addressed to all Christians, is even more cautious about describing the sins against nature than the Latin one. It includes the same vague description of sins against nature as those 'dont Dex fist tel vengement ke .v. cités en [furent fondues et arses] de feu puant' ('for which God took such vengeance that five cities were melted and burnt in a stinking fire'). But it omits the description of 'members' from the discussion of masturbation, and does not mention touching the genitals of others: 'quant li hons [u] la feme [fait] le pechié par soi et bien s'en apierchoit c'est contre nature' ('when the man or the woman commits the sin by himself or herself and knows well that it is against nature').[40] So, while both versions are circuitous in their descriptions of sexual sin, that addressed to a wider audience contains even fewer details. We cannot simply write this silence off as part of a wider tendency toward abridgement; although the French version omits several passages from the Latin, it also contains expansions, such as the lengthy section about penance at the end of the text.[41]

What emerges from the comparison thus far is that, out of the five discussions of lechery examined, those addressed expressly to clerical audiences — those by Grosseteste — are more explicit about sins against nature than those that address or imply both clerical and lay audiences — the *Compileision* and *Qui vult vere confiteri*. Moreover, of this latter work, the version that is addressed explicitly to both clerical and lay readers — the French one — is more

---

[37] Robert de Sorbon, p. 255.
[38] Robert de Sorbon, p. 255.
[39] There is, however, one copy of this text that goes into relatively explicit detail about the carnal acts that it purports to discourage. Diekstra writes that 'its elaborate dwelling on salacious details would appear to move far beyond the requirements of pastoral care' ('Robert de Sorbon', p. 224). However, because Robert is generally more cautious in his treatment of sexual sin, and because this version is only preserved in one manuscript, Diekstra concludes that this more explicit copy cannot be authorial ('Robert de Sorbon', p. 226).
[40] Robert de Sorbon, p. 255.
[41] Robert de Sorbon, pp. 258–59.

circuitous about 'sins against nature' than the Latin. This correlation suggests that trepidation around sexual sins is heightened in those works addressed to a general audience.

To test this theory, it is useful to turn to the *Somme le roi,* since it was written for courtly readers while Laurent was in the service of Philip III and has some material in common with *Qui vult vere confiteri.* In particular, the first two tracts of the *Somme le roi,* that on the Ten Commandments and that on the seven deadly sins, are derived from the *Mirroir du monde* (c. 1248–80), which, in turn, is indebted to *Qui vult vere confiteri.*[42] The treatment of sins against nature in the *Somme le roi* stands in stark contrast to that in either version of *Qui vult vere confiteri.* To illustrate the differences, it is worth quoting the relevant passage of the *Somme le roi* at length:

> Li derrains est li plus vilz et li plus orz, qui ne fet a nomer. C'est pechiez contre nature que li deables enseigne a fere a home ou a fame en mout de manieres qui ne font a nomer pour la matiere qui est trop abominable. Mes en confession le doit dire cil ou cele a cui il est avenu, car de tant comme li pechiez est plus granz et plus horribles, de tant vaut plus la confession, car la honte que on a dou dire est granz partie de la penitence. Cist pechiez desplait tant a Dieu que il en fist plovoir feu ardant et sofre puant sus la cité de Sodome et de Gomorre, et en fondi .V. citez en abisme.[43]

> The last is the vilest and the most putrid, which is not fit to be named. It is sin against nature, which the devil teaches man or woman to do in many manners that cannot be named, on account of the matter being too abominable. But in confession, he or she to whom [this sin] has befallen [*lit.* come] must say it, because the greater and more horrible the sin is, the more important confession is, because the shame that we have to say it is a big part of the penance. This sin displeases God so much that he made ardent fire and stinking sulfur rain on the city of Sodom and Gomorrah, and plunged five cities into the abyss.

Like Robert de Sorbon, Laurent avoids using the term 'sodomy', but Laurent's account of sins against nature is even more censored than Robert's. Gone is any discussion of touching genitals, and, aside from the cloaked reference to Sodom and Gomorrah, the account of 'sins against nature' is, in Laurent's text, reduced to an insistence that these are too horrible to be described.

Sexual Sin and Illicit Textual Pleasure

Other contemporary manuals for penitents addressed explicitly to lay readers voice equally powerful trepidation about sins done in private. An important text in this context is William of Waddington's Anglo-Norman *Manuel des péchés* (c. 1260), since this text survives in twenty-

---

[42] For the relationship between Robert de Sorbon's text and the *Mirroir de monde* (c. 1248–80), see R. R. Raymo, Elaine E. Whitaker and Ruth E. Sternglant, 'Introduction', in *The Mirroure of the Worlde: A Middle English Translation of Le Miroir Du Monde*, ed. by R. R. Raymo, Elaine E. Whitaker and Ruth E. Sternglant (Toronto: University of Toronto Press, 2003), pp. 3–42 (p. 7). For the relationship between the *Mirroir de monde* and the *Somme le roi*, see F. N. M. Diekstra, 'Introduction', in *The Middle English Weye of Paradys and the Middle French Voie De Paradis*, ed. by F. N. M. Dierkstra (Leiden: Brill, 1991), pp. 3–96 (pp. 215–16). Of course, for our present purposes, it would be valuable to examine how private sins are treated in the *Mirroir du monde*, but it has not been edited, and the wide divergence between its copies makes any analysis of it difficult at this stage.

[43] Laurent d'Orléans, *La Somme le roi*, ed. by Édith Brayer and Anne-Françoise Leurquin-Labie (Paris: Anciens Textes Français, 2008), p. 150.

eight manuscripts and fragments and therefore seems to have been popular in England, where it was written.[44] In the prologue, the text is positioned as a work for the laity:

> Pur la laye gent iert fet;
> Deu le parface, si ly plest,
> K'eus ver pussent apertement
> Kaunt eus trespassent, e kaunt nient.
> Si aukun de l'oyr seit asmendé,
> Deu de cyel en seit gracié.

> It is done for lay people;
> May God bring it to an end, if it please him,
> So that they can see clearly
> When they sin and when not.
> If anyone, from listening [to it], may be improved
> God in heaven may be thanked for it.[45]

William of Waddington first raises concerns about the treatment of private sins in the prologue. Here, William insists that none are described in his text: 'Des priuité3 n'i trouere3 ren, | Car mal peot fere, ou poi de bien' ('you will not find anything about private matters here | because it can lead to harm, or little good').[46] His choice of 'priuité3' here demarcates those sins that happen in secret from those that could be acquired through social observation.

The context behind William of Waddington's rejection of 'priuité3' is particularly suggestive. The lines just quoted follow from a passage about pleasure in reading. Immediately before William says that he will not include any 'priuité3', he writes: 'Ke plus en lisaunt seit delitus, | Cuntes nus mettrum vus aucuns' ('to make the reading delightful | we will add for you some stories').[47] These stories are supposed to help the reader hate sin: 'Sicum les sein3 nus unt cunté | Pur plus fere hayr pechié' ('[these tales are] just as the saints have told us | to make sin more hated').[48] This idea, that delightful ('delitus') stories will make us hate sin more, is consistent with many of the justifications of literary pleasure described by Glending Olson, that stress that literary pleasure supports a text's moralizing goals.[49] But the progression of ideas in the wider passage — from an insistence that stories are included to evoke a hatred of sin through literary pleasure, to an insistence that private sins are not included, because nothing good will come of them — is curious. The proximity of these two ideas might suggest a link between them, as if William is suggesting that 'private sins', like the stories he includes, could delight the reader, albeit in the wrong way.

Indeed, William often uses 'deliter' and its analogues in the context of sinful pleasures. So, for example, in the tale of the devil's confession, the devil states that various sins, including

---

[44] Dean and Boulton, pp. 349–51.
[45] Quoted and translated by Ulrike Schemmann in *Confessional Literature and Lay Education: The Manuel dé Pechez as a Book of Good Conduct and Guide to Personal Religion* (Düsseldorf: Droste, 2000), p. 229. For the question of whether these lines are authorial, see Schemmann, p. 324. Where possible, I quote passages from Schemmann's text, since the only edition of the *Manuel des péchés,* cited below, is out of date.
[46] William of Waddington, *Robert of Brunne 'Handlyng synne' and its French Original*, ed. by Frederick J. Furnivall, Early English Text Society, o. s. 119–23, 2 vols (London: Oxford University Press, 1901–3), I, ll. 83–84.
[47] Quoted and translated by Schemmann, p. 229.
[48] William of Waddington, I, l. 81–82.
[49] Glending Olson, *Literature as Recreation in the Later Middle Ages* (Ithaca: Cornell University Press, 1982), pp. 19–38.

lechery and gluttony, 'me delit mult' ('delight me very much').[50] There is, then, the possibility that William's fear as it is expressed in the prologue is not just that the description of private sins might provoke his audience to commit them — although this is clearly a central part of it — but that such description might prompt his audience to take the wrong kind of pleasure in his text.

William generally follows through on his promise not to include these sins. In his discussion of lechery he avoids the sins against nature, limiting himself to seven branches: fornication, adultery, incest, lechery between the ordained, taking a woman's virginity, rape of an unmarried woman, and the rape of another man's wife.[51] The descriptions of the branches of these sins are general and do not include specific sexual acts or body parts: 'Le premer est fornicaciun, | Ceo a dire, quant simples hom | E femme hors d'espusage | Se assemblent par fol corage' ('the first is fornication, that is to say, when single men and women meet by wanton desire outside of marriage').[52]

In his adaptation, *Handlyng Synne* (c. 1303–7), Robert Mannyng repeats William of Waddington's concern, but places it earlier than it appears in William's text: 'Of pryuytees speke y nouȝt: | Þe pryuytees wyle y nouȝt name, | For noun þarfore shuld me blame' ('Of private [sins] I will not speak, the private [sins] I will not name, for none therefore should I be blamed').[53] Avoiding private sins is, according to Mannyng, a way of avoiding guilt. The implication here is that including sexual sins in a text could make it offensive. The same idea appears in Henry of Lancaster's *Livre de seyntz medicines* (1354), where Henry explains that he will not describe his sins of lechery because if he did 'le livre feust plus haiez' ('the book might be the more loathed').[54]

Toward the end of the prologue, Mannyng repeats his intention to eschew descriptions of private sins: 'Þarfore may hyt & gode skyle why | Handlyng synne be clepyd oponly. | For hyt touchyþ no pryuyte | But opon synne þat callyd may be' ('Therefore may [this book], and with good reason, be called 'Handlyng Synne', and openly. For it touches on no private [things], but those sins that can be called 'open' [*i.e.* public]').[55] In other words, since it avoids private sins, it can be called by its title openly. The implication is that only in this way can a book be made fit for the public. Here, as in the *Livre de seyntz medicines*, books that include private sins are cast as suspect.

Like his source, Mannyng is generally true to his word, and avoids discussing private sins in any depth. He avoids the 'sins against nature' completely and describes the species of lechery without detail. Like its source, then, and like the *Somme le roi*, Mannyng's *Handlyng Synne* suggests significant unease surrounding private sins.

---

[50] William of Waddington, I, l. 11,198.
[51] William of Waddington, I, l. 5813–6070.
[52] William of Waddington, I, l. 5819–22.
[53] Robert Mannyng, *Robert of Brunne's 'Handlyng synne' and its French Original*, ed. by Frederick J. Furnivall, Early English Text Society, o. s. 119–23, 2 vols (London: Oxford University Press, 1901–3), I, l. 30–33.
[54] Henry, Duke of Lancaster, *Le Livre de Seyntz Medicines: The Unpublished Devotional Treatise of Henry of Lancaster*, ed. by E. J. Arnould (Oxford: Anglo-Norman Text Society, 1940), p. 69; translated in *The Book of Holy Medicines (Le Livre de Seyntz Medicines)*, ed. and trans. by Catherine Batt, Medieval and Renaissance Texts and Studies, 419/The French of England Translation Series (FRETS), 8 (Arizona: Arizona State University, 2015), p. 137.
[55] Robert Mannyng, I, 137–40.

Private Sin and 'Anxieties of Outreach'

The self-examination tradition of the *Manuel des péchés* and that of the *Somme le roi* had a significant influence on other self-examination texts, so the trepidation around private sins in these manuals is suggestive of contemporary views of the subject. A comparison of the treatment of sexual sins in these lay-oriented texts to that in Grosseteste's clerical texts, and to those intended for mixed audiences — the *Compileison* and *Qui vult vere confiteri* — reveals that authors addressing the clergy exclusively were more comfortable including details about sexual sin than authors addressing both the clergy and the laity. This might seem surprising when we consider that monks, and other members of the clergy, faced higher demands of chastity than layfolk.

Why, then, were authors more willing to describe private sins when addressing clerical audiences than lay ones? It is, of course, possible that it was because many of the sins in question were closely associated with monastic enclosure. James Brundage finds an emphasis on homosexuality and masturbation in pre-Lateran 'penitential' guides for priests and suggests that this reflects 'the experience and concerns of the monastic environment in which most penitential writers received their spiritual and intellectual formation'.[56] Jacqueline Murray, speaking of pastoral literature more generally, observes that 'confession had [...] evolved in the peculiarly masculine monastic environment of the early Middle Ages'.[57]

However, even if these sins were thought to be particularly common in monastic environments, this does not explain why they are censored in manuals that address both clerical and lay readers, like the *Compileison*. We would expect, rather, that these manuals that address clerical and lay readers would include these sins for the sake of the clerical ones. It seems more likely that authors were more open to listing private sins for clerical audiences because they worried that lay ones were more prone to trying new sins than were clerical ones. It is not hard to imagine that Grosseteste, writing for a monastic community, was less worried about introducing new sins to his readers than Laurent would have been. Moreover, authors like Grosseteste might have been less concerned about being accused of producing illicit content than those like Laurent. This is certainly suggested by Mannyng's statement that his not mentioning private sins will shield him from blame.

It would seem, then, that fears that the confessional interrogation could inadvertently teach penitents new sins spilled over into manuals for penitents, especially into those texts addressed explicitly to the laity. This matters, because it shows that the wave of manuals for penitents written for lay audiences in the wake of the Fourth Lateran Council raised concerns among those who produced them; their authors recognized that, while extending the confessional apparatus, they were also losing some control over how this apparatus would be used by their audiences.

On one hand, the creation of manuals for penitents that address a wider readership, such as the *Compileison*, is suggestive of a demand that reflects how far the changes in confessional practices that culminated in the injunction to confession of 1215 had been internalized by penitents and had permeated society. These texts represent the same widening of the Church's

---

[56] James A. Brundage, *Law, Sex, and Christian Society in Medieval Europe* (Chicago: University of Chicago Press, 2009), p. 174.

[57] Jacqueline Murray, 'Gendered Souls in Sexed Bodies: The Male Construction of Female Sexuality in Some Medieval Confessors' Manuals', in *Handling Sin: Confession in the Middle Ages* ed. by Peter Biller and A . J. Minnis (Woodbridge: York Medieval, 1998), pp. 79–94 (p. 81).

power that Payer and others find in manuals for confessors. But, at the same time, the concerns that would seem to be reflected in manuals addressed to general audiences over sexual sin suggest that members of the Church feared that the extension of this power could inadvertently introduce new sins — or even remind penitents of old ones — and point to the heightened tension that emerged as religious education became increasing removed from the institutional Church.

Aside from illuminating a new aspect of distance penitential education, the findings here shed new light on the medieval mind. Michel Foucault once declared, in *La volonté de savoir* (1976), that anxiety about sexual discourse emerged after the Council of Trent (c. 1545–63), and that this growing unease around the language of sexual sin in the Early Modern period was part of an emerging self-reflexivity.[58] In this model, anxiety about speaking of sex is a symptom of, and contributes to, the complex self-awareness of the modern subject — one generally absent from the medieval world. The findings presented here, by highlighting the significant unease about sexual discourse in manuals for penitents, contributes to a growing awareness of the forms of self-knowledge available to the medieval mind and, in so doing, to a broader movement of challenging a progressivist narrative that locates the emergence of self-reflexivity in the Early Modern period.[59]

---

[58] 'Consider the evolution of the Catholic pastoral and the sacrament of penance after the Council of Trent. Little by little, the nakedness of the questions formulated by the confession manuals of the Middle Ages, and a good number of those still in use in the seventeenth century, was veiled.' *The History of Sexuality*, trans. by Robert Hurley, 3 vols (New York: Vintage, 1990), I, 18–19, 70.

[59] For critiques of the tendency to locate the emergence of self-knowledge in the Early Modern period see, for example, Caroline Walker Bynum, 'Did the Twelfth Century Discover the Individual?' *The Journal of Ecclesiastical History*, 31 (1980), 1–17, and David Aers, 'A Whisper in the Ear of the Early Modernists; or, Reflections on Literary Critics Writing the "History of the Subject" ', in *Culture and History, 1350–1600: Essays on English Communities, Identities, and Writing*, ed. by David Aers (Detroit: Wayne State University Press, 1992), pp. 177–202.

The Wounded Beloved: Affective Wounding in *Ancrene Wisse* and the *Wooing Group*

A. S. Lazikani[1]

In her *Seven Manieren van Minne* (*There are Seven Manners of Loving*), the Flemish nun and prioress Beatrice of Nazareth (1200–68) describes the protracted violence that love inflicts on the heart:

> at times love becomes so boundless and so overflowing in the soul, when it itself is so mightily and violently moved in the heart, that it seems to the soul that the heart is wounded again and again, and that these wounds increase every day in bitter pain and in fresh intensity.[2]

This 'fifth manner of loving' is likened to a process of continual wounding. Affective wounds also mark six English texts composed during Beatrice's lifetime: the anchoritic guide *Ancrene Wisse*, and a related group of lyrical meditations known as the *Wooing Group*.[3] Whilst the guide and meditations should not be treated uncritically as a cohesive unit, they may be viably connected in a study on wound imagery. For the female readers of these texts, wound-images are at once signifiers, thresholds, weapons, bodily 'effluvia', protective alcoves, and points of intersection.[4] The images form the borderline between penetration and sensation— between weapon and agony—yet also correspond with the weapon itself.[5] A reader thinks upon images of wounds, inflicts imagined wounds on herself in sin and in penitence, and glimpses the potential for *Brautmystik* ('bridal mysticism') as she enters imaginatively into wounds. The first section of this article provides a framework rooted in the theory of conceptual metaphor and the anchoritic readership of the texts, while the second section offers an overview of wound devotion during this period. The third, fourth, and fifth sections will examine the wounds of Christ, the wounds of love, and the wounds of sin respectively.

---

[1] I would like to thank Dr Annie Sutherland and the anonymous reviewers of this article for their very valuable feedback.

[2] *Mediaeval Netherlands Religious Literature*, trans. by E. Colledge (New York: London House & Maxwell, 1965), p. 23.

[3] This article studies the following four *Wooing Group* texts, referring to each with an abbreviated title: *Ureisun of God, Lofsong of ure Lefdi, Lofsong of ure Louerde*, and *Wohunge*.

[4] The description of wounds as bodily 'effluvia' is Karma Lochrie's. See her *Margery Kempe and Translations of the Flesh* (Philadelphia: University of Pennsylvania Press, 1991), p. 40.

[5] See Elaine Scarry's comment on torture: 'what atrocities one's own body, muscle and bone structure can inflict

I. Conceptual Metaphors for the Female Recluse

Burgeoning scholarship on wounds has demonstrated their status as 'potent signifiers' in medieval European cultures.[6] Research into Christ's wounds, in particular, has foregrounded their role in 'devotional literacy'; two articles in the sole collection of essays on the *Wooing Group* have also highlighted the importance of devotion to Christ's blood in the texts' sensorial and purifying strategies.[7] Situated in this scholarship, the present article argues that the female reader's engagement with wound imagery is a fundamental aspect of her 'affective literacies', to use Mark Amsler's term: her constellation of emotional, somatic, and behavioural responses to texts.[8] It addresses this component of her affective literacies in *Ancrene Wisse* and the *Wooing Group* in much more detail than has yet been attempted, and thus seeks to contribute to nuanced knowledge of thirteenth-century reading practices. This study especially negotiates the ways in which flesh-based wounds act as 'conceptual metaphors' for affective pain. The conceptual theory of metaphor, pioneered by Mark Johnson and George Lakoff, affirms that metaphors are not inessential and deceptive ornamentations to meaning; rather, they are central to its formation. This is closely related to Paul Ricoeur's work.[9] Indeed, Sarah Covington aligns herself with the Ricoeurian notion of metaphor in her monograph on the imagery of wounds in the seventeenth century.[10] Writing on emotion, Zoltán Kövecses also explains how metaphors do not 'simply reflect a pre-existing, literal reality', but rather work to 'create or constitute our emotional reality'.[11] Medieval writers were not oblivious to the idea that metaphor can create affective meaning.[12] The work of Johnson, Lakoff, and Ricoeur would thus not have been unthinkable to the authors of *Ancrene Wisse* and the *Wooing Group*. For these authors and their readers, wounds act as conceptual metaphors for love, compassion, and remorse.

A clarification is needed on the readership of these texts. The *Wooing Group* comprises five English Passion meditations, now concretized in Catherine Innes-Parker's recent edition.

---

on oneself': *The Body in Pain: The Making and Unmaking of the World* (New York: Oxford University Press, 1985), p. 48.

[6] *Wounds in the Middle Ages*, ed. by Anne Kirkham and Cordelia Warr (Farnham: Ashgate, 2014), p. 1; and The Blood Project: Interdisciplinary and Collaborative Theories of Blood (http://www.thebloodproject.net).

[7] For wounds in 'devotional literacy', see Anne Kirkham and Cordelia Warr, 'Introduction: Wounds in the Middle Ages', in *Wounds in the Middle Ages*, ed. by Kirkham and Warr, pp. 1–14 (p. 3). For the articles on the *Wooing Group*, see Susannah Mary Chewning, 'Speaking of Flesh and Soul: Linguistic and Spiritual Translation in the *Wooing Group*', and Michelle Sauer, ' "Þe blod þ[at] bohte": The Wooing Group Christ as Pierced, Pricked and Penetrated Body', in *The Milieu and Context of the Wohunge Group*, ed. by Susannah Mary Chewning (Cardiff: University of Wales Press, 2009), pp. 48–65 and 123–47.

[8] See Mark Amsler, *Affective Literacies: Writing and Multilingualism in the Late Middle Ages* (Turnhout: Brepols, 2011), especially pp. 103, 113–16.

[9] For key works on the cognitive/conceptual theory of metaphor, see George Lakoff and Mark Johnson's classic *Metaphors We Live By* (Chicago: University of Chicago Press, 1980); Zoltán Kövecses, *Metaphor: A Practical Introduction* (New York: Oxford University Press, 2002); and Paul Ricoeur, *The Rule of Metaphor: The Creation of Meaning in Language*, trans. Robert Czerny with Kathleen McLaughlin and John Costello (London: Routledge, 2003).

[10] Sarah Covington, *Wounds, Flesh, and Metaphor in Seventeenth-Century England* (Basingstoke: Palgrave Macmillan, 2009), especially p. 5 and chapters four and five.

[11] See Zoltán Kövecses, *Metaphor and Emotion: Language, Culture, and Body in Human Feeling* (Cambridge: Cambridge University Press, 2000), p. 1.

[12] See *Medieval Literary Theory and Criticism c. 1100–1375: The Commentary Tradition*, ed. by A. J. Minnis and A. B. Scott, with the assistance of David Wallace, rev. edn (Oxford: Clarendon Press, 1988; repr. 1991), especially pp. 205–6 and 239–40.

All but one of the texts are found in the same manuscript (London, British Library, Cotton Nero A. xiv). These meditations are still under-studied, though scholarship in the past few years has begun to address this neglect. Their textual association with the anchoritic guide *Ancrene Wisse*, along with references within the texts that strongly allude to enclosure, suggest that the meditations are likely to have been read by anchoresses.[13] However, whilst the groundbreaking work by Caroline Walker Bynum, Amy Hollywood, and Karma Lochrie has shown that medieval female spirituality is powerfully and painfully embodied, it must be remembered that both *Ancrene Wisse* and the *Wooing Group* had a wide-ranging readership in their transmission history.[14] Despite the focus of this article, it must be remembered that wound devotion was not the terrain of female readers alone.

II. Wound Devotion in the Twelfth and Thirteenth Centuries

It is now a scholarly commonplace that by the early thirteenth century, Christ's body was imaged in both textual and visual cultures as being scarred and torn, bloodied and wounded.[15] From this Wounded Body emerged five wounds of special significance. This devotion to the Five Wounds — in the two feet, two hands, and side — did not originate in the thirteenth century. The five jewels adorning the Cross in *The Dream of the Rood*, for example, is only one instance of the wider use of the Wounds in Anglo-Saxon textual and visual imagery.[16] But devotion based on the Five Wounds did intensify in the twelfth and thirteenth centuries. Bernard of Clairvaux (†1153) was centrally involved in this process, and the devotion was also encouraged and propagated by Francis of Assisi's (1182–1226) stigmatization on Mount Alverna in September 1224.[17] The most cataclysmic and precious Wound became that inflicted on Christ's Heart due to the Side Wound. A distinct devotion to the Sacred Heart of Jesus evolved, entering the Benedictine, Cistercian, Carthusian, Franciscan, and Dominican orders.[18] Devotion to the Heart expanded in the thirteenth century, with the two Helfta nuns Gertrude the Great (†1301/2) and Mechthild of Hackeborn (†1298) being major players in the development of this devotion.[19] John Bainvel posits that it is in the writings of these two women, along with the *Vitis mystica* by Bonaventure (1221–74), that devotion to the

---

[13] For the recent edition, see *The Wooing of Our Lord and the Wooing Group Prayers*, ed. and trans. by Catherine Innes-Parker (Peterborough, Ontario: Broadview Press, 2015), For a recent overview of the readership of and scholarship on the *Wooing Group*, see pp. 17–23 and pp. 45–56 of Innes-Parker's edition; and A. S. Lazikani, *Cultivating the Heart: Feeling and Emotion in Twelfth- and Thirteenth-Century Religious Texts* (Cardiff: University of Wales Press, 2015), pp. 8–10.

[14] See especially Caroline Walker Bynum, *Fragmentation and Redemption: Essays on Gender and the Human Body in Medieval Religion* (New York: Zone Books, 1991); Amy Hollywood, *Sensible Ecstasy: Mysticism, Sexual Difference, and the Demands of History* (Chicago: University of Chicago Press, 2002); and Lochrie, *Margery Kempe and Translations of the Flesh*.

[15] See further chapter 2 of Ellen M. Ross, *The Grief of God: Images of the Suffering Jesus in Late Medieval England* (Oxford: Oxford University Press, 1997). For caution against combining wound and blood devotion carelessly, see Caroline Walker Bynum, *Wonderful Blood: Theology and Practice in Late Medieval Northern Germany and Beyond* (Philadelphia: University of Pennsylvania Press, 2007), p. 14.

[16] *The Vercelli Book*, ed. by G. P. Krapp, Anglo-Saxon Poetic Records, 2 (London: Routledge, 1932), 61: 7–9. See further Barbara Raw, *Anglo-Saxon Crucifixion Iconography and the Art of the Monastic Revival* (Cambridge: Cambridge University Press, 1990), for example plates ii, ivb, vb, viii, ix, xi, and xiv.

[17] See *New Catholic Encyclopedia*, ed. by Berard L. Marthaler and others, 2nd edn, 15 vols (Detroit: Thomson/Gale, 2003), XIV 860, cols 1–2; and Gougaud, *Dévotions et pratiques*, pp. 79–80.

[18] *New Catholic Encyclopedia*, XII 499.

[19] Bynum, *Wonderful Blood*, p. 14.

Heart 'seems to acquire substance'.[20] Written during this period of intensifying devotion to Christ's wounds and the Wounded Heart, *Ancrene Wisse* and the related *Wooing Group* show unmistakable marks of influence from this climate, as I will now discuss.

III. Christ's Physical-Affective Wounds

Christ's wounded body pervades the English anchoritic texts, including the anchoress' prayer-routine. Early in Part I of *Ancrene Wisse*, the anchoress is told: 'falleð o cneon to ower crucifix wið þeos fif gretunges ine munegunge of Godes fif wunden: *Adoramus te, Christe, et benedicimus tibi quia per sanctam Crucem redemisti mundum*' ('fall on your knees to your crucifix with these five greetings in memory of God's five wounds: We adore you, Christ, and bless you because through the sanctified Cross you redeemed the world').[21] A simplified version is also provided: '[h]wa-se ne con þeose fiue segge þe earste, *Adoramus te* [We adore you], cneolinde fif siðen' ('whoever does not know these five, say the first, *We adore you*, kneeling, five times'; 8: 56–57).[22] It is also likely that Christ's wounded body was visually prominent for the anchoress, with the author adjuring his anchoritic reader to kiss the 'wundestuden' (wound-places) on the crucifix in her anchorhold (54: 250–52).

Crucially, however, Christ's wounding on the Cross is portrayed in *Ancrene Wisse* and the *Wooing Group* as both physical and affective in nature, a fact recently observed by Elizabeth Robertson in her work on 'touch'. In Part II of *Ancrene Wisse*, Christ is wounded not only in his flesh, but also in his 'seli sawle' (innocent soul) through three 'spears of sorrow'. Sorrow is likened to a process of wounding.[23] After revealing Christ's sorrow-wounded soul, the text portrays Christ weeping through his entire body, basing its account closely on Bernard's third sermon *In Ramis Palmarum*:[24]

> ant her seið Sein Beornard þet he ne weop nawt ane wið ehnen, ah dude as wið alle his limen. *Quasi, inquit, membris omnibus fleuisse uidetur.* For se ful of ango[i]sse wes þet ilke ned-swat þet lihte of his licome, agein the angoisuse deað þet he schulde þolien, þet hit þuhte read blod. [...] On oðer half, swa largeliche ant swa swiðe fleaw þet ilke blodi swat of his blisfule bodi, þet te streames urnen dun to þer eorðe. (45: 971-978)
>
> And here Saint Bernard says that he does not weep only with his eyes, but, as it were, with all his limbs. *It seems as though, he says, he wept with all limbs.* For so full of anguish was

---

[20] John Bainvel, *Devotion to the Sacred Heart of Jesus: The Doctrine and its History*, trans. by E. Leahy (London: Burns Oates and Washbourne, 1924), p. 134. For a detailed assessment of the religious of Helfta, see Mary Jeremy Finnegan, *The Women of Helfta: Scholars and Mystics* (Athens, GA: University of Georgia Press, 1991), especially chapter 9.

[21] *Ancrene Wisse: A Corrected Edition of the Text in Cambridge, Corpus Christi College, MS 402 with Variants from Other Manuscripts*, ed. by Bella Millett, Early English Text Society, o. s. 325–26, 2 vols (Oxford: Oxford University Press, 2005–6), pp. 7–8 (ll. 34–55); all subsequent references (to page and line numbers respectively) are to this edition.

[22] Quoting E. J. Dobson, Millett clarifies the liturgical context of these salutations (*Ancrene Wisse*, ed. by Millett, II 18: 1/37–40). For the liturgical context see also *Ancrene Riwle: Introduction and Part I*, ed. and trans. by Robert W. Ackerman and Roger Dahood (Binghamton, NY: Medieval & Renaissance Texts & Studies, 1984), p. 93, n. 13ff.).

[23] For detailed examination of this passage, see further Elizabeth Robertson, '*Noli me Tangere*: The Enigma of Touch in Middle English Religious Literature and Art for and About Women', in *Reading Skin in Medieval Literature and Culture*, ed. by Katie L. Walter (New York: Palgrave Macmillan, 2013), pp. 29–55; see also Lazikani, *Cultivating the Heart*, pp. 17–18.

[24] See *Sancti Bernardi Opera*, ed. by J. Leclercq, C. H. Talbot and H. M. Rochais, 8 vols (Rome: Editiones

that same sweat of distress that descended from his body, about the anguished death that he should suffer, that it seemed red blood. [...] Moreover, so abundantly and so intensely flowed that same bloody sweat from his blissful body, that the streams ran down to the earth.

Sweat, blood, and tears converge.[25] As Christ releases moisture from all the orifices of his body, his porous physicality is aligned with his affective vulnerability. Such an image is a perfect recreation of Christ's sacrifice, since his blood and his shame both give succour to humanity—the Church itself born from his Wounded Side.[26] In his commentary on St John's Gospel, Augustine (354–430) affirms:

> dormit Adam, ut fiat Eva: moritur Christus ut fiat Ecclesia. Dormiente Adam, fit Eva de latere: mortuo Christo, lancea perforatur latus, ut profluant Sacramenta, quibus formetur Ecclesia.[27]

> Adam sleeps so that Eve may exist; Christ dies so that the Church may exist. Eve is born from the side of the sleeping Adam; the side of the dead Christ is pierced so that the sacraments may flow forth, from which the Church is formed.

In the same vein, a passage in the *Wooing Group* text *Lofsong of ure Lefdi* deconstructs the chronology of the Passion to form an array of multivalent images. The 'hokerunge' ('mocking') and the 'scornunge' ('scorning'), repeated twice, develop into more direct indications of affective pain: 'bi hi schome' ('by his shame'), 'bi his sor' ('by his sorrow/pain').[28] These affective stirrings are interspersed among the references to Christ's bodily wounds. In the anchoress' reading, Christ's affective pain thus becomes merged with and indistinguishable from his wounded anatomy (pp. 17–18, ll. 40–67).[29]

In *Ancrene Wisse* and the *Wooing Group*, Christ's physical-affective wounds are not sites of a painless attack, as Hilary of Poitiers (c. 315–67) attempted to suggest in his *De Trinitate*.[30] Christ's passible nature is unquestionable for the anchoritic authors. As seen in the passage quoted above, his sorrow-wounded soul feels 'pine', and he suffers a pang ('stiche' (45: 958–62)). In Part IV, the *Ancrene Wisse*-author explores the depth and breadth of Christ's physical wounds:

> ant he, o Munt Caluaire, steah ȝet o rode herre, ne ne swong neauer mon se swiðe ne se sare as he dude þet ilke dei þet he bledde o fif half brokes of ful brade wunden ant deope, wiðuten þe eþren capitale þe bledden on his heaued under þe kene þornene crune, ant wiðuten þe ilke reowfule garces of þe luðere scurgunge ȝont al his leofliche lich, nawt ane o þe schonken. (98: 1147–53)

Cistercienses, 1957–77), v 54–55; all subsequent references are to this edition.

[25] On the interchangeability of bodily fluids in medieval medical thought, see Elizabeth Robertson, 'Medieval Medical Views of Women and Female Spirituality in the *Ancrene Wisse* and Julian of Norwich's *Showings*', in *Feminist Approaches to the Body in Medieval Literature*, ed. by Linda Lomperis and Sarah Stanbury (Philadelphia: University of Pennsylvania Press, 1993), pp. 142–67 (p. 150).

[26] See Louis Gougaud, *Dévotions et pratiques ascétiques du moyen âge* (Paris: Desclée de Brouwer, 1925), p. 93; and Bynum, *Fragmentation and Redemption*, pp. 92–101.

[27] *PL* XLV, 1888. See further Raw, *Anglo-Saxon Crucifixion Iconography*, p. 119, and n. 53.

[28] *Þe Wohunge of ure Lauerd*, ed. by W. Meredith Thompson, Early English Text Society, o. s. 241 (London: Oxford University Press, 1958), p. 17, ll. 49, 50, 52, and p. 18, l. 65; all subsequent references to *Wooing Group* texts are to this edition. Abbreviations (with the exception of the *Tironian nota*) are expanded, word-spacing is modernized, and *p* is rendered *w*.

[29] See also *Lofsong of ure Louerde* (pp. 10–11, ll. 1–30).

[30] See further Kevin Madigan, *The Passions of Christ in High-Medieval Thought: An Essay on Christological*

And he, on Mount Calvary, ascended on the Cross even higher; no man toiled so fully nor so painfully as he did that same day that he bled on five sides, brooks of wounds so broad and deep — not to mention the head veins which bled on his head under the sharp crown of thorns, and not to mention the same pitiful gashes from the wicked scourging all over his lovely body, not only on the legs.

Apart from his wounds being 'brade' and 'deope', Christ toils 'sare'; the thorn-crown is 'kene', and the gashes of the scourging are 'reowfule'. In the images of the Passion in *Lofsong of ure Lefdi*, Christ's wounds are modified with the adjective 'sore' (p. 17, ll. 54–55, p. 18, ll. 60–61). And in *Lofsong of ure Louerde*, the speaker explicitly mentions Christ's pains and shames after mentioning the five wounds in her incantatory list of Passion moments: 'þurh þine vif wunden. ⁊ þe eadie flod þet of ham fledde. þuruh ðe irene neiles ⁊ þe þornene crune. ⁊ þuruh þe pinen ⁊ þe schomen' ('through your five wounds, and the blessed flood that flowed from them, through the iron nails and the crown of thorns, and through your pains and your shames', p. 10, ll. 9–12).

Wohunge, in particular, focuses on the pain of Christ's wounding. The meditator is brought close to the nailed hands and feet on the Cross, and Christ's agony is made plain (p. 23, ll. 137–38; p. 34, ll. 511–14). He does not utter a word in self-defence, declares the speaker in an invocation of Isaiah 53:7, despite his *'pinfule* wundes' (p. 25, ll. 199-205, emphasis added). The wounds are 'pinfule' and Christ experiences 'wa'; affective and physical pain are once again interlinked with 'schome' and 'pinfule wundes' juxtaposed. There is an outflow of blood when the scourging is enacted, and the meditator watches the blood issuing from Christ's nails as they are bound fast, invoking the testimony of saints to ratify the image: 'ha þe bunden swa hetelifaste þat te blod wrang ut at tine fingerneiles as halhes bileuen' ('they bound you so fiercely [or, scornfully] tight that the blood wrung out from your fingernails, as saints believe', pp. 32–33, ll. 467–82).[31] Later, the anchoress perceives Longinus cleaving Christ's side; like the *Ancrene Wisse*-author's concentration on the breadth and depth of Christ's wounds, here the centurion creates a '*wide* wunde' (p. 34, ll. 541–43, emphasis added). Though immersed in the pain of the Wounds, the meditator of *Wohunge* cannot forget its cause. The wounding process reveals the means by which the healing balm of Christ's blood is gained: 'cumes flowinde ut of þat wide wunde. þe blod þat bohte. þe water þat te world wesch of sake ⁊ of sunne' ('comes flowing out of that wide wound the blood that bought, the water that washed the world of sickness and of sin', p. 34, ll. 543–46).

On Calvary, Christ is not alone in his vulnerability to painful wounds. Those who observe him, though physically whole, are susceptible to violent affective wounding. The greatest sufferer of affective wounding is the Holy Mother herself. Her affective wounding is made explicit in *Wohunge*, where her 'moderliche herte' suffers a wound in conjunction with her Son's, a powerful recollection of Simeon's Sword of Sorrows (Luke 2:35): 'lauedi moder ⁊ meiden þu stod here ful neh ⁊ seh al þis sorhe vpo þi deorewurðe sune. was wiðinne martird i þi moderliche herte. þat seh to cleue his heorte wið þe speres ord' ('lady, mother and maiden, you stood here so near and saw all this sorrow upon your precious son. You were martyred within, in your motherly heart, which saw His heart cleaved with spear's point'; p. 35, ll. 554–59). Sorrow ('sorhe') is upon Christ, yet the Virgin is wounded within. Sorrow becomes externalised, visible on Christ's skin, whilst the wounding takes place far below the skin,

---

Development (Oxford: Oxford University Press, 2007), particularly chapters 5 and 6.
[31] See also *Lofsong of ure Lefdi*, p. 18, ll. 61–64.

within the recesses of the Mother's heart. This direct transferral of wounding, Christ's flesh-wound to Mary's wounded heart, is demonstrated perfectly in an image on fol. 53 of Glasgow University Library, MS Hunter 231 (U. 3. 4), later in date than *Wohunge* c. 1325×35).[32] It is a decorated initial beginning a tract on Mary's compassion ascribed to Bernard (though likely to be pseudo-Bernard), and comes opposite a page of anonymous hymns on Mary's sorrows. In this image, a sword protrudes from Christ's Side Wound, piercing Mary's chest at the place of her heart. Mary's sorrow is conveyed through her hand gestures: one hand clutches at the place where the Sword struck, the other is opened up by her side, with her arm dangling in a gesture of agony. The connection between Christ's and Mary's wounds in *Wohunge* also features in an anonymous thirteenth-century English lyric. Dated to the second half of the thirteenth century by Carleton Brown, the lyric is given the editorial title 'A Light is Come to the World'. It is found in Trinity College, Cambridge, MS 323, fols 32b–33a, a trilingual 'miscellany' in Carleton Brown's terms.[33] Mary's heart bleeds as she is forced to see the wounding of her Son: 'Hire herte bi-gon to bleden, | Teres hoe wep of blod' ('her heart began to bleed, | tears she wept of blood', p. 36, ll. 81–90). Her heart is so severely wounded that she cries tears of blood, much like Bernard's and the *Ancrene Wisse*-author's Christ, whose body weeps all moistures. In this image, the boundary separating physical and affective wounding is blurred. Tears are one somatic response to affective suffering, and blood is the sign of physical trauma. But in the realm of Mary's pain, the two coalesce.

The anchoress' own affective wounding is less explicit. No meditator can experience the Mother's Sword of Sorrows; this affective wound is preserved for Her alone. In his *Liber confortatorius*, Goscelin of Saint-Bertin (c. 1035–1107) affirms the uniqueness of the Mother's experience as the Sword pierces her, merging the voices of Psalm 142:4, Jeremiah 23:9, Lamentations 2:11, and Lamentations 1:12 into one anguished statement by Mary of her unparalleled sorrow. Aelred of Rievaulx (1110–167), in his anchoritic guidance text *De institutione inclusarum*, suggests only that the anchoress should weep in response to the Lady's Sword.[34] The uniqueness of Mary's Sword does not entirely deter the meditator in Anselm of Canterbury's (1033–1109) 'Oratio ad Christum'. The meditator's agonized spectatorship of Christ's piercing is referred to as an affective wounding: 'cur, o anima mea, te praesentem non transfixit gladius doloris acutissimi, cum ferre non posses vulnerari lancea latus tui salvatoris?' ('why, oh my soul, were you not present to be pierced by a sword of most acute sorrow, when you could not endure to see the piercing of the side of your saviour with a lance?').[35] But even here, the meditator only imagines her own sword of sorrow, lamenting that she has not yet been wounded by it. Instead, the meditator engages in a two-layered spectatorship, witnessing Christ's slaughter from Mary's anguished viewpoint (8). Despite the uncomfortably voyeuristic appraisal of Mary's face, the Anselmian meditator does attempt to capture the

---

[32] This is a deluxe compendium of devotional and philosophical writings. Its contents include works by Augustine, Anselm, and Hugh of Saint-Victor, as well as work by Seneca and Aristotle. For a reproduction of the image, see Ross, *The Grief of God*, p. 52; dating follows that given in Ross' footnotes (p. 149, n. 50).

[33] See further *English Lyrics of the Thirteenth Century*, ed. by Carleton Brown (Oxford: Clarendon Press, 1932), p. xx. References are to this edition.

[34] Goscelin of Saint-Bertin, 'The *Liber confortatorius* of Goscelin of Saint Bertin', ed. by C. H. Talbot, *Studia Anselmiana*, 37 (1955), 1–117 (31); and Aelred of Rievaulx, *De institutione inclusarum*, in *Aelredi Rievallensis Opera Omnia: 1 Opera Ascetica*, ed. by A. Hoste and C. H. Talbot, Corpus Christianorum Continuatio Mediaevalis, 1 (Turnhout: Brepols, 1971), 671. All subsequent references are to these editions.

[35] Anselm of Canterbury, *Orationes sive meditationes*, in *S. Anselmi Cantuariensis Archiepiscopi Opera Omnia*, ed. by F. S. Schmitt, 6 vols (Stuttgart: Frommann, 1968), III 7; all subsequent references are to this edition.

mother's response to the Passion — and in so doing, to come closer to her affective wound. The anchoress also imagines her own affective wounding by adopting Mary's perspective in the *Wooing Group*. In an indication that the anchoress is progressing closer to the Holy Mother's Sword of Sorrows, the meditator of *Ureisun of God* observes the nails being driven into Christ from his mother's viewpoint: 'þi sune was ituht on rode. þurh driuen fet 7 honden. wið dulte neiles. blodi his side' ('your son was tied on the Cross, blunt nails driven through [his] feet and hands, bloody his side'; p. 9, ll. 152–53). In *Wohunge*, as the anchoress watches Christ's torture, her heart breaks and water flows from her eyes: 'nu min herte mai to breke. min ehne flowen al o water' ('now my heart may break; my eyes overflow with water'; p. 33, ll. 489–91). Within the pervasive imagery of the broken and torn Christ, the anchoress' affective response is depicted as a form of wounding. Her heart breaks, causing, instead of the flow of blood, a flood of water from her eyes. Christ's painful physical-affective wounds inspire the anchoress' own affective wounding; in the anchoress's reading, flesh-wounds act as potent conceptual metaphors for compassion and sorrow. Wounds are fundamental to the anchoress' amorous bond with the Spousal Lamb, a significance to which I now turn.

IV. Love-Wounds

Like (if also unlike) the Holy Mother who endures the Sword of Sorrows, the anchoress is susceptible to affective wounding in her imaginative participation at Calvary. Both women are affectively wounded through love. *Ancrene Wisse* in Part VII cites as an example of immense love the human mother who is willing to offer a salvific 'beað of blod' (bath of blood) to save her dying child, as Christ did (149: 156). The Mother-Christ's blood is shed from Love and carries the potential for life; hewn from Love, Christ's wounds are imbued with Love's potency. Throughout *Ancrene Wisse* and the *Wooing Group*, the pain suffered by Christ and the anchoress through his wounds is bound with love, delectable and nurturing. In emphasizing the 'transformative potential' of love across a range of religions, Nancy M. Martin and Joseph Runzo have stressed its anguish and violence, as witnessed in the opening of this article with Beatrice of Nazareth's writings:

> love at times bewilders and overwhelms the soul, overtaking it in an experience of piercing pain or burning conflagration. St. Teresa of Avila speaks of such love piercing her like 'an arrow... driven into the very depths of the entrails, and sometimes into the heart'.[36]

For the anchoress, love and pain cannot be disentangled: love is painful, and the way to love is pain. However, whilst Teresa of Avila (1515–82) may have been pierced by the arrow of Love, our anchoresses are not. Although *Lofsong of ure Louerde* does cite the Song of Songs (2:6/8:3), and both *Ureisun of God* and *Wohunge* are infused with the Canticles' imagery of sweetness, Song of Songs 4:9 ('thou hast wounded my heart, my sister, my spouse, thou hast wounded my heart') is never directly quoted as a description of the anchoress' affective response in *Ancrene Wisse* or the *Wooing Group*. Though love and pain are melded for the anchoress within Christ's wounds, this *sponsa Christi* love-wound is not applied to her.

The precise meaning of being 'wounded in Love' warrants further attention. Gertrude the Great has an entire chapter entitled 'De Vulnere Amoris' (On the Wound of Love, Book

---

[36] Nancy M. Martin and Joseph Runzo, 'Love', in *The Oxford Handbook of Religion and Emotion*, ed. by John Corrigan (Oxford: Oxford University Press, 2008), pp. 310–32 (p. 319). The term 'transformative potential' is Martin and Runzo's (p. 318).

II, Chapter 5). In a painting of the crucified Christ in a book ('depicti in folio'), Gertrude perceives a ray of sunlight with a sharp point like an arrow ('in modum sagittae acuatus') spread out and then draw back. Christ appears unexpectedly ('ex improviso'), implanting a wound in her heart and bidding it to be stabilized in his love ('infigens', 'stabiliantur in amore meo').[37] For Gertrude, the Wound of Love is thus a higher step in her evolving relationship with Christ. After receiving the Love-Wound, Gertrude's Love for Christ reaches a greater level of confidence and maturity. Through the Wound, she ensures that all the stirrings of her heart are organized and secured in Christ's love. Goscelin also envisages love-wounding at the core Eva's anchoritic existence: 'plora coram Domino, utque unam tantum petitionem peteres a domino id est, ut solum Christum uulnerata caritate concupisceres, ipsumque solum in directione cordis et in tota anima tua in dotem expeteres' (' "weep before the Lord." That is, only one thing you should desire as petition to the Lord, which is that you may desire Christ alone in wounded love, and him alone you may with the full concentration of your heart and your whole soul wish for as your dowry'; 28). Like Gertrude, Goscelin understands wounded love as an confident, mature, unfaltering love for Christ, and an impetus for spiritual development. He recognises Eva's sensitivity to affective response: her heart is ready to feel such soreness of wounded love ('caritatis uulnerata'), as he does. Her heart, full of the Lord's arrows ('plenum sagittis Domini pectus'), is characterized by raw sensitivity (41). Aelred, on the other hand, never cites Canticles 4:9 or refers to being 'wounded' in love in his anchoritic guidance text.

Like Aelred, the *Ancrene Wisse* and *Wooing Group*-authors never refer to Love-Wounds; yet the love is no less sophisticated than that explained by Gertrude and Goscelin. In a passage based on Deuteronomy 11:24 in Part VII of *Ancrene Wisse*, love has the power to subsume every entity into itself:

> luue haueð a meistrie biuoren alle oþre, for al þet ha rineð, al ha turneð to hire ant makeð al hire ahne. *Quemcumque locum calcauerit pes uester—pes videlicet amoris—uester erit.* Stretche þi luue to Iesu Crist, þu hauest him iwunnen. Rin him wið ase muche luue as þu hauest sum mon sumchearre, he is þin to don wið al þet tu wilnest. (153: 325-335)

> Love has a mastery above all others, for all that it touches, it turns it all to her and makes it all her own. *Whichever place your foot treads on — that is to say, the foot of love — will be yours.* [...] Reach [out] your love to Jesus Christ, and you have won him. Touch him with as much love as you had one time for some man, and he is yours to do with all that you want.

Focused on this all-powerful love, Part VII reveals the many actions of love within the heart. Love 'schireð' ('shines') and 'brihteð' ('brightens') the heart; the anchoress can 'tilie' ('cultivate') love in her heart; love bestows the heart with 'briht sihðe' ('bright sight'; 145: 3, 14–15, 20); the anchoress can 'ontenden' ('kindle') love within her heart, repeated in an extensive passage which likens God's Love to Greek Fire (151: 232, 249ff); and despite all this tumult, love can even make the heart 'griðful' and 'cleane' ('peaceful and clean'; 153: 325). The anchoress' love can do all this — and yet, it is never said to wound.

Perhaps Love-Wounds are too closely aligned for these early Middle English writers with visionary experience, of which the *Ancrene Wisse*-author is deeply suspicious (IV, 86: 660–61). A reference to being 'wounded in Love' seems out of place in the consciously tempered

---

[37] Gertrude the Great, *Œuvres spirituelles*, ed. by Pierre Doyère, 5 vols (Paris: Les Éditions du Cerf, 1967–86), II

devotion they seek to cultivate in the anchoress. She is, nevertheless, encouraged to seek out Christ's own wounds. In her affective engagement with Christ's wounds, the anchoress propels herself imaginatively towards them. She enters into these areas of love, and once inside or nearly inside, nurtures her own powerful affection for her Spouse. After the *Ancrene Wisse* galvanises the anchoress to banish the flea-bitten 'helle-dogge' (hell-dog) in Part IV, Christ's wounds are invoked as protective alcoves in which she can hide (110: 1614). The author encourages the anchoress to fly to the wounds as she continues her offensive against that 'dogge-deouel' (dog-devil): 'nempne ofte Iesu; cleope his passiunes help; halse bi his pine, bi his deorewurðe blod, bi his deað o rode; flih to his wunden' ('call often to Jesus; cry out for his passion's help; beseech by his pain, by his precious blood, by his death on the Cross; fly to his wounds'; 111: 1627–29). Christ's broken body is imaged as a sanctuary from a harsh environment. It is cultivated with wounds born from love: 'muchel he luuede us þe lette makien swucche þurles in him forte huden us in. Creop in ham wið þi þoht — ne beoð ha al opene? — ant wið his deorewurðe blod biblod[g]e þin heorte' ('greatly he loved us, he who let such holes be made in him, in which to hide us. Creep in them with your thought — are they not all open? — and with his precious blood bloody your heart'; 111: 1629–31). With her 'thought' harnessed as she enters these spaces, the anchoress 'bloodies' herself with Christ's blood. Although it has been translated as 'drench', the verb 'biblodge' can more literally be translated as 'bloody'.[38] Placed directly after the 'blod' of Christ, this verb appears to explicitly merge the anchoress with Christ in the arena of his Wounds; she becomes bloodied by her blood-immersed Lover.[39]

This image of Christ's Wounds — especially his Wounded Side — as indestructible refuges 'al opene' for the anchoress finds its source in Canticles 2:14: 'my dove in the clefts of the rock, in the hollow places of the wall'. *Ancrene Wisse* employs this well-known image in the post-Bernardine sense of Christ's Wound, in lieu of Origen's general 'rock of Christ'.[40] In his sixty-first sermon of the *Sermones super Cantica Canticorum*, Bernard describes the protection and nurturance of Christ's Wounds, invoking Psalm 83:4: 'in his passer invenit sibi domum, et turtur nidum ubi reponat pullos suos; in his se columba tutatur, et circumvolitantem intrepida intuetur accipitrem' ('within them the sparrow finds a home, and the turtle-dove a nest where she may rest her chicks; in them the dove is protected, and fearlessly observes the circling hawk'; II, 149). Canticles 2:14 is also appropriated to this effect by Aelred (671). Isaiah 2:10 is used in *Ancrene Wisse* to illustrate the protection offered by Christ's wounded body, immediately following the 'bloodying' of the anchoress' heart: ' "*Ingredere in petram, abscondere fossa humo.*" "Ga into þe stan", seið þe prophete, "ant hud te i þe doluen eorðe", þet is, i þe wunden of ure Lauerdes flesch' (' "*Enter in the rock, hide in the buried trench.*" "Go into the rock", says the prophet, "and hide yourself in the dug up earth", that is, in the wounds of our Lord's flesh'; 111: 1631–34).[41]

250.

[38] *Guide for Anchoresses: A Translation Based on Cambridge, Corpus Christi College, MS 402*, trans. by Bella Millett (Exeter: Exeter University Press, 2009), p. 111.

[39] Instances cited in the *MED* of the verb 'biblodge' are all from the *Ancrene Wisse* Group [accessed 14 October 2011].

[40] See E. Ann Matter, *The Voice of My Beloved: The Song of Songs in Western Medieval Christianity* (Philadelphia: University of Pennsylvania Press, 1990), p. 137.

[41] As Millett notes, Isaiah 2:10 and Psalm 21:17 are also connected in Bernard's sixty-second sermon of his *Sermones super Cantica Canticorum* in the context of Christ's wounds. See *Ancrene Wisse*, ed. by Millett, II 197/4 1631–32. For the source-text, see *Bernardi Opera*, II, 159.

From the basis of Psalm 21:17, the author delineates the spatial dimensions of the Wounds. Through this Psalm, he emphasizes two key aspects of the wounds: their nature as habitable spaces, and the agony that Christ suffers in them. The painful process of wounding is made worse through the verb *duluen*:

> *foderunt manus meas et pedes meos*, þet is, 'Ha duluen me baðe þe vet ant te honden.' Ne seide he nawt 'þurleden'; for efter þis leattre, as ure meistres seggeð, swa weren þe neiles dulle þet ha duluen his flesch ant tobreken þe ban mare þen þurleden, to pinin him sarre. (111: 1635–39).[42]

> *They dug my hands and my feet*. That is, 'They dug holes in me, both the feet and the hands'. He did not say 'pierced', for according to the letter [i.e., literally], as our masters say, the nails were so dull that they dug into his flesh and broke the bones more than 'pierced', to pain him more sorely.

Based on both Isaiah 2:10 and Psalm 21:17, Christ's agony and the anchoress' protection within these wounds become inextricably joined. He suffers greater pain — with the holes 'duluen' (dug) rather than 'þurleden' (pierced) in his body — for the anchoress' sake. The *Ancrene Wisse*-author quotes and translates Canticles 2:14, informing the anchoress that Christ 'calls' her to these wounds, in an apparent invocation of Canticles 1:3: 'he him seolf cleopeð þe toward teose wunden. "*Columba mea, in foraminibus petre, in cauernis macerie*": "mi culure", he seið, "cum hud te i mine limen þurles, i þe hole of mi side" ' ('he himself calls you towards these wounds. "*My dove, in the cleft of the rock, in the hollows of the wall*". "My dove", he says, "come hide yourself in the holes of my limbs, in the opening of my side" '; 111: 1639–42). The love contained in these speaking sites of pain is clear: 'muche luue he cudde to his leoue culure, þet he swuch hudles makede' ('much love he makes known to his dear dove, that he made such refuges'; 111: 1642–43). Like Bernard's sparrow and turtle dove, the dove-anchoress envelopes herself in the protective and love-generated space of the Wounds, alcoves in which she can enable her evolving intimacy with Christ. In Thomas of Cantimpré's *Vita* of the Benedictine/Cistercian Lutgarde of Aywières (c. 1182–1246), the holy woman hears Christ's wounds calling to her and draws near to drink in their sweetness.[43] Unlike Lutgarde, the anchoress reading *Ancrene Wisse* and the *Wooing Group* does not drink from the Wound. But given that she is implored to 'biblod[g]e' her heart with Christ's blood, she receives the moisture's nurturance by other means (111: 1631).

The Side Wound as a gateway to Christ's Heart — that richest of spiritual arenas — is seen in *Wohunge* with Longinus' violence: 'he þurles his side cleues tat herte' ('he pierces his side, cleaves that heart'; pp. 34–35, ll. 542–43).[44] In the vocabulary of Christ's wounded body in *Ancrene Wisse* and the *Wooing Group*, his agony and his self-disclosure become inseparable, a coupling evident in texts throughout the Middle Ages.[45] The Side Wound formed by Longinus' spear is linked immediately with the accessibility of the heart it cleaves (p. 34, ll. 543–44). The Wounded Heart enables the anchoress' entrance, and we witness a spectacular gesture towards *Brautmystik*: 'A swete iesu þu oppnes me þin herte for to cnawe witerliche ⁊ in to

---

[42] On the parallel with a Lombardian gloss, see *Ancrene Wisse*, ed. by Millett, II 197: 4/1636–39, drawing on E. J. Dobson.

[43] *AASS*, III June 16, 239E, 244F.

[44] Caution is needed when applying the label of 'mysticism' to this passage: cf. Gougaud, *Dévotions et pratiques*, p. 106.

[45] See further Gougaud, *Dévotions et pratiques*, p. 95.

redden trewe luue lettres. for þer i mai openlich seo hu muchel þu me luuedes' ('Ah sweet Jesus, you open (for) me your heart to know truly, and to read in it true love letters. For there I may openly see how much you love me'; p. 35, ll. 546–51). It has been suggested that this image in *Wohunge* is inspired by the romance motif of epistles shared between lovers.[46] Given the centrality to *Wohunge* of the romance motif of Christ as wooer, romance texts are most probably the ultimate source. However, it is not certain that the *Wohunge*-author is dependent on romance traditions directly; he may be using an image found in the common source he shares with Parisian sermons.[47] Christ's 'herte' in *Wohunge* becomes a space that nurtures sophisticated reading skills, invoking the unique spatial world of the anchorhold. The anchoress' home is recast as a space in which she can read — and reach — Christ's love.[48]

This moment in *Wohunge* is famously paralleled in Part VII of *Ancrene Wisse*: 'his leofmon bihalde þron hu he bohte hire luue: lette þurlin his scheld, openin his side, to schawin hire his heorte, to schawin hire openliche hu inwardliche he luuede hire' ('his lover beholds there how he bought her love: [he] lets his shield be pierced, opens his side, to show her his heart, to show her openly how inwardly he loved her'; 148: 125–27). In both images of the Wounded Heart, love and woundedness become intertwined: the point of Christ's most extreme wounding is also the site where the most profound mysteries of his Love can be sought. Both these images engage with the tradition in which the 'wound of Christ caused by the lance of Longinus was interpreted as the gateway to his heart and as a precondition for the union with God'.[49] The emphasis in the anchoritic texts is not on mystical union, but on affective entrance into Christ's body.[50] There is no *annihilatio*: the anchoress is still present with her love, bound with pain, inside this space. Both texts refer to Christ's love being shown 'openlich' — an adverb with a range of possible meanings. In both cases it could mean 'unobstructedly', which is supported in *Wohunge* with the use of the adverb 'witerliche'. The sense of 'visibly' is also possible, as in *Wohunge* it is coupled with the act of seeing ('seo'), and in *Ancrene Wisse* with the act of showing ('shawin'). Yet there is also the possible sense of 'publicly' in both cases, in *Ancrene Wisse* juxtaposed with the adverb 'inwardliche'. With this sense, Christ's 'inward' love, and the anchoress' 'inward' meditation on this love, is opened up for public view.[51]

A crucial difference between the two images is also apparent. In *Wohunge*, the Heart itself is wounded; in *Ancrene Wisse*, it is not itself wounded, and is only visible through the Wounded Side. Whilst one explanation may be that the two texts are appealing to different points in the transition from devotion to the Wounded Side to the Wounded Heart, this divergence seems to be of greater significance.[52] In *Ancrene Wisse*, though the love within the Wound is 'openliche' available to her, the anchoress remains external to the Heart. *Wohunge* moves her

---

[46] Eric Jaeger, *The Book of the Heart* (Chicago: University of Chicago Press, 2000), p. 91. Jaeger's description of *Wohunge* as a 'mystical text' is not adopted in this article.

[47] See Bella Millett, 'The "Conditions of Eligibility"' in *Þe Wohunge of ure Lauerd*', in *The Milieu and Context of the Wohunge Group*, ed. by Susannah Mary Chewning (Cardiff: University of Wales Press, 2009), pp. 26–47.

[48] See further Denis Renevey, 'The Moving of the Soul: the Functions of Metaphors of Love in the Writings of Richard Rolle and Antecedent Texts of the Mediaeval Mystical Tradition' (unpublished doctoral thesis, University of Oxford, 1993), p. 91.

[49] Wolfgang Riehle, *The Middle English Mystics*, trans. by Bernard Standring (London: Routledge & Kegan Paul, 1981), p. 46.

[50] See further *Guide for Anchoresses: A Translation Based on Cambridge, Corpus Christi College, MS 402*, trans. by Bella Millett (Exeter: Exeter University Press, 2009), p. 178, n. I. 100; and Renevey, 'The Moving of the Soul', p. 70.

[51] These are all cited among the possible senses in the *MED* entry for 'openli'.

[52] On the two traditions, see Gougaud, *Dévotions et pratiques*, pp. 98–99.

a step closer. The Lover no longer shows his heart from the shield of his body, but now invites her to infiltrate it. The *Wohunge*-image also refers to the act of reading (whereas in *Ancrene Wisse* it is only *beholding*), dependent upon the tradition of Christ as a book.[53] Unlike the later *Charters of Christ*, these love letters in *Wohunge* are amorous documents that foster an intimate interaction between Bridegroom and Bride.[54] The anchoress is invited to read the amatory inscription with the same insight as the speaker in the thirteenth-century *Stimulus amoris*, blinded by the flowing blood of the Wounded Heart.[55] As Catherine Innes-Parker hypothesizes, *Wohunge*'s account of the lover-knight 'represents its author's perception of the way in which an anchoress would read the parable', a representation that involves a higher level of participation from the anchoress.[56]

A further parallel can be drawn with a passage in Bonaventure's *Vitis Mystica*. Given that Bonaventure lived slightly later than the assumed compositional date of *Ancrene Wisse* and the *Wooing Group*, he is not treated as a source here, but as an important indicator of affective devotion to the Wounded Side and Heart during this period.[57] Three reasons are given for the wounding of Christ's side: access to Christ; the formation of a protective space of habitation; and finally and most crucially, the ability to perceive beyond the visible wound, what Bonaventure calls the 'invisible wound of love'. Lover and Beloved are united in a vocabulary of woundedness, not unlike the Lover who is bloody and the Beloved who is bloodied in *Ancrene Wisse*:

> quis illud cor tam vulneratum non diligat? Quis tam amantem non redamet? Quis tam castum non amplexetur? Diligit profector vulneratum quae mutuo illius amore vulnerata clamat: *Vulnerata caritate ego sum*. Redamat Sponsum amantem quae dicit: *Nuntiate dilecto, quia amore langueo*. Nos igitur adhuc in carne manentes, quantum possumus, amantem redamemus; amplectamur vulneratum nostrum, cuius impii agricolae *foderunt manus et pedes*, latus et cor; oremusque, ut cor nostrum adhuc durum et impoenitens amoris sui vinculo constringere et iaculo vulnerare dignetur.[58]

> Who would not love a heart so wounded? Who could forbear to respond to a heart so loving? Who would not embrace a heart so chaste? The lover thus wounded can only accept as true a love that proceeds from one who is herself wounded by love, who can cry *I am wounded with love*. The loving Bridegroom accepts a return of love from one who says, *Tell my beloved that I languish for love*. So we who are yet carnal must give back as much love as we can to our Lover. We will embrace our wounded Bridegroom, whose feet and hands, as also his side and heart, have been dug into by those wicked husbandmen.

---

[53] For this tradition, see Vincent Gillespie, *Looking in Holy Books: Essays on Late Medieval Religious Writing in England* (Turnhout: Brepols, 2011), pp. 124–26. See also Jaeger, *The Book of the Heart*, p. 108.

[54] For an edition of the *Charters*, see *The Middle English Charters of Christ*, ed. by Mary Caroline Spalding (Pennsylvania: Bryn Mawr, 1914).

[55] Cited from Walter Hilton's (†1396) translation and adaptation of the original text. See *The Goad of Love*, ed. and trans. by Clare Kirchberger (London: Faber and Faber, 1952), p. 51 (Latin given in n. 1).

[56] Catherine Innes-Parker, '*Ancrene Wisse* and *Þe Wohunge of Ure Lauerd*: The Thirteenth-Century Female Reader and the Lover Knight', in *Women, the Book and the Godly*, ed. by Lesley Smith and Jane H. M. Taylor (Cambridge: Brewer, 1995), pp. 137–48 (p. 138).

[57] As Gougaud notes, passages from the *Vitis Mystica* were presumed to have been composed by Bernard of Clairvaux (*Dévotions et pratiques*, p. 98); see also the remarks on authorship by an 1889 translator of the *Vitis Mystica*: *The Mystic Vine (Vitis Mystica)*, trans. by Samuel John Eales (London: Sonnenschein, 1889), p. iii.

[58] *Vitis Mystica*, in *S. Bonaventurae Opera Omnia*, ed. by A. Lauer and others, 10 vols (Quaracchi, Florence: Ad Claras Aquas, 1898), VIII 164–65.

Let us pray that our hearts, still so hard and impenitent, may be found worthy to be bound by the chain of his love, and to be wounded by his spear.[59]

For Bonaventure, woundedness and true love are indistinguishable. Prior to the contemplative's wounding by the spear, she or he has not gained entrance into the intricacies of Christ's Heart. Christ is unable to love an un-wounded self — and vice-versa — since his nature is defined by his wounds. The anchoress who enters Christ's Heart in *Wohunge* does not voice such woundedness. Slightly later, however, she desires to hang with Christ on the Cross, anticipating a crucifixion within her enclosure: the affective-literate goal of her reading (p. 36, ll. 590–95). She is never said to receive the mystical love-wound of the Canticles, but she is 'wounded in love' through her affective crucifixion. Through this wounding, she is able to move towards — and at times into — her Spouse. Such imagined entrance or near-entrance into the openings of his body is crucial to the anchoress' affective literacies, as it is vital to her intimacy with him. Whilst mystical union within the Wounded Heart may not be the focus of *Ancrene Wisse* and the *Wooing Group*, the anchoress' love for Christ is no less intense, and no less distinguished.

V. Sin-Wounds

Christ's Wounds to Sinner's Wounds

Although she does not receive a mystical love-wound to the heart, the anchoress does sustain wounds of sin. This is a major goal of her affective literacies: healing the sin carved in her soul. Whilst the previous section examined the role of love-wounds in the anchoress' relationship with Christ, this section turns to the ways in which the anchoritic reader employs sin-wounds to rationalize her penitential existence. It should be noted at this point that the image of a 'sin-wound' is not unique to these anchoritic texts. Pre-1215 penitential and theological texts contain images of sin-wounds and priest-doctors, as in Hugh of Saint-Victor's (c. 1096–1141) *De sacramentis Christianae fidei*: 'Peccata sunt quasi vulnera' (Sins are like wounds).[60] These images form part of what Naoë Kukita Yoshikawa has termed the 'unique interface between medicine and religion' in spiritual healing, created by the pre-Cartesian connection of body and soul.[61] Such imagery was given impetus by the Fourth Lateran Council of 1215; the mandatory confession laid down in Canon 21 is expressed through a simile/metaphor of wounding and surgical healing:

> sacerdos autem sit discretus et cautus, ut more periti medici superinfundat vinum et oleum vulneribus sauciati, diligenter inquirens et peccatoris circumstantias et peccati, per quas prudenter intelligat, quale illi consilium debeat exhibere et cuiusmodi remedium adhibere, diversis experimentis utendo ad sanandum aegrotum.[62]
>
> The priest shall be discreet and cautious, so that like a doctor he may pour wine and oil on the wounds of the wounded one. Let him diligently inquire about the circumstances of

---

[59] *The Mystical Vine: A Treatise on the Passion of our Lord by S. Bonaventure*, trans. by a friar of S. S. F. (London: Mowbray, 1955), pp. 21–22.
[60] *PL*, CLXXVI 1150C.
[61] See especially Naoë Kukita Yoshikawa, '*Post-mortem* Care of the Soul: Mechtild of Hackeborn's the *Booke of Gostlye Grace*', in *Medieval and Early Modern Literature, Science and Medicine*, ed. by Rachel Falconer and Denis Renevey (Tübingen: Narr Verlag, 2013), pp. 157–70 (p. 157).
[62] 'Concilium Lateranense IV 1215', in *Conciliorum Oecumenicorum Decreta*, ed. by Albergio Giuseppe (Basil:

both the sinner and the sin, so that he may prudently discern what sort of council he must give and what remedy to apply, using diverse experiments to heal the diseased person.

This medicinal discourse for sin and confession, bolstered though by no means invented by Canon 21, permeates the Lambeth and Trinity homilies — texts which are geographically and linguistically associated with the *Ancrene Wisse* Group.[63] Most notably, in Trinity 6, the devil is described as inflicting wounds on Adam's five organs as he consumes the forbidden fruit (pp. 33–35). Christ comes to Earth so that he may heal the burdened sinner of his or her 'synwunden', a term occurring twice in this sermon (pp. 35, 41). This is a crucial compound word of Old English origin.[64] By it, sin is no longer simply likened to a wound: sin becomes a wound. In this conceptual metaphor, sin is a painful and life-threatening disease, yet also an ailment that can be remedied.

Indeed, wounds are not arbitrary signifiers of sin — a fact again given credence by the growing body of scholarship on medicinal language in spiritual healing. M. K. K. Yearl has remarked on the 'concept of medicine as duplex', with particular reference to Hugh of Fouilloy (d. c. 1172) and William of Saint-Thierry (c. 1075–1147/1148): 'knowledge of the body was thought to provide a useful tool for those engaged in treating the wounded soul because of a prevailing cosmology that accepted correlations between all aspects of the universe'.[65] And as Jeremy J. Citrome asserts, the image of sin-wounds also had a basis in medieval physiology. For a medieval patient, 'wounds and other signs of illness are not merely metaphors for spiritual corruption, but they are the material substance of sin manifest upon the flesh'.[66] As he rightly notes, the confessor 'encourages the internalization of a pained and wounded self-image'.[67] Our texts encourage the anchoress to develop a 'wounded self-image' in the nurturance of her affective literacies. She feels the pain of her sin-wounds, regarding these with the same urgency as wounds suffered on her flesh.

There is a linkage between Christ's woundedness and the anchoress wounded in sin. As Jocelyn Wogan-Browne observes, there is no consistent gap between the anchoress' permeable body and 'the exudings and openings' of Christ's. She cites in particular the *Ancrene Wisse*-author's connection of Christ's bleeding on the Cross to the anchoress' bloodletting, partly quoted earlier in this article (98: 1146–50).[68] Wogan-Browne's case for connection is fundamental to reading the sin-wounds in *Ancrene Wisse* and the *Wooing Group*. In these texts,

---

Herder, 1962), p. 221.

[63] See Bella Millett, 'The Pastoral Context of the Trinity and Lambeth Homilies', in *Essays in Manuscript Geography: Vernacular Manuscripts of the English West Midlands from the Conquest to the Sixteenth Century*, ed. by Wendy Scase (Turnhout: Brepols, 2007), pp. 43–64. See *Old English Homilies, First Series*, ed. by Richard Morris, Early English Text Society, o. s. 29, 34, 2 vols (London: Trübner, 1867–68), pp. 23, 29, 83. See also *Old English Homilies, Second Series*, ed. by Richard Morris, Eearly English Text Society, o. s. 53 (London: Trübner, 1873), pp. 33–35, 41, 57, 77–79.

[64] This compound word occurs in the Old English *Christ II* and in a late Old English confessor's handbook. *Christ II* expands on the sin-wound metaphor: *The Exeter Book*, ed. by George Philip Krapp and Elliott Van Kirk Dobbie, Anglo-Saxon Poetic Records, 3 (New York: Columbia University Press, 1936), 24: 756–57; for the full development of the sin-wound image, see ll. 756–71a. See also Roger Fowler, 'A Late Old English Handbook For the Use of a Confessor', *Anglia*, 83 (1965), 1–34 (27: 319).

[65] M. K. K. Yearl, 'Medicine for the Wounded Soul', in *Wounds in the Middle Ages*, ed. by Kirkham and Warr, pp. 109–28 (p. 110).

[66] Jeremy J. Citrome, *The Surgeon in Medieval English Literature* (New York: Palgrave Macmillan, 2006), p. 7.

[67] Citrome, *The Surgeon*, p. 17.

[68] Jocelyn Wogan-Browne, 'Chaste Bodies: Frames and Experiences', in *Framing Medieval Bodies*, ed. by Sarah Kay and Miri Rubin (Manchester: Manchester University Press, 1994), pp. 24–42 (p. 30). Wogan-Browne is

there is a transactional mapping from one wounded body to the other: Christ's wounds heal the anchoress' sin-wounds.

In Part I of *Ancrene Wisse*, Christ's five wounds are said to cleanse the 'blodi sawle' ('bloody soul') of all the sins with which it is 'iwundet' ('wounded'), in subtle employment of the *Christus medicus* concept (11: 152–53).[69] In *Ureisun of God*, Christ's lesions harbour an indispensable healing balm.[70] The meditator also observes 'þe large broc' ('the large brook') flowing down his 'softe side' (p. 7, ll. 98–99). By emphasising Christ's softness, the speaker draws attention not only to Christ's injuries, but also to the ease with which he can be wounded. As in Part II of *Ancrene Wisse*, he suffers wounds due to the raw sensitivity inherent in his flesh and soul. From his tender side, the brook of blood becomes an infallible healing liquid:

> nes hit forto waschen sunifule soulen? nes hit forto saluen seke ine sunnen? hwoa is þeonne unweaschen. þet aueð þis halwende wet inwið his heorte? hwoa þerf beon unsalued . þet haueð so mihti salue. ase ofte ase he þerto haueð treoue bileue? (pp. 7–8, ll. 100–6)

> Is it not to wash sinful souls? Is it not to heal (those) sick in sin? Who is then unwashed, who has this healing moisture inside his heart? Who remains unhealed who has so great a salve, as often as he thereto has true belief?

God is referred to as the anchoress' 'heouenliche leche' ('heavenly doctor'), even transforming himself into a form of medicine: 'makedest us of þi seolf so mihti medicine' ('you made of yourself so mighty a medicine'; p. 8, ll. 106–7). It is medication of the highest potency, for 'a drope of þine deorewurðe blode. muhte weaschen awei alle folkes fulðe' ('a drop of your precious blood can wash away the filth of all people'; p. 8, ll. 111–12). From this crowd, the anchoress emerges to reveal the transactional wounding from Christ to her permeable body:

> þeoilke fif wellen of þine blisfule bodie sprungen 7 striken dun strundes of blode. weasch mine fif wittes; of alle blodie sunnen. of al þet ich habbe misiseien mid eien 7 mid min earen iherd. wið muðe ispeken. oðer ismauht 7 wið noese ismelled . wið eni lim mis iueld. 7 wið fleschs isuneged. (p. 8, ll. 113–19)

> Those same five wells of your blissful body spring and strike down streams of blood, wash my five senses of all bloody sins, of all that I have wrongly seen with eyes, and with my ears heard, with mouth spoken, or sensed and smelt with nose, with any limb wrongly felt and with flesh sinned.

The wounds of Christ's body, sources of a medicinal balm, are mapped onto the anchoress' body, appallingly burdened with sins. Christ's wounds are directly transferred onto the wounded soul in an affective-literate process: 'þine wunden helen þe wunden of mine soule' ('your wounds heal the wounds of my soul'; p. 8, ll. 119–20).

Several of these images also occur in *Lofsong of ure Louerde*. In the incantatory opening, Christ's 'iblescede blode' ('blessed blood') is one of the images by which the meditator pleads, stressing the medicinal value of Christ's wounds (p. 10, ll. 25–26):

responding to Lochrie, *Margery Kempe and Translations of the Flesh*, pp. 23–27, 26. See also Lotta Sigurdsson, 'Death Becomes Her: Writing and Reading the Mortified and Dead Body in the *Ancrene Wisse* and Related Works', in *Fleshly Things and Spiritual Matters: Studies on the Medieval Body in Honour of Margaret Bridges*, ed. by Nicole Nyffenegger and Katrin Rupp (Newcastle Upon Tyne: Cambridge Scholars Publishing, 2011), pp. 141–63 (pp. 150–52).

[69] On the healing power of Christ's wounds and blood, see Yoshikawa, '*Post-mortem* Care of the Soul', pp. 159–60. See also her earlier article 'Holy Medicine and Diseases of the Soul: Henry of Lancaster and *Le Livre de Seyntz Medicines*', *Medical History*, 53 (2009), 397–414; on background to *Christus medicus*, see p. 399.

[70] On the Side/Heart Wound as 'eucharistic [*sic*] medicine as revealed in the sacrament of the Mass', see Yoshikawa,

> [as]e a drope of þine deorewurðe blode þet tu o rode scheddest were inouh to weaschen alle folkes fulðe. þeo sterke stremes 7 þet flod þet fleaw of þine wunden. moncun uor to helen; clense 7 weasch mine sunfule soule þuruh þine fif wunden iopened o rode . wið neiled uor driuene 7 seoruhfulliche fordutte. hel me uor-wunded þuruh mine fif wittes wið deadliche sunnen. 7 opene ham heouenliche king touward heouenliche þinges. (p. 11, ll. 43–53)

> As a drop of your precious blood that you shed on the Cross was enough to wash all people's filth, the strong streams and that flood that flowed from your wounds (were) to heal mankind. Cleanse and wash my sinful soul through your five wounds opened on Cross, nailed, driven in and sorrowfully closed up. Heal me, all wounded through my five senses with deadly sins, and open them, heavenly king, towards heavenly things.

Christ's 'eadie flod' ('blessed flood'; p. 10, l. 10) of blood is directly placed on the sin-wounds of the anchoress in a process of healing: 'þeo sterke stremes 7 þet flod þet fleaw of þine wunden. moncun uor to helen'. The meditator implores Christ to cleanse her soul through his five wounds 'iopened o rode', to heal she who is 'uor-wunded þuruh mine fif wittes wið deadliche sunnen'. Through the opening of the wounds on the Cross, the dangerous gateways of the senses/organs are instead exposed to 'heouenliche þinges'. As touched upon above, the emphasis remains on Christ's body as the source of healing liquid, rather than nourishment.[71] Through the anchoress' affective literacies, Christ's wounds are mapped onto the sinner's wounds in a curative process. But this is not an easy transaction, which poses another challenge in her affectively literate reading.

Sin-wounds are repeatedly characterized by their aggression. In Part IV, the *Ancrene Wisse* proclaims that a God-sent illness heals the wounds of sin: 'þus is secnesse sawlene heale, salue of hire wunden, scheld þet ha ne kecche ma, as Godd sið þet ha schulde ȝef secnesse hit ne lette' ('thus is sickness the healing salve of the soul's wounds, a shield so that she does not get more, as God sees that she should if sickness did not prevent it'; 69: 68–70). In the *Ancrene Wisse*, bodily disease becomes a shield to prevent sin-wounds, infinitely more perilous than any physical ailment. As Part IV progresses, the author formulates a taxonomy of sin-woundedness. He differentiates bodily and spiritual temptations or sins as a 'fot-wunde' (foot-wound) and 'breost-wunde' (chest-wound) respectively (74: 204–6). This conveys not only the greater danger in the chest-wound — its 'peril' as the author says (74: 205) — but also its heightened painfulness. The taxonomy is later expanded: 'prude ant onde ant wreaððe, heorte sar for worltlich þing, dreori of longunge, ant ȝisceunge of ahte — þeose beoð heorte wunden, ant al þet of ham floweð, ant ȝeoueð deaðes dunt anan buten ha beon isaluet' ('pride and envy and wrath, heart-sorrow for (a) worldly thing, dreariness from longing, and coveting possessions — these, and all that flow from them, are heart-wounds, and give death's blow immediately unless they are treated'; 104–5: 1398–1402). The author has moved from breast-wounds to 'heorte wunden', inching closer to the point of fatality. It is also in Part IV that the author investigates the possibility of rotting or infecting wounds, based on the well-known third penitential Psalm, 37:6:[72] '*Putruerunt, et cetera.* "Weilawei! mine wunden, þe weren feire ihealet, gederið neowe wursum, ant foð on eft to rotien" ' ('*They rot, etc.* "Alas! My wounds,

---

'*Post-mortem* Care of the Soul', pp. 159–60 and pp. 165–66.

[71] On Christ's blood as nourishment, see Rudolph M. Bell, *Holy Anorexia* (Chicago: University of Chicago Press, 1985), p. 25; Caroline Walker Bynum, *Holy Feast and Holy Fast: the Religious Significance of Food to Medieval Women* (Berkeley: University of California Press, 1987), pp. 177–79; and Ross, *The Grief of God*, p. 50.

[72] See also Psalm 37:3 and 18.

that were beautifully healed, collect new pus, and begin to rot again" '; 104: 1373–74). Whilst carnal temptation is imaged as the enemy hurting the anchoress 'o þe vet' ('on the feet'), there is still the risk of inflammation 'up toward te heorte' (104: 1392–94), due to renewed sin (104: 1368–75) and failure to confess (V, 124: 373–74). This image reminds the anchoress that a bodily wound is not a passive mark, a sign of pain already inflicted and passed. A wound can be infected and thus harbour further danger in itself. Virtues can protect the soul from being 'i-wundet', a protection shunned at the risk of the sinner (91: 873–74).

As is clear in this statement, the sinner's agency is essential both to sin and to its remedy. According to Abelardian precepts, all sin is harmless without the agency of the sinning self.[73] As the sinner wounds herself in sin, so must she harness the agency of confession to reveal these wounds. The emphasis on revealing sin-wounds during confession is particularly strong in Part V of *Ancrene Wisse*, as would be expected. The second dimension to the Lateran image — the priest-doctor — is invoked in the condition of confession as 'ihal' ('whole'). The confessant who does not disclose all her sins places herself in mortal peril, becoming 'ilich þe mon þe haueð on him monie deadliche wunden, ant schaweð þe leche alle ant let healen buten an, þet he deieð upon as he schulde on alle' ('like the man who has on him many deadly wounds, and shows the doctor all and lets him heal all but one — from which he dies, as he should from all'; 119: 220–22). The Pharisee is presented as the epitome of an unsuccessful confessant due to his failure to reveal 'hise wunden' (124: 409–11).

The speaker in *Lofsong of ure Lefdi* draws attention to the wounds of sin being 'fastened' onto her, an image with no obvious epistemology: 'luðre men and deoflen. heo habbeð monie wunden on me ifestned; þet acwelleð mine soule' ('wicked men and devils; they have fastened on me many wounds, which slay my soul'; p. 16, ll. 12-14). This unusual use of the past participle 'ifestned' seems, at first glance, to show a sinner lacking in agency. She is wounded by her inattentiveness rather than the creation of sin in her soul, paralleling the concept of 'sins of omission'.[74] But the sinner's agency is not entirely absent from this meditation: 'flesches fulðe ifuled me. þus ich am lodliche ihurt ine licame. 7 ine soule; wið alles cunnes sunnen. for þauh þet werc nere in þe bodie; þe wil was in þe heorte' ('flesh's filth befouled me. Thus I am horribly hurt in body and in soul, with all kinds of sin, for though the deed was not in the body, the will was in the heart'; p. 17, ll. 30–34). The 'wil' that exists in the heart, urging the meditator on to forbidden thought or deed, plummets her into mortal sin. This erases any possibility of a passive 'fastening': the anchoress' own will — or, in Abelardian terms, her consent to her will — causes her sin-wounds.

The centrality of her will underscores the need for agency in the counter route of confession; the anchoritic speaker immediately affirms to the Virgin Mary, 'þis ich i *cnouelechie*' ('this I confess/acknowledge to you'; p. 17, l. 34, emphasis added). In the confessional passage of *Lofsong of ure Lefdi*, the anchoress admits that she has enabled her five senses, those gateways of iniquity, to facilitate her wounding. Sins have wounded her: 'prude 7 wilnunge of pris; me habbeð sore iwunded' ('pride and desire for renown have sorely wounded me'; p. 16, ll. 21–22). It is a wounding with reference to the pain of sin; she is '*sore* iwunded' (emphasis added). The aggression of sin-wounds demands agency in the reading process. The anchoress aggresses against sin-wounds through her affectively literate reading, as I will now consider.

---

[73] See *Peter Abelard's Ethics: An Edition with Introduction, English Translation and Notes*, ed. by D. E. Luscombe (Oxford: Clarendon Press, 1971), pp. 22–24.
[74] See Odon Lottin, *Morale fondamentale* (Paris: Desclée, 1954), p. 479.

A. S. Lazikani

The Anchoress' Penitence

Penitence is represented in the texts as self-laceration, but the modern scholar must not assume an overly literal reading. Self-mutilation without clerical approval is expressly prohibited in Part VIII of *Ancrene Wisse*, particularly in its revised version in Cambridge, Corpus Christi College, MS 402, intended for a broader anchoritic readership (158: 121–27). Furthermore, the anchoress is never shown to receive stigmata, and her heart is never said to be emblazoned with the sign of the Passion.[75] This does not prevent the author from employing the conceptual metaphor of wounds to describe the potency of the anchoress' penitence, however.[76] In Part III's account of the 'wreaðful' pelican, confession is a process of self-wounding. After slaying its 'ahne briddes' ('own chicks'), the pelican is so overcome by remorse that it resorts to wounding itself, resuscitating its chicks through its own blood (48: 7–11). Like the enraged pelican, the anchoress must attack her own breast with her beak:

> þet is, wið schrift of hire muð þet ha sunegede wið, ant sloh hire gode werkes, drahe þet blod of sunne ut of hire breoste, þet is, of þe heorte, þet sawle lif is inne; ant swa schulen eft acwikien hire isleine briddes, þet beoð hire gode werkes. Blod bitacneð sunne; for alswa as a mon bibled is grislich ant eatelich i monnes ehe, alswa is þe sunfule biuore Godes ehe. On oðer half, na mon ne mei iuggi wel blod ear hit beo icolet. Alswa is of sunne. (48: 14–21)

> That is, with confession of her mouth by which she sinned and killed her good works, draw that blood of sin out of her breast, that is, of the heart, in which resides the soul's life; and thus after, (she) shall awaken her slain chicks, which are her good works. Blood signifies sin; for as a man stained with blood is grisly and horrible in man's eye, so is the sinful before God's eye. In addition, no man may judge blood well before it is cooled. So it is with sin.

Wounding herself in confession, the anchoress heals herself by removing the blood of sin. Through its unattractiveness and its heat, blood is associated with sin and death, set against Christ's curative and resuscitative fluids.[77]

This metaphorical wounding is also employed in relation to penitence more broadly, beyond spoken confession. After exploring the need for both physical pain and shame in the penitential processes (134–35), the *Ancrene Wisse*-author develops an image of the 'torn' penitent body based on his reading of Isaiah 18:7. These torn people are equated with a victorious castle:

> eise ant flesches este beoð þes deofles mearken. Hwen he sið þeos mearken i mon oðer i wummon, he wat þe castel is his, ant geað baldeliche in þer he sið iriht up swucche baneres, as me deð i castel. I þet totore folc, he misseð his merken, ant sið in ham iriht up Godes banere, þet is heardschipe of lif, ant haueð muche dred þrof, as Ysaie witneð. (137: 222–27)

---

[75] See further Bynum, *Fragmentation and Redemption*, p. 187, n. 28; and Lochrie, *Margery Kempe and Translations of the Flesh*, p. 13.

[76] On metaphorical versus physical beating, see further Sigurdsson, 'Death Becomes Her', pp. 154 and 160.

[77] The association of blood with death has parallels with medieval attitudes to menstruation: see further Joan Cadden, *Meanings of Sex Difference in the Middle Ages* (Cambridge: Cambridge University Press, 1993), p. 174. On arguments for the significance of menstrual blood in the anchoritic existence, see Sauer, ' "Þe blod þ[at] bohte" ', pp. 123–47, and Kristen McQuinn, ' "Crepe into that blessed syde": Enclosure Imagery in Aelred of Rievaulx's

Ease and gratification of the flesh are the devil's marks. When he sees these marks in man or woman, he knows the castle is his, and goes boldly in where he sees such banners raised up, as one does in a castle. In the torn people, he cannot find his marks, and he sees in them God's banner all raised up (that is, hardship of life), and he has much fear of it, as Isaiah witnesses.

The tearing does not cause fissures in the 'castel': it rather fortifies its defences. As Christiania Whitehead observes on the architectural image of the virgin body in *Ancrene Wisse*, the anchoress in Part VI becomes an unassailable fortress; the tearing of penitential shame and pain seals her from penetration.[78]

Within the wider discussion of the 'totoren folc' ('torn folk') in Part VI, the author forms an image of 'þornes' of hardships. These 'thorns' cradle the promise of wholesome, penitential 'wounds' on the anchoress. It is a wounding that protects her from the devil's schemes: 'þet te beast of helle, hwen he snakereð toward ow forte biten on ow, hurte him o þe scharpschipe ant schunche aʒeinwardes' ('so that the beast of hell, when he snakes towards you to bite you, they [i.e. the thorns] hurt him sharply and drive him back'; 143: 436–40). Although the anchoress is among those torn people ripped apart by penitence, the thorns actually face the attacking devil. The thorns' reversal of direction here adds to their functionality, forming, as Wogan-Browne says, 'a protective girdle turned *outwards*'.[79] The thorn-wounds of penitence thus become not only a form of protection, but also a form of weaponry. The anchoress does not passively withdraw into this pre-prepared space. Both Wogan-Browne and Lochrie have spotlighted the concept of 'sealing' as male control of the dangerous excretions and entrances in the female's porous bodily spaces.[80] The anchorhold itself has been reinterpreted as a representation of the undamaged hymen of the virginal body, sealed or 'opened' as desired by a man.[81] In this wounding space safeguarded by thorns, however, the anchoress herself devises and enforces the sealing. The anchoress nourishes her affective literacies so that she can image herself wounded in sin, yet also image herself as one of the 'torn folk' who so alarm the devil. The conceptual metaphor of the wound again fosters a proactive reader.

Conclusions

Unlike Beatrice of Nazareth, our anchoritic readers are never said to receive a *sponsa Christi* love-wound (Canticles 4:9), but their engagement with wound imagery is no less vigorous. The present study has responded to recent research which conveys the 'myriad ways in which [wounds] functioned in medieval society', interrogating their multifaceted affective readings in *Ancrene Wisse* and the *Wooing Group*. It has sought to examine wound imagery in these

---

De Institutione Inclusarum', in *Anchorites, Wombs and Tombs*, ed. by Liz Herbert McAvoy and Mari Hughes Edwards (Cardiff: University of Wales Press, 2005), pp. 95–102 (especially p. 99).

[78] Christiania Whitehead, *Castles of the Mind: A Study of Medieval Architectural Allegory* (Cardiff: University of Wales Press, 2003), p. 91. See further Christopher Cannon, *The Grounds of English Literature* (Oxford: Oxford University Press, 2007), p. 159.

[79] Jocelyn Price ' "Inner" and "Outer": Conceptualising the Body in *Ancrene Wisse* and Aelred's *De Institutione Inclusarum*', in *Medieval English Religious and Ethical Literature: Essays in Honour of G. H. Russell*, ed. by G. Kratzmann and J. Simpson (Cambridge: Brewer, 1986), pp. 192–208 (p. 205); emphasis added.

[80] Jocelyn Wogan-Browne, 'The Virgin's Tale', in *Feminist Readings in Middle English Literature: The Wife of Bath and All Her Sect*, ed. by Ruth Evans and Lesley Johnson (London: Routledge, 1994), pp. 165–94 (pp. 168–69); Lochrie, *Margery Kempe and Translations of the Flesh*, p. 127.

[81] Wogan-Browne, 'The Virgin's Tale', pp. 168–69.

texts more closely than has yet been attempted. I have argued that, in her reading of wounds as 'potent signifiers' — as representations of physical trauma as well as conceptual metaphors for affective pain — the anchoress enriches her sophisticated 'affective literacies'.[82] Such findings support scholarly awareness, reinvigorated by Amsler, of the active nature of thirteenth-century reading practices. Sections I–II of this study offered a critical framework and an overview of wound devotion during the twelfth and thirteenth centuries. Section III then demonstrated that Christ's painful wounds stimulate the anchoress' own affective wounding as she meditates on him. The anchoress' Lover is wounded for her both physically and affectively; in engaging with his wounds, she cultivates her own woundedness, coming close to the Holy Mother's Sword of Sorrows (Luke 2:35). Section IV examined the anchoress' entrance (or near-entrance) into Christ's wounds. Whilst the anchoritic reader does not receive the mystical love-wound, she undergoes an affective crucifixion in her reading that brings her nearer to her Spouse. Through this form of love-wounding, she cultivates a sophisticated intimacy with him. Finally, Section V highlighted the aggressive nature of the sin-wound metaphor, an aggression fought through the anchoress' penitential 'wounding' or 'tearing'. As a miscreant, she feels her sins as wounds in her soul, yet she also heals these injuries with penitential thorns. It is clear that the anchoritic reader of *Ancrene Wisse* and the *Wooing Group* is not an inert figure dragged into wounds against her will; she is not a feeble combatant of her sin-wounds, nor does she remain placid as her heart is immersed in Her Lover's blood. She tirelessly flies to and enters the Wounds — in *Wohunge*, dwelling within the Wounded Beloved himself.

---

[82] For the quotations, see Kirkham and Warr, 'Introduction: Wounds in the Middle Ages', pp. 1 and 11.

Also published by *Leeds Studies in English* is the occasional series:

LEEDS TEXTS AND MONOGRAPHS

(ISSN 0075-8574)

Recent volumes include:

Approaches to the Metres of Alliterative Verse, edited by Judith Jefferson and Ad Putter (2009), iii + 311 pp.

The Heege Manuscript: a facsimile of NLS MS Advocates 19.3.1, introduced by Phillipa Hardman (2000), 60 + 432pp.

The Old English Life of St Nicholas with the Old English Life of St Giles, edited by E. M. Treharne (1997) viii + 218pp.

Concepts of National Identity in the Middle Ages, edited by Simon Forde, Lesley Johnson and Alan V. Murray (1995) viii + 213pp.

A Study and Edition of Selected Middle English Sermons, by V. M. O'Mara (1994) xi + 245pp.

Notes on 'Beowulf', by P. J. Cosijn, introduced, translated and annotated by Rolf H. Bremmer Jr, Jan van den Berg and David F. Johnson (1991) xxxvi + 120pp.

Úr Dölum til Dala: Guðbrandur Vigfússon Centenary Essays, edited by Rory McTurk and Andrew Wawn (1989) x + 327pp.

Staging the Chester Cycle, edited by David Mills (1985) vii + 123pp.

The Gawain Country: Essays on the Topography of Middle English Poetry, by R. W. V. Elliot (1984) 165pp.

For full details of this series, and to purchase volumes, or past numbers of *Leeds Studies in English*, please go to <http://www.leeds.ac.uk/lse>.

www.ingramcontent.com/pod-product-compliance
Lightning Source LLC
Chambersburg PA
CBHW080940300426
44115CB00017B/2888